I0130656

# Deconstructing Toxic Masculinity

This accessible book explores toxic masculinity, looking at how to define it, and how we can and should challenge its spread.

This book draws on Derrida's deconstruction, using the philosophical lens to deconstruct what toxic masculinity means and to better understand its significance for our society. It focuses on how harmful aspects of masculinity spread, infiltrate, and intoxicate our societies and how existing structures allow aspects of harmful masculinity to become toxic. This book also features discussions and analysis of participants' lived experiences of masculinities, alongside the author's reflections. It explores the relevance of toxic masculinity in work environments, politics, relationships, and gender roles and seeks to challenge and mitigate its damages for everyone.

Encouraging critical thinking and understanding of healthier ways of being for all, this timely book will be of interest to therapists, counselors, teachers, and practitioners of family studies. It will also be useful reading for students in the fields of psychology, gender studies, sociology, and related fields.

**Carlos Perez** is an Associate Professor and departmental chair of a Behavioral Sciences department at a liberal arts university. He is also a Licensed Marriage and Family Therapist and a Licensed Professional Counselor.

# Deconstructing Toxic Masculinity

A Redefining for Society

**Carlos Perez**

Routledge
Taylor & Francis Group

NEW YORK AND LONDON

Designed cover image: Getty © ByM

First published 2025
by Routledge
605 Third Avenue, New York, NY 10158

and by Routledge
4 Park Square, Milton Park, Abingdon, Oxon, OX14 4RN

*Routledge is an imprint of the Taylor & Francis Group, an informa business*

ISBN: 9781032734415 (hbk)
ISBN: 9781032734392 (pbk)
ISBN: 9781003464228 (ebk)

DOI: 10.4324/9781003464228

Typeset in Times New Roman
by codeMantra

*To my wonderful bride, Ali, whose endless patience and support with this conversation made this book possible. To Noah, you teach me so much about what it is to be a man and a father. To Dad, I wish you were here to read this.*

# Contents

# Figures

# Preface

I became a father in August of 2016. Around the same time, there seemed to be countless examples of men doing horrendous things to women and other men. Perhaps I was sensitive to it because of my newfound fatherhood, but I felt there were too many examples of masculinity I did not (and still don't) want my son to grow up around. I started to deeply discern what it meant to be an example of masculinity to my son.

In that year, several public figures, all men, were brought to light for acts they had committed. Matt Lauer, the very popular lead anchor for the Today Show on NBC, had been fired for sexually harassing co-workers. Around that time the Harvey Weinstein scandal started to take hold of the media, where he was found to have sexually assaulted multiple women. It was discovered that not only was Weinstein an abuser, but there was a deeper culture of abuse within Hollywood, a culture that mistreated women and kept men in positions of power. The discovery of this culture gave way to the #metoo movement, where women took to social media to say they, too, had been treated (many had experienced much worse) in inappropriate, sexual ways. Several Hollywood actresses paved the way for other women, confessing to their experiences of being mistreated.

This was known as the Weinstein effect; there was a wave of response across multiple industries where hundreds and thousands of women shared their victimization, and in turn made known their abusers. It was a wave of reckoning for women. It was also a wave of discovering for men. There was a silent, toxic display of masculine power that had gone unchecked, and it was coming to light.

It was a dark time for men. It was a time of overt toxicity. And women, along with society, were trying to fight it. As a new father, I was trying my hardest (and still am) to protect my son and my family from it.

But this is still happening. Even today there are allegations, over and over again, of men being sexually inappropriate with women, making public sexist jokes, and taking advantage of their male power. There is a subtle, and sometimes overt, display of toxic masculinity in movies and Hollywood; how men are usually portrayed as the stoic hero who saves the damsel in destress. Or, for example, religions that still hold to and respect a patriarchy – not to mention the numerous incidences of young boys being abused by bishops and priests which have failed to be corrected. From overt physical violence we see in American football (and I grew up watching football, I've always enjoyed watching it, but my views of it have changed since writing this book), to "locker room talk," to inappropriate jokes about women, this toxicity permeates our cultures.

There are things in our societies keeping these toxicities alive, in their status quo. The above examples are only a few ways in which our world today (specifically from Western America) keeps toxic masculinity alive. The longer we have men and women who uphold these beliefs, values, and toxic characteristics, the longer we will keep producing toxic masculinity. There are people today who still hold to the ideals of a masculinity, ideals that are not equal between genders, dominant, even hegemonic, which are oppressive to women and other men.

\*\*\*

The purpose of this book, then, is to explore what toxic masculinity is, define it as a scholar and as a consumer of secular ideas, study the ways in which it's kept alive, and to research other's ideas (both women and men) and experiences with it. Parts of this book will show you what men and women want to change about toxic masculinity. The task at hand is to also deconstruct, in the classical Derrida sense, and to approach toxic masculinity with such a lens and with the intention of changing the harmful narrative. The need to re-story masculinity is overdue. With the help of deconstruction, we can explore the possibilities that lie beyond the toxic narrative.

We could argue the ways to fix or change toxic masculinity and offer ideas of what a healthy form of masculinity would look like. There are plenty of works which already offer that. In my mind, that's only half the battle. Even though giving solutions is useful and has its place, there is a different understanding and process with deconstruction. We might offer solutions at some point in the process, but the goal here is to offer more than just advice.

The first section of this book will focus on definitions of toxic masculinity found in secular news, journalism, and scholarship. We will also study society through theories and theorists to see how toxic masculinity is kept alive. We will then go through the strategy of deconstruction with the help of research participants. I mix qualitative inquiry with the deconstruction strategy to provide a new approach to deconstruction, one which I hope makes the philosophy more approachable.

My data collection has consisted of collecting surveys and conducting interviews. As of now (Spring 2025), I have over 500 survey responses and have conducted 13 interviews. This is an ongoing data collection. Participants consist of men and women with various educational backgrounds and economic statuses – from high school diplomas to doctoral degrees. The ages of participants range from 18 to 57. Ethnicities vary slightly – Latin, Asian, and Black participants comprise the minority demographic. Most participants were of some European White descent. Chapter 4 discusses the collected data. I intentionally don't organize data in terms of participants' demographics. I am only interested in everyone's views of toxic masculinity for this project. Future studies and iterations of this work will focus more closely on the demographics of participants.

The final portion of this work will theorize on what society at large can do to change the future narratives of toxic masculinity, as well as how we can apply deconstruction to our own lives.

The main concepts I'll be focusing on in this work are Deconstruction, Toxic, Gender, and Toxic Masculinity. Gender is used intentionally because both men and women can be considered masculine. I don't want to limit the phenomenon of toxic masculinity to only men, that wouldn't be fair or true. Therefore, the way I will be using all three will is prefaced below.

## Deconstruction

My feminist beliefs are a large driving force behind this work. These beliefs have also led me to the task of deconstruction. bell hooks (2004) argues that feminists have been guilty of a one-sided argument against men; even feminist activists have been on the side of change but, change for the sake of reclaiming power for women. This is largely needed. There is one piece missing, though. If we are to reclaim power for women, we also need to educate men. And this is where hooks (I do, too) believes some feminist thought has lacked. In my feminist beliefs, both men and women are equal, regardless of gender, race, class, or anything else. Only reclaiming power is half the battle. The rest of the battle lies in the conversation about men, with men, for men. Men need to educate men about their histories in dominating women, and men need to have the conversation with men about what it means to be that sort of man who lives equally with women. This is where deconstruction is useful. By deconstructing toxic masculinity, we can begin these conversations.

To deconstruct toxic masculinity, we need to do several things. First, we need to establish all definitions: toxic, masculinity, and then toxic masculinity. We cannot do this without defining gender and its complications, spectrums, and evolutions. We also need to visit the philosophical practice of deconstruction. Derrida's deconstruction is the base of this conversation. Although this is not a new practice, the philosophical intent behind deconstruction will give us a different approach to the conversation of gender, masculinity, and toxicity. I believe some scholars and educators have misused the term deconstruction to signify something it wasn't originally intended to do. Deconstruction has taken on a meaning that is not quite true to its philosophical inception. It's been used to describe things, such as deconstructed clothes, housing styles, and decor. It's also been used to describe a process of intellectually "breaking down" something to "rebuild" it. This process gets closer to what deconstruction was intended to do, but it's still missing the mark. We will establish the traditional philosophical practice of deconstruction as it was intended by Derrida before we begin the process of deconstruction on toxic masculinity.

## Toxic

The term toxic is also up for debate. Not quite an academic term, this phrase has become popular in mainstream, secular nomenclature. I understand that to mention the phrase "toxic masculinity" is itself problematic and perhaps toxic. This is where the difficulty of writing this book lies: to approach the phrase itself, the one in which society at large has used to describe some men, and to give it the right attention and space to have a genuine conversation with it. Few scholars, journalists, and mainstream personalities are attempting to have a true, open-minded, honest understanding of toxic masculinity. We are quicker to condemn it and to fix it. Even though the potential harm of toxic masculinity needs to be condemned and corrected, I believe we are missing half of the solution. The other half comes with true exploration and understanding. Derrida's deconstruction gives us a way to understand toxic masculinity and to explore what lies beyond the phenomena into what we can do to change the experience itself. When done well, deconstruction leads to deep change.

The use of the term toxic, therefore, is intentional. Referring to it as something else misses the overall tenor of the phenomenon. "Problematic" masculinity comes close, but the phrase does not give way to ideas, multilayered effects, narratives, or deeply rooted beliefs that are sown within the minds and behaviors of men of all ages. As we will see in Chapter 1, toxic refers to an infiltration, a virus-like happening that infects its host, like toxic algae, toxic blood, and a poison. Referring to masculinity as problematic is a fair understanding of potential damages masculinity can cause. This book goes further into the potential poisonous influence masculinity can have.

"Toxic masculinity," then, will be defined as such. I will refer to harmful, dangerous, or problematic forms of masculinity. These forms and traits of masculinity are very commonly referred to as toxic masculinity. As a descriptor, it may be accurate, but this has taken away from the true danger of toxicity. We have overused the term toxic masculine (you'll probably feel like it's being overused in this book), and we have become too dull to what it really means. Rather than a phrase describing men, or women, we don't like, this book intentionally uses it differently.

The spread, infiltration, and systematic ways harmful traits of masculinity seep into society is the focus for our definition. This gives the phrase a different focus altogether. Therefore, we are not deconstructing harmful or problematic masculinity – which will be a part of the process. Instead, we are deconstructing the phenomena of the toxicity of masculinity, the process of intoxicating society with harmful masculinity.

America's recent election is a good place to start with this definition, that of spreading and intoxicating. A political tactic, in my opinion, is emotional riling. Politicians are good at making people angry and getting them to a place where they are angry with other people. This works very well. It works so well, things like sexism, racism, and misogyny seem to blend in with it. When people at rallies get riled up on border control, they seemingly ignore or dismiss the racist part of political rhetoric. It's as if racism and sexism and misogyny are subliminally offered and accepted. But this is how these harmful masculine traits are spread, through this subliminal emotional strategy, all the while throwing in derogatory comments that seem to be normal in the "heat of the moment." People become *intoxicated*, quite literally, through the emotional riling, and the disparaging words might as well be honey in their ears.

When thinking about toxic masculinity by this definition, one where harmful aspects of masculinity spread and infiltrate, it becomes a different conversation. To think critically (which is not deconstruction) about the harmful parts of masculinity is a good and needed effort. However, if we're choosing to use the definition of toxic masculinity as a process, one which intoxicates society, then we need to be asking questions about how societies keep problematic masculinity alive, how it's taught, and how it spreads. How have dangerous forms of masculinity been a part of societies, and how have they structurally and systematically been fed to our young men and women? Electing a leader who shows these harmful traits is a good way to make something toxic.

To deconstruct this, as the way Derrida envisioned deconstruction, cannot be done in one book. We can start here and lay the "groundwork" for the deconstruction process. To truly deconstruct toxic masculinity, it "ends" not in a book but when the deconstruction process convinces you, the reader, and me, the initiator of the conversation, to change. This book ends, then, with you.

## Gender

How does one begin to approach the conversation of gender? We live in a post-gender world where gender is something questioned, challenged, and thought critically about when it comes to identity. I use the term post-gender intentionally because gender is being questioned by individuals who try to live beyond their biological sex. The experience of "traditional" gender tends to lend itself toward aspects of toxicity, though. Therefore, the notion of post-gender is a factor in our deconstruction by way of challenging traditional ways of identifying and classifying gender, and opposing the societal structures that define masculinity and what it means to be a man. I'm using gender to intentionally include all possibilities of masculine.

## What to Expect

This book is a small conversation in much larger ones. Masculinity, and its potential damages, is not an easy equation to solve. As a society, we've taken steps in the right direction when it comes to equality, squelching oppression of women, and accepting "new" forms of manhood. But we are a long way from being where I think we need to be. This work tries to further the conversation, to think philosophically about issues at hand, and to come to a place where we can all benefit from it. You might be offended; you might be relieved. You might wish there were other aspects covered; you might think one area of focus was overdone. This tends to be the case when we approach these topics and try to change the narratives surrounding them. This is also the case when the right or wrong things are being said. It is my hope to say the right things, which means some of us might be offended along the way.

I have also kept memos to make this process as transparent as possible. These memos primarily show how I have wrestled with this conversation. These are unfiltered and raw, sharing this struggle with readers like you. I hope my struggles will be relatable as well. You will find these memos dispersed throughout this book at the end of Chapters 1–7, relating to and in proximity of specific content, so you can see exactly where I have had to mentally and emotionally process (extra) what I'm writing about.

***

The danger of sticking with the phrase toxic masculinity is the narrative it carries. I consider myself a postmodern thinker, and for me that means not adhering to destructive labels. My background is in marriage and family therapy, where I also practice as a postmodern therapist. A big part of my practice is believing in the danger of narratives and the potential destruction they can cause to one's mental health. I believe people internalize problematic narratives, to the point where they believe what narratives say about them to be truth. For example, someone diagnosed with depression. Depression holds a certain narrative in today's rhetoric; someone who's depressed is commonly seen as someone who cries a lot, can't manage their emotions, they even look a certain way, they might even be "crazy." The narrative also comes with its own solutions. If someone is depressed, then the "right" thing to do is to get on medication so your emotional state can be "fixed." The biggest problem with the Depression narrative, I think, is it communicates something is wrong; therefore, it needs to be changed. What's wrong with being depressed?

The same is true for the narrative of toxic masculinity. The narrative comes with things that may or may not be fair: toxic masculinity is machismo, violence, womanizing, sexism, homophobia, patriarchy. Even though some, if not all of those may be true, we still run the risk of grouping *all* men into that narrative. We also run the risk of generalizing these narratives to things that are not toxic. Not all men are toxic; not all forms of masculinity are toxic.

Now, I believe violence is wrong. I believe sexism and homophobia are wrong. There are certain things that are destructive and toxic. There are also certain things about depression that are also destructive. There is a line in the sand needing to be drawn on things that are not acceptable. Where we go wrong is when a narrative becomes so dominant it excludes other narratives from being accepted, which arguably puts masculinity at a lose-lose. Toxic masculinity is being condemned (and there are forms of masculinity that ought to be), and at the same time, the narrative has become so strong there is no room for other forms of masculinity. If you are toxic, then you a dick. If you are not toxic, then you must be a pussy, which is an entire other harmful narrative for men. If you aren't a hard ass, then you're the opposite: emotional, soft, girly, a sissy, fruity, gay, weak...I can go on. There is a chasm that exists between narratives, and both are and can be internalized. Both can be destructive.

By using the phrase toxic masculinity, I don't want to support it. I also don't want to further the narrative. But there is a need to loosen the power this narrative has in and on our world today.

As deconstructionists, we are living in a very philosophical time; a time that questions what it means to be human, what it means to be any given gender, and what it means to hold more than one identity. We are living in a time where truth is constantly being questioned, and where "facts" are a mere illusion based off algorithms on your TikTok feed. We are living in a time where sources of information are standards for information, more so than the information itself. We are living in a world where we like bite-sized bits of information, where attention spans are shrinking by the generation. Truth, and what it means to pursue it, has never been more fragile than it is today. Which is why this conversation is so important.

Toxic masculinity, the "truth" of what it means for men and women, has never been more pronounced. If Fox news says something about toxic masculinity, or if The Atlantic says something about it, the two sources will receive different responses. Our biases are slowly becoming our filters for information, what's true, and therefore what we believe. Our sense of belief has never been shallower than it is now. Whether you are a democrat or republican, whether you are a Christian or not, whether you are educated or not, *everyone* has their own way of using the information given to them. And *everyone's* way is "right." Be it the latest poll or what it means to be a man; our lives are driven by the philosophical assumption of what is true. This epistemic time we're living in has never been more "toxic" than it is now.

## Critical Theory

What is it that needs to change about toxic masculinity? There is no shortage of news articles and stories about its damage and harm, victimizations and repercussions. If we are going to answer the question of what needs to change, we need to begin a conversation that is more than simple advice or saying what/how not to be. Deconstruction is one part of this conversation. An additional part of this is to share my philosophical stance to approaching this endeavor. I also believe something needs to change. I also believe we, as a society, haven't had the patience or space to entertain a dialogue with toxicities. To do this, I take a Critical Theory approach to asking questions and writing on toxic masculinity.

A critical theorist believes in a socially constructed reality. Our collective lived experiences create the reality in which we live. "Truth" is created when enough people believe in the same thing: politics, religion, gender, masculinity, etc. Ideas and thoughts are largely the same across people; we socially create the ideas which we believe in. Sometimes, these ideas and beliefs can be damaging or oppressive. For example, some find ultra conservative politics to be a threat to human rights, oppressing decisions woman can make over their own bodies. Some conservative areas of the United States fundamentally disagree with same-sex marriage, oppressing the LGBTQ community and their rights to matrimony. A collective whole believes in such philosophies and stances, therefore making the social aspect of a belief that can harm someone else.

The critical theorist recognizes the power of a socially constructed reality; one that is harmful to another group of people. At the same time, the intention behind critical theory is to change such power, advocate for marginalized groups, and what I believe is to deconstruct such realities. I believe there are people who have been

harmed by toxic masculinity, both men and women. I also believe there is a collective group of people who still believe in such masculinity, therefore creating the
socially constructed reality of toxic masculinity. As such, my goal is to recognize
the power of such a socially constructed reality, advocate for those whom it has
harmed, and attempt to change such power and victimization. This is no small task.
To deconstruct toxic masculinity is difficult enough. Which is why we need the
help of the power of a collective whole.

***

There is a larger reason and impetus behind this book, which consists of what gender has become in our world today. Judith Butler argues that gender has become a
threat to humanity, civilization, "man," and nature (2023). And if this threat is true,
then gender is essentially the equivalent of a nuclear disaster, something that can
potentially annihilate who we are, not as individuals, but as larger peoples. I agree
with this position; gender has become something weaponized, a source of severe
conflict, and a way to ignite conflicts of power through political and social means.
To take the point further, toxic masculinity has become one of those weapons, used
by those who live it, and feared by those who try to fight against it. When we conceptualize gender in those terms, and when we specifically place toxic masculinity
as a weapon, it creates a sense of urgency in me. It is time something was done
about it, yes, for the sake of gender as a whole. Gender should not be the demise of
society. But even more so, masculinity should not be toxic.

I believe we are on the right path to change. I also think deconstruction plays
a large part in this conversation, one which has not been had yet. Gender has
been de-constructed and reconstructed and critically examined by feminists and
non. Masculinity, specifically the toxic and dangerous forms, has not been deconstructed. This is what we aim to do here this book.

# 1    Why Deconstruction? Why Toxic Masculinity?

Deconstruction, as Derrida intended it to be, is one of the ways we can have conversations with toxic masculinity that is not being done today. There is no shortage of writings on how men *should* change so they can be less toxic and less harmful. Deconstruction doesn't tell people how they should or shouldn't be, nor does it point the finger and blame men for how they act. Even though there are aspects that seem to originate from masculinity we shouldn't tolerate, like abuse and violence, deconstruction allows us to approach all areas of toxic masculinity that others are not doing. This is not easy. It takes a large amount of open mindedness, humility, courage, and willingness to be open to possibilities when it comes to deconstructing toxic masculinity.

When done well, deconstruction not only gives us the space to have these conversations, it also provides a roadmap in having the conversations themselves. With it, we are doing more than only thinking critically about a subject and more than giving critique. We are also doing more than simply offering our advice on how to change harmful forms of masculinity. Yes, this may be a part of the process of deconstruction, but it is not the goal. Instead, deconstruction helps us look past what has already been done and debated about. It helps us investigate toxic masculinity in a way that will help us think differently about it. Deconstruction helps us make sense of the world, and as a result convicts us to change something about it. Deconstruction also helps us to think past the "normal" ways of thinking about toxic masculinity. It helps us escape the back and forth of what *is* and what *should be*. As we will see in the following chapters, this is a venture which hopefully will convict us into approaching thoughts and people differently.

Why toxic masculinity? Men are struggling. Even though the narrative might be changing for men, Western society has done an excellent job (said with sarcasm) of raising boys to be a certain kind of boy. Pollack's (1998) work tells us about the "boy code," where boys are taught how emotional expression and vulnerability are not acceptable. The entire idea of "boys don't cry" has done extensive damage to the boys and men we've raised in our societies. By default, the boy code also teaches boys to be violent and aggressive. It is the rule of thumb: don't cry, be tough. This rule of thumb is the root of a lot of harm for young boys and men.

There are serious consequences to the generations of men who have grown up in this boy code. Now more than ever, men are living with high rates of anxiety,

DOI: 10.4324/9781003464228-1

depression, and suicide. According to the American Foundation for Suicide Prevention and the Centers for Disease Control and Prevention, men have a higher suicide rate than women, which is directly linked to men's emotional suppression. In 2022, the United States recorded 49,449 deaths by suicide. For men, every 23.1 per 100,000 deaths were committed by suicide, as opposed to 5.9 for every 100,00 for their female counterparts.

In addition to suicide, men who tend to adhere to traditional masculine norms, which include not feeling free or safe to express emotions, also report high amounts of psychological distress, like anxiety, depression, and self-esteem issues (Mahalik et al., 2003). Oliffe and Han (2014) share similar findings, reporting how traditional masculinity can exacerbate mental health issues in men by discouraging emotional expression along with help-seeking attitudes that might give men support. It is because of these masculine norms and expectations placed on men that they are less likely to seek mental health help (Addis & Mahalik, 2003). According to the American Psychological Association, men's anxiety and depressive symptoms are also commonly shown through other behaviors like anger and aggression (Weir, 2017). If traditional masculine norms like violence, domineering, and emotional suppression are considered harmful, and if they manifest as anxiety and depression, then there is something deeper and psychological that needs to be uncovered.

Carl Whitaker, a well-known therapist and theorist on experientialism (1975; 1976), believes the root of all psychological problems is the act of emotional suppression and denial of impulses. If this is correct, and I believe this theory holds significant weight even today, and if Pollack's "boy code" still exists in how boys respond to emotions, we are setting up our boys for a lot of emotional problems. Boys not being able to cry, feel, and express emotions is exactly what Carl Whitaker describes: the denial of impulses. *It is in our nature to emote. To deny that is to deny ourselves.*

Boys and men not being able to express emotion leads to other harmful manifestations of emotional states. When we are conditioned to deny our impulses and to suppress emotions, we compensate with other aspects of our emotional catalog. In the case of masculinity, if it's masculine not to show emotions, then the normal compensation is the release of "acceptable" expressions: violence, anger, aggression, all the traits known to be toxic in men. A central argument for the root cause of toxic masculinity, like Carl Whitaker posits, is the denial of the parts of men that are unacceptable to show and how men have been conditioned to do so.

We cannot continue this for men.

I want to help the conversation of toxic masculinity, and I want to help men approach masculinity by not being afraid of who they are. I want others who have been hurt by oppressive forms of masculinity to feel hopeful about the changing narrative of toxic masculinity, and masculinity as a whole. My hope is to help get us closer to that with this book.

**Origins**

Before we define toxic masculinity for our conversation, we will review some of the wide-ranging definitions and writings associated with the term. Even though this review is not meant to be exhaustive, and for the purposes of this work, we will be reviewing literature that defines the phrase itself: toxic masculinity. We will dissect it in the following chapter.

The phrase "toxic masculinity" originated within the decades of 1980 and 1990. The term was arguably first used by Shepherd Bliss in the late 1980s. He was using the phrase to characterize his father's militarized, authoritarian masculinity (Gross, 1990). In those decades, there was a particular interest in men to re-establish their masculinity given the industrial and economic changes to family life. This era was known as the Mythopoetic Men's Movement. The movement consisted of a reaction to feeling "trapped" by the rise of the industrial revolution and urban society (Messner, 2000). Men felt as if they had lost their "deep masculinity" to the then modern lifestyle, therefore needing to replenish it. According to Messner, men felt as if they did not have comrades or friends, specifically in the workplace. As a reaction, men began to see men as other competitors. Because of the shift in labor force, men were also spending more time in their homes with their families. This shift caused men to feel as if they were not realizing their full potential in their internal masculinity. And because of the rise of the feminist movement, men felt as if their voices had been stifled and muted.[1]

To preserve masculinity, men formed self-help groups to support each other in their efforts to keep their masculinity alive. These groups were rooted in Jungian Psychology, the Swedish psychotherapist Carl Jung. The philosophy behind the self-help groups was based off Jung's archetypes. Jung believed each human being was made of internal parts of themselves, key parts, that made up their entire psyche. One of the common archetypes, or parts, was known as the *puer aeternus,* which translates to the "eternal youth." This archetype is believed to contain characteristics such as creativity, charm, affection, and pursing of one's dreams. The Mythopoetic Men's Movement attempted to capture these internal qualities and foster them through groups of support.

The self-help groups were common places which held spiritual practices, where men would gather and try to re-experience, or reclaim their sense of masculinity that was lost. It was in these efforts to regain their masculinity that the term toxic also began to emerge. Because of the changes of labor force, and because men were now seen as competition (women were as well, but the MMM movement's sense of competition was only with other men), toxic traits were considered those which showed to be overtly competitive and aggressive. These traits were referred to as characteristics which men lived and practiced as part of their masculinity, therefore creating a new rhetoric for men: toxic.

The phrase itself was originally used by other men to describe men. The feminist movement spurred controversy in this debate because both movements happened during the same decades. While the MMM movement tried to regain their original, masculine voice, the feminist movement was fighting for equality between men and women, which also included women's voices being heard. The feminist movement critiques the MMM movement as being anti-feminist. Other scholars argue how both movements were simply happening at the same time (Brod, 1987; Faludi, 1999).

A central feminist critique of the MMM movement came from the Jungian approach to the movement's drive. Jung's archetypes were believed to be essential to our internal being, including the way our gender is formed. The MMM believed the *puer aeternus* archetype to mean a man's essential qualities of masculinity, making gender essential and rooted in biology; men are "hardwired" to be masculine. The critique argues how inherent traits, according to our biological sex, are not definitive; there is room for all gender traits to be experienced by both (all) genders. Therefore, they want to be masculine, even though in a non-toxic way according to the MMM movement, was considered unequal to the women's voice.

**Definitions in Secular Literature**

After the Mythopoetic Men's Movement and the Feminist Movement, secular and academic circles started to grab hold of the phrase to describe men and masculinity. For example, there are accounts of mainstream celebrities that have been accused of being toxic. Recently (I write this in the Spring of 2023), the Hollywood celebrity and podcaster Russel Brand was accused of demeaning some of his female workers, commenting on their appearances, and shaming them for not "giving into" the nomenclature of his humor; this is only one of his examples. In 2019, The New York Times published an opinion piece called What is Toxic Masculinity (Salam, 2019). Certain behaviors are highlighted as toxic according to Salam: suppressing emotions, maintaining an appearance of "hardness," or violence associated with power, the "tough guy" behaviors. Again in 2019 (Salter, 2019), The Atlantic published an article titled The Problem with a Fight Against Toxic Masculinity, where they included sexism and misogyny in their definitions. Similarly, Verywell Mind, an online hub for mental health run by mental health professionals, includes three core components: Toughness, being physically aggressive and emotionally callous; Antifemininity, men should reject anything feminine; and Power, men must work hard to obtain power, status, and respect (Morrin, 2022).

Jennifer Rubin (2022) wrote an opinion piece for The Washington Post called The GOP: An Unending Display of Toxic Masculinity, where she calls Republicans bullies, which she argues is a manifestation of their manliness:

> Whether they are separating children from their parents, spying on and infringing on women who do not want to be compelled to complete their pregnancy, or threatening to take away transgender children whose parents seek appropriate medical care, manliness as bullying has been the Republican's defining feature of late.

She goes on to write about how men in politics tend to spur on violence and divisions through their own policies and even their outright support of other's political policies.

In 2020, Yvonne Abraham wrote an opinion piece for the Boston Globe called Trump's Toxic Masculinity. She claimed the toxic trait Trump displayed was when he was recovering from COVID-19, ripping his mask off, saying that masks are for sissies – overt sexism and degrading behaviors, like wearing a mask, as they pertain to a woman's characteristic.

As recent as 2023, Vox published an interview with Christine Emba called The New Crisis of Masculinity (Illing, 2023). The interview briefly referenced the above masculine behaviors and characteristics, but Emba references the phrase "manfluencers," where more and more men in the spotlight are gaining attention: Andrew Tate, Jordan Peterson, and Joe Rogan, for example. Manfluencers is seen as a spectrum from benign behaviors, like Jordan Peterson's abrasiveness in his talks and writings, to destructive behaviors like Andrew Tate, sometimes referred to as Tateism – behaviors associated with Andrew Tate.

WebMD , the popular online source for medical information, diagnosis, and treatments, also has a list of toxic masculine behaviors. They include homophobia, need for control, promiscuity, refusing to help with household duties, risk-taking, sexual aggression toward women, stoicism, and violence. WebMD even lists toxic masculinity risk factors: dysfunctional family environment, exposure to social norms that encourage violence and male dominance, exposure to violence at home, lack of access to mental health services, lack of behavioral control, and social rejection by peers.

In 2019, the American Psychological Association published its first-ever guidelines for psychologists working with boys and men where they also reference dangerous aspects of masculinity. Even though the phrase toxic masculinity is never mentioned in their guidelines, they do recognize the issues of harmful masculinity. For example, one guideline aims to understand how boys and men run the risk of developing sexism and sexist ideals based on their privilege, where sexism is a byproduct of male privilege. The guideline warns mental health professionals that sexist ideals may be deeply engrained in a boy's construction of masculinity (O'Neil, 2015), and that boys can suffer negative consequences for violating those masculine norms (Reigeluth & Addis, 2016). The guidelines also recognize how boys and men who do not fit the mainstream ideal of masculinity do tend to suffer from mental health illnesses like depression and self-esteem, and those boys and men tend to become marginalized.

There have also been major movements aside from the Feminist Movement to try to fight against toxic masculinity. In 2020, the #metoo movement opened a chain of women who stood against the mistreatment they had experienced in workplaces, marriage, and relationships. The movement was spurred by women saying that they, too, had been victims of sexual misconduct, slander, and inappropriate behavior, all from men. This was a turning point for women and the feminist movement because it showed how women, and some men, were determined to stop the threat of toxicity. Even though many women had been trying to change the narrative of genders and oppression,[2] the #metoo movement was one of the first in which men advocated for women, and where men's maltreatment of women was put on public display. Man after man was "found out" about how they had treated women, sexually abused them, or dominated them in psychologically demeaning ways.

The #metoo movement brought to light the ways in which women were being treated, giving other areas of social media the ability to bring awareness to what toxic masculinity is and what can be done about it. There are also multiple pod-casts[3] that speak to breaking the cycle of toxicity, encouraging men to be nurturing, caring, and all the opposites of toxic.

Mainstream media like movies and Netflix shows have also joined the fight against toxic masculinity. The popular documentary, The Masks We Live In (Newsom, 2015), speaks to the way in which society has raised young boy and how we're setting them up to be toxic. According to the film, it is all too common for boys to be told, "don't cry, don't be a pussy," "be a man, fight," "suck it up, buttercup," or "that's for girls, are you a girl?" The documentary shows how expectations placed on boys at such a young age, to not show emotions and to not be gentle, and in fact to be the opposite of that, is what creates a generation of men that we see today; men who won't cry, who are afraid to treat women as equals, and who will gravitate to other men like them because they have been living the same experiences. The result of this is a society in which these characteristics give way to deep behavioral patterns and expectations that are difficult to break.

## Academic Literature

The phrase toxic masculinity is not as favorable in the academic world, despite its popularity and usage in mainstream secular literature. Most academics prefer the term hegemonic masculinity. Even though the word hegemony was not origi-nally associated with masculinity, social scientists paired it with the phenomenon of dominance that comes with masculinity.

### Hegemonic Masculinity

Before we understand toxic masculinity, we need to define the broader concept of hegemonic masculinity. In American and European societies, this can arguably be seen as the "standard" for masculinity; unfortunately, this commonly means domi-nation over women, hierarchy, homophobia, dysfunctional competition, inability to express emotion, opposition to "weakness," and devaluing any form of feminine attributes (Brittan, 1989). Even though there are many forms and experiences of masculinity, some of which do not adhere to the conventional norms of masculine expectations, the above attributes tend to be the dominate notion.

Hegemony was originally a contribution to Marxist thinking, where a society holds power and the way it forms social groups. This points to the idea that the rul-ing class will find a way to establish and maintain dominance (Donaldson, 1993). "Hegemony involves persuasion of the greater part of the population, particularly through the media, and the organization of social institutions in ways that appear 'normal,' 'ordinary,' 'natural'" (p. 645). Hegemonic masculinity was made popular by Australian sociologist R. W. Connell (1987), where it was paired with masculin-ity through sociological research on power structures. Hegemonic masculinity was seen as a practice that kept men's dominance in society, specifically dominance over women (Connell, 1987, 1995, 2005). It was not that most men were a part of this dominance, rather it was a small minority of men. This required men who were not a part of the dominate role of a man to be subordinate to it, positioning themselves in relation to hegemonic masculinity.

This was commonly seen in patriarchal practices. Both men and women tended to show a complicity to dominate masculinity, therefore making it the "desired" way of being a man. Even though this form of masculinity was not violent, it usually meant a sort of ascendancy, or being "better than." What made this idea controversial is that Connel (1987) also argued that there were cultural and institutional influences that helped keep this specific form of masculinity one to be desired, and therefore dominate. For example, Connel gives the instance of Rambo or John Wayne. I think today's examples could be Dwayne Johnson, or Andrew Tate. He argues that the media plays a large role in fantasizing these forms of masculinity. It is the very fact that they are being fantasized over that keeps them dominating. The institution of media, then, is an easy example of the strategies that keep that specific form of masculinity dominate.

What makes these masculine traits hegemonic, or dominate, is their relationship to other masculine traits. Connell (1987) argues that hegemonic masculinity is formed, or constructed, by way of its subordinate masculinities, this also includes women. Meaning that for a type of masculinity to be dominate, it needs other forms that are not as dominate to "support" it. In a masculinity competition, the dominant will always win over the lesser form. In today's case, lesser forms of masculinity tend to be dysfunctional, homophobic, and devalue women.

Hegemonic masculinity, then, is a certain strategy employed by the dominate group (men) to subordinate others (women). Not only that, other forms of masculinity can also be considered subordinate to the dominant form of masculinity. This is played out in multiple ways on a large scale: dominate heterosexuality where patriarchy exists, homophobia, misogyny, overt sexism, and violence, are all upheld and kept alive by other men. Staying with the Marxist thought, men are the dominate social group, and their ploy for dominance is played out through the above acts. Connell (1987) adds the gender aspect by arguing how societal structures, like politics, religion, even specific cultural aspects like machismo in Mexican culture, all keep masculinity dominate.

Consider the following distinctions provided by Connell (1987):

In the concept of hegemonic masculinity, "hegemonic" means a social ascendancy achieved in the play of social forces that extends beyond contests of brute power into the organization of private life and cultural processes. Ascendancy of one group of men over another achieved at the point of a gun, or by the threat of unemployment, is not hegemony. Ascendancy, which is embedded in religious doctrine and practice, mass media content, wage structures, the design of housing, welfare/taxation policies and so forth, is.

(p. 186)

What makes this difficult to analyze is the fact that hegemony is not only a word to describe a certain group of people, but also the factors that play into the process of making a group dominate, or the factors that bring a group to ascendancy. What are the factors that make one group dominate? Specifically, what are the factors that make masculinity dominate? Or, perhaps more accurately, who keeps forms of masculine dominant? This needs to be considered before we begin to understand toxic masculinity.

It is safe to point out the difference between hegemonic masculinity, and other forms that are not. This is where our conversation of toxic comes into play. In the above example, Connel points directly to violence *not* being a form of hegemony – gunpoint or overt power by threatening unemployment. If institutions like religion and media are guilty of fantasizing masculinity and keeping the narrative alive of "women submit to your husband," and if that is considered hegemony, what then is considered toxic? This is a very fine line to draw, but there are some key differences we'll discuss here.

This is a double-edged sword. On the one hand, we have men who overtly display their patriarchal positionings through homophobia and misogyny to dominate other social groups. On the other hand, we have institutions like religion that praise and even in some cases admonish the subordinate role of a woman. Therefore, we have generations of men and women who live in such a way; in a way that keeps women subordinate, and men dominate. This creates a very particular challenge, also a double-edged sword challenge. Not only is the fix for problematic or harmful masculinity to change men, but it might also include a different narrative for subordination, in particular, the narrative of women being submissive to their husbands – a narrative deep in some religious traditions.

It is possible, though, for the dominant form of masculinity to not be destructive. Hegemonic masculinity does not delineate between good and bad, destructive, or not, it only calls into play the dominant form of masculinity. This is where the word *toxic* is useful.

Toxic masculinity separates the forms of masculinity that are specifically destructive, hegemonic, or otherwise, from the ones that are not. Violence, devaluing women, and homophobia are examples of destructive when coming from forms of masculinity. The fear of expressing emotions and appearing to be weak are also traits that have the large potential to be destructive. But not all forms of masculinity need to be toxic. Competition is not in itself destructive, nor is physical strength and want to be a "protector." Pride, arguably one's downfall, is also not inherently destructive.

The fact that harmful masculine traits also tend to be dominant masculine traits points to the construction of hegemonic. There are enough powers at be to support such traits and keep them alive. There are enough people who live such dominate traits and support others who do. If there is a dominator, there will always be a subordinate. The "subordinate" traits of masculinity, too, are constructed as such. If the dominate traits are constructed, then the toxic ones are, too.

### Critiques of Hegemonic Masculinity

Before we turn to toxic masculinity, let us first review the feminist critique to hegemonic masculinity. This term has been revisited by multiple disciplines, including social sciences and women and gender studies. In the recent decades, feminist scholars have expanded on the concept, as well as Connel himself. While getting a lot of attention, both positive and negative, the term has evolved, specifically within the feminist literature.

To begin with, Connel and Messerschmidt (2005) responded to Connel's (1987) original thesis on hegemonic masculinity. In their response, they noted several critiques that needed to be addressed. One major critique was the idea of masculinity itself being vague (Hearn, 2004). Masculinity, as an idea, is flawed because it is ultimately unnecessary to understand power (as the term hegemonic implies). With the lack of post-structuralist analysis of gender, suggested by Whitehead (2002), masculinity had not, and has not, reached a state of fluidity; masculine identity still lies in its dominant narrative, furthering the male-female opposite. Therefore, the concept of masculine is still respected by biological sex, and not the cultural and socialized experiences of gender.

The biological argument complicates the idea of hegemony because masculinity is not solely a biological act. There is nothing essential about masculinity and which gender can live it – women (or biological females) can also hold masculine traits. As mentioned before, this complicates not only the hegemonic argument but the overall masculine experience.

There is also a relational component to consider within this critique. The critique lies in the traditional research that has focused narrowly on analyzing men in relation to men (Brod & Kaufman, 1994), which also argues how women tend to be left out as part of the masculine analysis. This critique comes from the hegemonic practice of exclusion and subordination of homosexual men. The relational argument believes that masculinity needs to be studied between all genders, in relation to each gender. Doing so only among and between men is a lopsided way of studying masculinity.

Another central critique of hegemonic masculinity is in the ambiguity of what and who classifies as masculine, and therefore what makes it hegemonic, and the fact that there is overlap in those choices. There is confusion about what and who is and can be a hegemonic man. The examples today of what a man is, how they act, and what they do, are all very fluid and flexible, even among definitions of a "man's man." What adds to the ambiguity is again the fact that biological men and women can live masculinity. Therefore, the fact that overlap can exist in definition, gender, and examples, all lead to the confusion of the use of hegemonic. More than the ambiguity of masculinity is its multiplicities, which complicates even further the idea of hegemony. It is not one single form of masculinity that people experience – both men and women.

Perhaps the most important critique of hegemonic masculinity, in relation to this current work, is that hegemonic masculinity reduces masculinity itself to a reification of power. Or, masculinity is treated as inherit power, just because of the masculine traits shown by men. Holter (2003) argues how this is also a part of the patriarchal power men have over women and furthers the construct of men being "powerful" over women. This critique of reification of power is a central critique of Collier's (1998), where hegemonic masculinity comes to be associated with negative characteristics. Given the inherent power men are given through patriarchy, this leads to depicting men as unemotional, independent, non-nurturing, and aggressive (Connell & Messerschmidt, 2005).

This critique is important to us because of the argument of power that can lead to certain behaviors mentioned above. Since the term hegemonic masculinity refers to the practices and beliefs that allow men's dominance over women (and other men), there are cases where hegemonic masculinity may be seen as toxic (Connel & Messerschmidt, 2005). This is an important point of distinction: there is a difference between hegemonic and toxic. Even though there are times when hegemonic masculinity can be toxic (like violence, for example), and since there are so many different forms and levels of hegemonic masculinity, it is not always the same as toxic.

## Toxic Masculinity

Which brings us to our definitions and current work. To define toxic masculinity presents a problem, of which the very title of this work is up for discussion. The problem with the very effort to define such a phenomenon is the knee jerk reaction, the automatic response, or the unconsciousness of the images we generate in our minds. When I say, "toxic masculine," most, if not all of us, will have an idea of what that means, who that looks like, and what this person does. That, in and of itself, is quite limiting. This is the first problem. The second problem is how toxic masculine unfairly assumes gender. Yes, women can be toxic masculine, but the automatic assumption of toxic masculine tends to be placed on men. To define it, then, is to create a multi-layered definition: (1) Toxic masculine as it pertains to men, and (2) Toxic masculine as it relates to everyone outside the gender box of "man." As part of our definition, we will intentionally stick to the masculine aspects which are considered harmful to others. Is a woman "masculine" if she's violent or aggressive? Maybe sometimes. Therefore, our definition will aim to include both men and women that can potentially be toxic masculine.

Defining toxic masculine also includes distinguishing it from hegemonic masculine. We are establishing here the difference between toxic and hegemonic, where hegemonic implies a structure, system, or strategies that are complicit in what is required of a dominate and a subordinate group. How the group becomes dominate is important to what toxic is – through beliefs, practices, indoctrination, or even media. But in these examples, there are complicit parties. There are both men and women who believe in the narrative of "wives submit to your husband." Even though there may be infectious components to dysfunctional beliefs, on their own they are not toxic.

What makes toxic masculinity toxic is something arguably forced or exerted through power (more on this in the next chapter). There is a clear perpetrator and victim to toxic. Hegemonic can lead to toxic, but on their own, they are two different aspects of masculinity.

Even among academic scholars, the definitions of toxic masculinity vary. With such limited quantitative and qualitative data supporting the phenomenon, it is difficult to define it with clarity. Having been primarily derived from Marxist hegemony, the term toxic evolved to refer to certain practices. These practices resulted in the oppression of specific groups of people, including women, men, and trans and gender-diverse populations (Conell & Messerschmidt, 2005). These toxic practices are believed to give way to aggressive heterosexual behavior, commonly resulting in domestic violence perpetrated by men (Bhana, 2012). This also tends to result in men suppressing their emotions, leading to emotional and mental health issues (Kupers, 2005). Other toxic practices include homophobia, physical and political violence, and men's rights activism (Banet-Weiser & Miltner, 2015).

Similarly, Kupers (2005) defines toxic masculinity as the "constellation of socially regressive male traits that serve to foster domination, the devaluation of women, homophobia, and wanton violence" (p. 15). This definition came within the context of men who were imprisoned, arguing how prison brings out the toxic aspects of masculinity.

Some scholars believe toxic masculinity to be a subset of hegemonic masculinity (Parent et al., 2019). As such, Kupers (2005) further defines it as characterized by the enforcement of rigid gender roles, but also enforces the need to "aggressively compete and dominate others" (p. 713). Parent et al. also mention how social media has become a place for such toxic masculine behaviors. They argue how there is a certain amount of disinhibition that leads to more volatile, negative interactions. Those interactions are often seen in antifeminism, opposing opinions in general, and domination through online platforms.

The difficulty with solely relying on toxic masculinity to be a definition of behaviors or toxic practices is that it directs us away from other contributing factors. There are other biopsychosocial factors, like developmental delays, cultural expectations, and the performance of gender, that can also complicate the definition of toxic masculine (Corvo & Golding, 2022).

My favorite academic definition of toxic masculinity is provided by (Rotundi, 2020). Toxic masculinity is defined as such,

> It is named as toxic because it stifles and prevents a man from being human, from feeling and expressing emotions common to all human being, and it forces to him to be constantly strong, even if he eventually needs to be supported or comforted.

This definition brings to attention the specific idea of limitations, or masculinity in a box as I'll call it. The power behind the expectations to be a certain kind of masculine creates an inclusion/exclusion experience for men. It is a masculinity without choice, one dimensional. And because of that one dimension, the one choice of masculinity, men who experience otherwise are left out at best and internalize their failure as men at worst. This exclusion is widespread through different forms, institutions, and powers at be.

Let us next look into the individual definitions of the phrase: toxic, masculine, and then the combination of toxic masculine. Separating each term will give us validity in the use of the phrase itself, despite it not being a strictly academic, or favorable phrase. I myself am not the biggest supporter of the phrase, but the definitions provide us with specific context and framework from which we can think about the potential harms of masculinity.

## A Closer Look

For our purposes, we need to examine the phrase closer and break down (not deconstruct) each term to have a closer look at what each can mean. Let us first define the term *toxic* before we combine it to the phrase. The Oxford English Dictionary defines toxic as: poisonous; harmful or dangerous to health or life. The Merriam-Webster Dictionary defines toxic as: Containing or being poisonous material especially when capable of causing death or serious debilitation; exhibiting symptoms of infection; extremely harsh, malicious, or harmful. The Collins Dictionary defines toxic as: of, or affected by, or caused by a toxin, or poison; acting as a poison, poisonous.

*Poison* is the common phrase between most definitions of toxic.

The Collins Dictionary further defines poison as: anything harmful or destructive to happiness, welfare, such as an idea or emotion. The Oxford English Dictionary defines poison as: material that causes illness or death when introduced to; a principle, doctrine, influence, etc., which is harmful to character, morality, or the well-being of society; something which causes harm; something which is detested.

What then, is considered toxic, or poisonous? There are many chemicals that are considered poisonous to our bodies that can cause serious damage, even death. There are also biological functions, or failings, that can turn our blood toxic; our liver failing, our appendix bursting inside of us. When gone untreated, our toxic blood can cause brain damage, heart failure, and even death.

When contacted with poison, our bodies shut down, become unable to function, and cause serious harm. What then is considered harmful to character, morality, or the well-being of society?

## Masculinity

Masculinity is also straightforward to define in its form of a descriptive. The Merriam-Webster Dictionary defines masculine as: marked or having qualities, features, etc. traditionally associated with men. What are those qualities and features?

There are several traditional and stereotypical features associated with masculinity: tall, muscular, strong, facial hair, or a deep burly voice. Men tend to be associated with sports, such as American football, basketball, golf, and American soccer, or rugby. Sports populated by men also tend to be more aggressively driven; the stronger you are, the harder you hit, the better you are at the sport. Even though the women's equivalent exists for most sports, save American football, the pairing with physical strength is held in high esteem, even preferred.

What makes these traits toxic, though? To refer to their definitions, how do masculine traits and masculinity become poisonous? Causing destruction to welfare? Causing illness? Like poison, or a substance that is toxic to our bodies, how is masculinity potentially poisonous to ourselves? What are some examples of such a phenomenon?

*When generation after generation of boys are taught to be toxic, we create a society infected by emotionless, violent, and misogynist ways. Masculinity becomes toxic when it infects the character of our society, politics, media, or entertainment.*

Characteristics like misogyny, sexism (specifically against women), and acts of violence toward men and women are seen as toxic in our society because of the damage they have created. By way of our definition, these characteristics have *poisoned*, infecting our politics, entertainment, and even our religions with systemic structures that keep these alive. Structures like unequal pay between men and women, the public display of misogyny from the former (now current) president of the United States of America, and the support it is given; it happens to be men who are in some form of power that are the catalyst for toxicity.

## Systems at Play

The idea of masculinity infecting society raises the question of the state of society itself. What is it about society in which it can so easily be infected with toxic masculinity? Just like a cell is infected with a virus, how is it that societies can be infected with harmful aspects of masculinity? This question also brings us back to hegemonic masculinity. Its conceptualization of a certain type of masculinity that became a form of male dominance in a patriarchal society still has implications for how we live today. There are arguably systems in today's world that keep a certain type of male dominance alive. What I am arguing here is that we still live in a world that not only keeps masculinity hegemonic, but one that also keeps toxic masculinity hegemonic, or one where toxic masculinity is the dominant form of masculinity. There are several ways in which this happens.

A key area of thought for this book is to intentionally hone on not only the problem with harmful masculinities but also to contextualize them, to see how they are being kept alive. I mention being kept alive on purpose; I believe societies have enforced laws, standards, and expectations, and kept strategic ideals in place so that harmful aspects of masculinity are kept dominating. This is either done intentionally or not, but as we will see, there are ways to conceptualize and contextualize toxic masculinity and how it survives, which is how we will approach the need for deconstruction.

I do not want to communicate that men and women who may be considered toxic are inherently bad. By saying "you should change this," we are also saying "there is something wrong with you." Yes, there are things that people do that are considered wrong, and we should not tolerate these things – violence, abuse, and misogyny. But I believe people can change and are worthy of being helped to reach that change. This is where deconstruction comes in, offering us a different conversation from the common "here's how you change your toxic ways" narrative.

What follows are multiple parts to deconstructing toxic masculinity. First, we will outline the deconstruction process or put it into steps so we can follow it closely. Chapter 4 enters the research done for this project – and is still being done.

This is an ongoing project for me. At this point, I've collected surveys and conducted interviews. The data chapter will analyze surveys along with the interviews conducted, which will give us thoughts and experiences from individuals who have lived with and thought about toxic masculinity. Chapter 5 will give us a "new concept" of masculinity. As part of the deconstruction process, one of the outcomes is to produce a new concept beyond what is being deconstructed – this will be explained in the next chapter. The following chapters discuss societal implications after having deconstructed toxic masculinity, and what we can do about changing the narrative of harmful, destructive masculinity.

### *Memo #1 On Interpreting Masculinity*

I've used several different platforms to gather surveys. In doing so, I've stumbled across comments, critiques, and feedback. One platform specifically, Reddit, was where I found all sorts of interesting comments. Once subreddit in particular, the r/Christianity sub, was full of spiteful things to say about the survey, masculinity, toxic masculinity, and even god (or if you prefer: God). Several comments mentioned how the term toxic masculinity doesn't exist, that it's gay men who have been coddled by their mothers who created the term, and how they can't handle "real" masculinity, therefore it becomes toxic. Others said that masculinity doesn't exist, and to place the term in relation to g(G)od, it's taking it to a place where masculinity isn't even a thing.

And then others said that the term toxic shouldn't be associated with masculinity. And how masculinity isn't inherently bad, or toxic. But it's how people respond to masculinity that makes it toxic. There are several things that are wrong with this logic.

To say it's the response to masculinity that makes it toxic is to relieve men, and women, of their characteristics that can be harmful to others. For example, Andrew Tate is only toxic because I'm offended by it, never mind his demeanor, misogyny, or disrespect toward women. To say that toxic is in the eyes of those perceiving is to say sexism doesn't come from men's attitude toward women, it only comes from women who either don't understand masculinity or take it the wrong way. Either way, that's the textbook definition of gaslighting… "I'm not toxic, you're just misinterpreting my masculinity. Therefore, you're in the wrong."

No, masculinity isn't inherently bad, nor is it gender specific. Both men and women can exhibit masculine traits. Both men and women can also exhibit toxic traits.

Whichever gender one identifies as, all genders have the potential to be toxic, even those genders that exhibit masculine traits.

I know this is difficult to parse out. Traditional masculine traits are the ones that tend to be toxic. Being overtly strong, not showing emotions, even condoning the lack of emotions, *machismo* that womanizes and treats women as inferior (or any cultural form of masculine that treats women as inferior), overt sexism coming from a place of "being a man." They are all toxic, and they all infect our world. All these traits aren't necessarily gender specific, but they are masculine by tradition.

It's the way in which we harbor these masculine traits, promote them, and don't do anything to change them, that makes it toxic…seeping into our social media, politics, narratives of fatherhood, or how we treat women.

The difficulty in this: there is no way to not offend someone. When it comes to gender, to masculinity, and then throw in the word "toxic," people are going to be very defensive. I've seen men, like the examples above, become very angry, even belligerent, in their comments about the phrase itself. It's ironic: men making homophobic comments about toxic masculinity is the very definition and display of toxic. To see men make derogatory comments about my study, the overall idea of the phenomenon, and to say things that belittle other's comments and my study, is a case in point, toxic.

To even say toxic brings out toxicity.

**Notes**

1 Although not a direct contradiction to feminist theory, the women's movement, by way of rising opportunity for women, resulted in the backlash and defensiveness of men. Some feminist scholars attribute this specific movement as antifeminist while others only refer to is as anti-women's right. The argument of oppression is what distinguishes these two sides. While men felt silenced, their reaction through the Mythopoetic Movement did not directly result in women's oppression, rather the support from men to keep masculinity alive.

2 For example, Susan B. Anthony who founded the National Woman Suffrage Association, Betty Friedan and her work The Feminine Mystique (1963), bell hooks, Judith Butler, or Rebecca Walker.

3 Man Enough by Justin Baldoni, The Guilty Feminist by Deborah Frances-White, Unladylike by Cristen Conger.

**References**

Abraham, Y. (2020, October 7). Trump's toxic masculinity. *The Boston Globe*. https://www.bostonglobe.com/2020/10/07/metro/trumps-toxic-masculinity/

Addis, M. E., & Mahalik, J. R. (2003). Men, masculinity, and the contexts of help seeking. *American Psychologist*, *58*(1), 5–14. https://doi.org/10.1037/0003-066X.58.1.5

Banet-Weiser, S., & Miltner, K. M. (2015). #MasculinitySoFragile: Culture, structure, and networked misogyny. *Feminist Media Studies*, *16*(1), 171–174. https://doi.org/10.1080/14680777.2016.1120490

Bhana, D. (2012). Understanding and addressing homophobia in schools: A view from teachers. *South African Journal of Education.* *32*(3), 307–318. https://doi.org/10.15700/saje.v32n3a659

Brittan, A. (1989). *Masculinity and power*. Basil Blackwell.

Brod, H. (Ed.). (1987). *The making of masculinities: The new men's studies*. Routledge.

Brod, H., & Kaufman, M. (1994). *Theorizing masculinities*. Sage.

Collier, R. (1998). *Masculinities, crime and criminology: Men, heterosexuality and the criminal(ised) other*. Sage.

Connell, R. W. (1987). *Gender and power: Society, the person and sexual politics*. Stanford University Press.

Connell, R. W. (1995). *Masculinities*. Polity Press.

Connell, R. W. (2005). Globalization, imperialism, and masculinities. In M. S. Kimmel, J. Hearn & R. W. Connell (Eds.), *Handbook of studies on men& masculinities* (pp. 71–89). Sage.

Connell, R. W., & Messerschmidt, J. W. (2005). Hegemonic masculinity: Rethinking the concept. *Gender & Society, 19*(6), 829–859. https://doi.org/10.1177/0891243205278639

Corvo, K., & Golding, P. (2022). Toxic masculinity and patriarchy: Barriers to connecting biopsychosocial risk for male violence to policy and practice. *Partner Abuse, 13*(4), 420–434. https://doi.org/10.1891/PA-2022-0020

Donaldson, M. (1993). What is hegemonic masculinity? *Theory and Society, 22*, 643–657. https://doi.org/10.1007/BF00993540

Faludi, S. (1999). *Stiffed: The betrayal of the American man.* HarperCollins.

Friedan, B. (1963). *The feminine mystique.* Norton & Co.

Gross, D. (1990) Toxic masculinity and other male troubles - The gender rap. *The New Republic, 202*(16), 11–14.

Hearn, J. (2004). From hegemonic masculinity to the hegemony of men. *Feminist Theory, 5*(1), 49–72. https://doi.org/10.1177/1464700104040813

Holter, Ø. G. (2003). *Can men do it? Men and gender equality: The Nordic experience.* Nordic Council of Ministers.

Illing, S. (2023, August 7). The new crisis of masculinity: What's the matter with men – and how do we fix it? *Vox.* https://www.vox.com/the-gray-area/23813985/christine-emba-masculinity-the-gray-area

Kupers, T. A. (2005). Toxic masculinity as a barrier to mental health treatment in prison. *Journal of Clinical Psychology, 61*(6), 713–724. https://doi.org/10.1002/jclp.20105

Mahalik, J. R., Locke, B. D., Ludlow, L. H., Diemer, M. A., Scott, R. P. J., Gottfried, M., & Freitas, G. (2003). Development of the conformity to masculine norms inventory. *Psychology of Men & Masculinity, 4*(1), 3–25. https://doi.org/10.1037/1524-9220.4.1.3

Messner, M. A. (2000). Essentialist retreat: The mythopoetic men's movement and the Christian Promise Keepers. In *Politics of masculinities: Men in movements* (pp. 17–23). AltaMira Press.

Morrin, A. (2022, December 8). *What is toxic masculinity?* Verywell Mind. https://www.verywellmind.com/what-is-toxic-masculinity-5075107

Newsom, J. S., & Anthony, J. (2015). *The mask you live in.* Kanopy Streaming.

Oliffe, J. L., & Han, C. S. E. (2014). Beyond workers' compensation: Men's mental health in and out of work. *Am J Mens Health, 8*(1), 45–53. https://doi.org/10.1177/1557988313490786

O'Neil, J. M. (2015). *Men's gender role conflict: Psychological costs, consequences, and a agenda for change.* American Psychological Association.

Parent, M. C., Gobble, T. D., & Rochlen, A. (2019). Social media behavior, toxic masculinity, and depression. *Psychology of Men & Masculinities, 20*(3), 277–287. https://doi.org/10.1037/men0000156

Pollack, W. S. (1998). *Real boys: Rescuing our sons from the myths of boyhood.* Random House.

Reigeluth, C. S., & Addis, M. E. (2016). Adolescent boys' experiences with policing of masculinity: Forms, functions, and consequences. *Psychology of Men & Masculinity, 17*(1), 74–83. https://doi.org/10.1037/a0039342

Rotundi, L. (2020). *The issue of toxic masculinity.* [Graduate thesis, Libera Universita Internazionale degli studi sociali]. https://www.academia.edu/84020042/The_Issue_of_Toxic_Masculinity.

Rubin, J. (2022, March 7). The GOP: An unending display of toxic masculinity. *The Washington Post.* https://www.washingtonpost.com/opinions/2022/03/07/republicans-trump-toxic-masculinity/

Salam, M. (2019, January 22). What is toxic masculinity? The concept has been around for-ever. But suddenly, the term seems to be everywhere. *The New York Times*. https://www.nytimes.com/2019/01/22/us/toxic-masculinity.html

Salter, M. (2019, February 27). The problem with a fight against toxic masculinity. *The Atlantic*. https://www.theatlantic.com/health/archive/2019/02/toxic-masculinity-history/583411/

Weir, K. (2017). The men America left behind. *Monitor of Psychology, 48* (2), 34. https://www.apa.org/monitor/2017/02/men-left-behind

Whitaker, C. A. (1975). Psychotherapy of the absurd: With a special emphasis on psychotherapy of aggression. *Family Process. 14*, 1–16. https://doi.org/10.1111/j.1545-5300.1975.00001.x

Whitaker, C. A. (1976). The hindrance of theory in clinical work. In P. J. Guerin (Ed.), *Family therapy: Theory and practice* (154–164). Gardner Press.

Whitehead, S. M. (2002). *Men and masculinities: Key themes and new directions*. Polity Press.

# 2 Constructions of Toxic Masculinity

There are many areas of our societies that keep toxic masculinity alive, ways in which toxic masculinity is constructed. From politics to fraternities and their cultures, to devaluing mental health services for men (Mahalik et al., 2007), our societies have enforced and normalized cultures in a way which fosters harmful aspects of masculinity. Those ideals and beliefs spread into the minds of young men, making them toxic. More on this in the next chapter. For more areas of our society that might keep the ideals of harmful, toxic masculinity alive, see Appendix 1 where I have a conversation with ChatGPT.

From beliefs to social theories, to aspects of our societies, there are clear ways in which harmful aspects of masculinity have been allowed to live, to be dominant. This chapter reviews several of those areas, starting with gender itself.

## The Power of Gender

Michel Foucault speaks of power and gender, specifically in terms of how gender is constructed. There are things structurally placed in society that lead to the making of power. To simplify what elsewhere is a larger thought, power is something made by people, specifically the people who hold that power. Politics, news, social media, and even academics, all contribute to the dominate discourses of our times. Dominate discourses are defined by the way in which society speaks of certain topics, the language used to describe certain things, or specific words chosen to communicate an idea. For example, in the dominant discourse of gender; what language is used to describe a certain gender? How are women described? With what words are they being described? What language is used to describe men? What words are specifically used to communicate masculine? In our conversation, toxic is one of those words used to describe some masculine traits of men. The phrase "toxic masculinity," then, is an example of a dominate discourse of our time. Who is it, however, that has given rise to such discourse?

Foucault (1977) believed in grand narratives, or narratives that encapsulate a certain discourse. When it comes to masculinity, there is a story we tell ourselves when we encounter such a phrase, even a person. When we hear the phrase toxic, we automatically have a set of preconceived ideas as to what that phrase means, or what that person is. These grand narratives and discourses are kept alive by people

DOI: 10.4324/9781003464228-2

in power. Foucault, and other postmodernists, aim to challenge the process of keeping dominate discourses alive.

If we are going to change the narrative of toxicity, or harmful masculinity, we need to question the structures keeping such discourses alive. The longer we hold onto these narratives, the more we further the experiences of toxicity. The longer those experiences survive, the longer society suffers.

Michel Foucault also believed in biopolitics (1975), which refers to the regulation of societies through established norms and policies. When it comes to gender, societies tend to organize and manage masculinity to serve the bigger picture of patriarchy. Foucault believed in ways societies developed and maintained the idea of gender, which encouraged men to take on certain roles. This results in societies creating a gender hierarchy. Scholars like Judith Butler (1999) and Raewyn Connell (1995) further the idea of biopolitics by arguing how power is created through gender hierarchies, specifically through institutions that privilege groups like men over women. Because institutions give power to men, they are then encouraged to take on the traditional roles of protectors, providers, and other labors – or lack thereof – around the family.

## Double Bind

Because of the traditional expectations placed on men, and because of the efforts to change those narratives of gendered power, there are multiple messages being conveyed to men. A double bind is defined as a form, mainly confusing form of communication embedded in a secondary layer of communication, or meta communication. This means two contradictory messages on two different levels of communication, direct and abstract. For example: do ___, or I will punish you. In a relational context, punishment can take the form of refusing love, abandonment, judgment, or in our case of masculinity, shame; the shame resulting from not meeting the societal or cultural expectations of being masculine. That message is harsh enough.

The second, abstract level of messaging, then, would be something like this: do ___, but do it because you want to and because you know it's the right thing to do. What makes this a double bind is the fact that the person cannot escape the expectations placed on them. They must do something to (1) not be punished, and (2) because on a different level, they're "supposed" to. This can become even more confusing if the individual does not want to do whatever it is they are being asked to do. The result is a confused state of mind with strain on the relationships from which they received these messages.

There is also a third part to the double bind, one that overtly prevents the individual from escaping the double bind. For example:

"Don't be a sissy, be a man instead. Don't you want to be a man?"

*"Well, I thought you told me to be more sensitive?"*

"Shut up, don't talk back to me. That's exactly what I mean."

The double bind lies in the inescapable response to different messages. When one tries to clarify, protest, or even refuse, they are placed back in the bind by manipulation, shame, guilt, or sometimes violence.

Is it possible that men are living in a double bind in which the outcome is toxicity?

According to original family systems research where double bind was first conceptualized, the outcome of these family and relational communication patterns that presented as a double bind was schizophrenia (Baetson, 1976). Even though the research is quite dated, the theory of being lost in a double bind is still accepted among social scientists.

What does this mean for masculinity, though? The narrative of gender is changing, but the expectations still range widely. Men are sometimes expected to fulfill their traditional gender roles of provider, being physically strong, and domineering.

*At the same time, men are expected to be kind, sensitive, and gentle. But not too much. And as soon as you speak out against the confusion of expectations, you're being toxic. So, stop that, too.*

Perhaps the outcome of double-bound gendered expectations is toxicity. When men cannot gather their bearings when it comes to their gender expectations, they easily fall back to what is comfortable and familiar. Unfortunately, aspects of the patriarchy are all too familiar to most men, even young boys. This may be especially true if the expectations, the double bind, are coming from women. bell hooks (2004) believes how some feminist thought is only an effort to regain control for women, and sometimes to disempower men. That is neither feminism nor equality. If women, particularly women who attempt to regain power and at the same time disempower men, create this double bind for men, then we are only furthering the push toward toxicity. And if we are concerned about what is keeping masculinity alive, then we cannot ignore the double bind in which men live in today.

## Patriarchy

Another mechanism that keeps toxic masculine alive is the ideals and practices of patriarchy. At a systemic level, patriarchal values are seen in different areas of our societies – politics, religion, policy, and law. This comes with consequences. bell hooks (2004) argues how patriarchy is damaging to boys even at a very young age. She defines patriarchy as:

> a "political-social system that insists that males are inherently dominates, superior to everything and everyone deemed weak, especially females, and endowed with the right to dominate and rule over the weak and to maintain that dominance through various forms of psychological terrorism and violence.
>
> (p. 18)

She goes on to argue that boys and men in a sense absorb the values of patriarchy, the values that both overtly and covertly dominate over others (hooks, 2004):

> ...sexist ideology enables men to falsely interpret this disturbed behavior positively. As long as men are brainwashed to equate violent domination and

abuse of women with privilege, they will have no understanding of the damage done to themselves or to others.

(p. 18)

This becomes dangerous because of the seemingly unawareness boys and men have when they live a life within expectations of patriarchy. They become numb, callous, and emotionally still to the point of not realizing the damage done to themselves to get to a place of dominance, and to others of whom are victims.

> Patriarchy demands of men that they become and remain emotional cripples. Since it is a system that denies men the full access to the freedom of will, it is difficult for any man of any class to rebel against patriarchy, to be disloyal to the patriarchal parent, be that parent female of male.
>
> (hooks, 2004, p. 27.)

When boys grow up in a world where men are overtly dominate over women, be it pay gaps, physical strength, lifestyle seen through gender roles, or political decisions made by men that greatly impact women, and that domination is never challenged, the beliefs about the patriarchy become a part of their internal world. Once that internal world is solidified, it is difficult to change it. It turns into a filter by which they see the world. It also becomes a standard for which and through which they enter relationships later in life, be it romantic or platonic.

Patriarchy also runs the risk of boys internalizing their hatred toward women. If young boys are not allowed to show emotions, cry; if they are taught the only way to be a man is to be the example of the above patriarchy, then we risk boys believing that women are less than they are. Taken one step further, boys might learn to demean women, even the feminine aspects of themselves. Therefore, even at a young age, boys are taught to hate themselves, the feminine aspects of themselves, as well as the overt hatred toward women.

*What a sad existence it is to be a boy that cannot embrace their own internal parts of themselves, the parts that may be feminine or at the very least not "manly." And then to be overtly cruel or better than a woman. It's almost as if boys are living a life of hate – hate toward their own selves and hate toward women.*

### Negative Feedback Loop

Patriarchy, though, is systemic. There are certain aspects of societies, whether intentional or not, that feed into patriarchy, which keeps masculinity toxic. What are the things societies implement, convey, believe in, or support that allow masculinity to become and stay toxic?

We can point to different aspects of our world that promote malicious forms of masculinity: media, movies, sports that favor violence, and even forms of religion that marginalize women. Religion is particularly important since it furthers the belief in certain doctrines that promote a specific type of gender role – "wives, submit to your husbands." There are many things that keep harmful masculinities alive.

If we conceptualize these in terms of systems, we can begin to point to an answer of what keeps things surviving. Systems theory has been adopted by several different disciplines and fields of study. Of the ones I'm most familiar with is its sociological use. A common term associated with systems theory (and among other theories of communication) is feedback loops. Feedback loops are used within systems to govern internal and external information. If a system gets a faulty message, the system itself sends error messages that reject that information. For example, a vehicle. The vehicles we drive are considered a system that has many different parts to it, and those parts are in communication with each other. If our oil needs to be changed, there is a light that displays on our dashboard which sends the message to us. This signal tells us that the system is not in its normal state of operation – status quo. Therefore, something needs to be done to bring it back to its normal state of operation.

Now, let's turn to masculinity as an example. Our societies at large can be seen as one giant system with many different parts to it. Let us focus on the example of masculinity and conceptualize that as a system itself. There is a status quo of masculinity – macho, strong, aggressive, even sometimes violent, dominate, all the toxic traits we've discussed. When the system receives information, it does not accept it, it rejects it, just like the car turns on the oil light on the dash. But what is the information rejected by the system of masculinity? To put it simply: any other form of masculinity that is not the status quo.

The rejection of masculine information from the system of masculinity is done through error messages (see Figure 2.1). What is the metaphorical oil light of masculinity that tells us there is something wrong and the system is not operating at its optimal level? I think there are several ways societies reject marginalized forms of masculinity, keeping the dominant form of masculinity alive. For example, when young boys cry, they are commonly rejected and are told to "be a man, don't be a sissy." Or "only girls cry, are you a girl?"

The messages young boys hear that force them to hide their inner experiences, the experiences that don't fall in line with the accepted form of masculinity, are the system's error messages. When someone from the "masculinity system" sees a form of masculine not in line with how they are living, they reject it. It is the rejection itself that is the negative feedback loop.

When young boys see male figures being idolized, male figures like professional wrestlers or professional athletes who are violent in their careers, this image becomes internalized. And when they experience something else, other than the idolized version of the man they watch, they become conflicted. This, in addition to the messages they received about "be a man," is a strong negative feedback loop, one that keeps boys' internal selves operating in a way where dominating masculinity is kept alive.

### Freudian Slip

Derrida, often portrayed as a poststructuralist, frequently claimed how structures, either political, moral, or linguistic, determine the order in which binary opposites

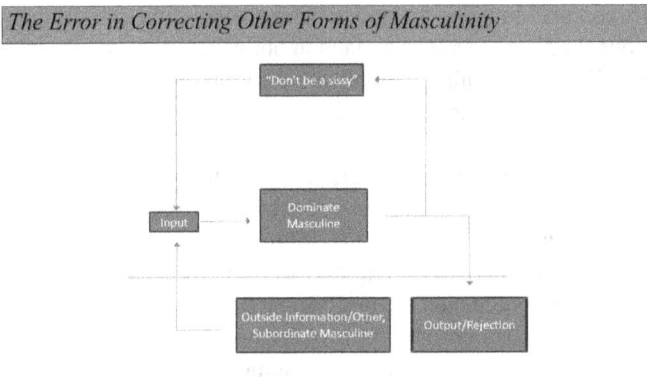

The Error in Correcting Other Forms of Masculinity

*Figure 2.1* The Error in Correcting Other Forms of Masculinity

exist (more on this in the next chapter). As a poststructuralist, he challenged the inherent structures that gave rise to power within binary opposites. For example, man/woman. There are structures in place that continue to make the space for "man" to commonly come before "woman." Be it the story of creation where in the book of Genesis God made Adam first, and then later made Eve from Adam, or the political landscape around gender neutrality and fluidity, there are structures that keep these narratives, or the order in which we place man/woman, living. And because the order of those is as such, we've come to treat both men and women in a specific way, organized by this very order of man/woman.

One of the ways we've come to treat men is through the expectations around emotions. It's been a common phenomenon for men to be emotionless – literally without emotion. If men become too angry, it is arguably harmful. If men cry, they're seen as weak. At the same time, men are expected to be sensitive, but not too much. The expectations placed on men are vast and can sometimes be confusing. It is not a social norm for men to be caring, soft, nurturing, or even to cry in public.

The famous psychoanalyst, Sigmund Freud, introduced a concept placed around expectations. Klein (1946) formulated Freud's concepts into what she called Projective Identification. This is where one person holds a certain regard toward someone else, usually negative in tone. In our case, someone who's toxic masculine. The person holding the regard toward someone who's toxic masculine will behave toward them to unconsciously communicate their negative regard. By way of their unconscious behavior, the toxic masculine person unconsciously responds with toxic behavior confirming the original person's negative regard toward the toxic male.

Therefore, if I believe you are an angry person, I will (unconsciously – everything with Freud is about the unconscious anyway) act toward you so that you will, as an outcome of my behavior and unconscious bias toward you, behave in that certain way. This may sound like placing the blame on the innocent bystander, the one holding the negative regard. After all, what fault do they have for unconsciously thinking a certain way about a certain person? But is arguably what society does. Do we not all have deep ways of thinking about someone, maybe even too deep to intentionally conjure? Imagine the power behind such a thought; a thought or belief about someone that is so deeply ingrained in our minds that we are not aware of it. And imagine the power behind the collective unconscious behavior we (innocent bystanders) display toward that certain person.

In this conversation, it is the man or men who we think (overtly or not) are toxic in their masculinity. Is it possible that toxic masculinity is a two-way street? The unconscious feelings toward toxic men and the non-explicit behaviors we exude to them, and then the inevitable response (fulfillment) of such behaviors?

If the dominate unconscious thought is for men to be without emotion (emotionless), then is it possible men are preforming that by following suit? Is the toxic masculine experience one brought on by a larger, collective expectation we have of men? So then, as soon as a man acts with some feelings, even negative feelings, they are shunned and criticized for being too angry, hostile, or any other word that describes extreme emotion. They then have no choice but to submit to their original emotionless state.

The same is true for the conversation of patriarchy. Patriarchal men believe certain things about women. As already noted, there is a certain "better than" belief when it comes to patriarchal standards. The unconsciousness of these beliefs is very dangerous to begin with. A lot of men do not know they are living with patriarchy in their belief systems. However, the unconscious behavior toward women is where Freud's concept becomes even more dangerous.

*If I expect something (usually negative) from you, I in turn, will act in a certain way toward you that will bring out certain expectations I have on you, in which you will fulfill those expectations.*

The patriarchy believes/expects women to be lesser than men; men in turn act a certain way toward women; those behaviors unconsciously bring out the behaviors in which women will fulfill those expectations. This is very, very dangerous.

It is easy enough to see how we (victims of toxic masculine) can unconsciously view toxic men and women. We have all read news stories about sexual aggression and hypermasculine attitudes of men in power. Therefore, our unconscious beliefs and behaviors toward men are somewhat easy to point out. However, the other side of that coin is somewhat challenging to see. If the patriarchy believes such things about women, and if men behave toward them based on their unconscious belief, how do women in turn unconsciously fulfill those expectations? Is it possible that some women will unconsciously fulfill the expectations of the patriarchy? This is not to say that women keep the patriarchy living. It is to point out the damaging effects unconscious beliefs have on individuals and their gender roles. I wonder how many women *believe* men are superior, and that they in fact are inferior?

Make no mistake, believing you are less than someone else is one of the most toxic traits we can harbor and spread through belief. Be it gender, race, class, or mental health, the toxicity lies in how our beliefs guide our lives to a place of destruction.

If Freud's and Klein's concept of Projective Identification is correct, then as long as we harbor negative sentiment toward toxic masculine, or just anyone in general, then our own beliefs keep these active.

## The Male Physique

For centuries, history has been fascinated by the male body. From ancient Greeks who made sculptures like The David to the modern sport of bodybuilding, the male body has always been something on display. The fascination, though, is arguably another societal factor that has promoted harmful aspects of masculinity. As we will see in the next chapter, the quality of being physically strong is a common response to a male quality. At the same time, it is also a positive aspect of being a male, when it is handled responsibly.

The act of being strong has also been a form of competition. When it comes to some sports like American football, or Rugby, being strong also represents an area of sport that is physically dominating, even violent. Although some might not argue American football to be violent, the physically aggressive aspect of the game is unmistakable. However, when men, and in some cases women, are driven to be stronger than someone else so they can be domineering on the field, the sense of "healthy competition" becomes somewhat blurred.

Being strong, having a strong physique, and looking a certain way are all forms of either deep insecurity or forms of being molded into a male-driven society. Being physically strong, when used as a form of intimidation, abuse, or superiority, becomes something more than only a physical trait; it is what makes masculinity toxic.

Once again, this becomes complicated because being physically strong, or the desire for an attractive physique is not gender specific. Even women can be strong; they play Rugby and American football. Both men and women can be physically strong and compete in bodybuilding contests. Strong is not harmful. It is, though, when both men and women use their physical strength in damaging ways, where it becomes toxic…even women can be toxic masculine.

When women bodybuilders work on their physique, they take supplements, frequent the gym, and become physically strong, are they aiming to "look like man?" When women want to grow their biceps to make them as big as possible, is that because they want to "look like a man?" The stereotype behind bodybuilding itself is an interesting gender study: is it that women want to look like men by being strong? Or is society's obsession with the male physique such a social construction that when women grow their biceps, we unfairly assume them to want to "look like a man."

If we are that deeply socially constructed to assume a woman wants to look like a man by bodybuilding, there is something infectious about how we are constructed to automatically think so. If it is that women *do* want to look like a man by bodybuilding, there is also something quite infectious about the obsession with the male body.

The media we surround ourselves with also has a part to play in not only the male physique but in feeding the harmful aspects of masculinity. Media, like film, advertising, and now social media, tends to perpetuate and glorify the male figure. At the same time by upholding the male figure, media has also created a culture in which the male physique also comes with certain attitudes toward women, objectification, sexism, and misogyny (Faber & Coutler, 2023).

Media that glorifies the male figure, along with dangerous traits that might come with it, creates unrealistic expectations for men and young boys. It is an expectation of exclusion, where one is either *that* kind of man, or they are not.

Even though media is changing, we still have hints of the "typical" male figure. For example, the TV comedy show Modern Family tries to blur the lines of the traditional male. Even though you have a patriarchal figure as a grandfather, Jay, who exemplifies the strong man who married a much younger beautiful woman, we also have a homosexual male couple who seem to have acceptance in the family. Regardless of the progressive efforts of media, it seems difficult to escape the examples of the traditional male figure.

## The Male Figure in Religion

Religion is also guilty of furthering a masculine narrative, in some cases, this male depiction can be harmful. This is not to place blame on any one set or form of religion. There are many different religions to consider, but there are some overarching similarities between religions that portray the male figure in a certain light. For example, most religions depict their god as male, a man, or something divine. Some religions also include an earthly figure, like Jesus or Muhammed, who are also said to be divine, sons of God. This narrative tends to uphold the idea and practice as man being superior to women, where men are "leaders" of their houses and families, and women are to be "submissive" to their leadership. Even though gender equality is changing throughout some religions, the image of a divine god, who is also shown to us as a male figure, still rings true for more people practicing their religion. When was the last time you saw an image of God who was a biological woman, with long hair, breasts, and crown on her head?

The belief and practice religions hold of choosing to humanize a god in a male form is not harmful. When people refer to God, they usually refer to their god as a "he." Assigning gender to a god has its own faults, but toxic masculinity is not one of them. If God were alive today, he/his/him would be forced upon its image. When our image of God, along with its divine characteristics, begin to influence the construction of men today, it can become problematic. When men use the excuse of religion, their faith traditions, or their "sanctity" in their gender because of Adam and Eve, then it becomes problematic. *Justifying dangerous masculine traits like power and dominance in the name of religion is at its core toxic.*

As we will see in the next chapter, Derrida (1977) refers to the Garden of Eden, where God created Adam and Eve in "his" image. According to the Old Testament, God created Adam first. And from his rib, God created Eve. This creation story has implications for deconstruction and for how toxic masculinity still lives. At the same time, the order in which God created Adam and Eve, and then Eve later tempted by the serpent, paints them both in a specific light. Adam, being created first, and being used to make a woman from his own flesh, can arguably be constructed to be the superior gender. Eve's creation story also constructs women in an unfavorable way; Eve was literally created second, she was the one who was tempted by the serpent, and she was the one who "tricked" Adam to eat of the fruit. The way we conceptualize, and there to internalize the hierarchy of gender, is commonly done by way of the story of creation. Both men and women are guilty of believing such narrative, such hierarchy. The belief system of gender (the hierarchy of gender where Adam comes before Eve) found in religion creates a group of people who uphold that certain value, where they strategize and demonstrate their beliefs. This tends to create a social group, a hegemonic group, that seeks to dominate others. This is all too common in religions and denominations, especially where one religion thinks they are the only one going to heaven. And therefore, everyone else is literally left out. *These beliefs, like a poison, infect and infiltrate people's lives. Not only that, but it also tries to get others to believe in it, too.*

Again, the creation story by itself is not inherently bad when it comes to gender. The story is quite fascinating and entertaining. It is when men use the story to justify and solidify gender roles where it becomes toxic. This is especially true for the construction of women; when a woman is "secondary" to man because God made them "for a man," and when women are "weak" because the serpent so easily tempted Eve.

When religions and other faith-oriented institutions use their traditions, bible stories, and own rules to promote masculinity, and then justify their harmful uses of masculinity by their own faith traditions, the outcome furthers dangerous forms of masculine and oppresses women. When religions spread harmful ideals, teach them, and when young men and women believe them, it becomes toxic, infiltrating their belief system. Religion has the potential to poison minds with distorted beliefs of gender.

*Religion, then, is one example of how social institutions create not only hegemony but toxic hegemony. It is particularly toxic in that the belief of the hierarchy of gender, where one is subordinate to the other, plays out in the way the institution functions, and in their indoctrination of those who follow those beliefs. It is found in the masculinity that is homophobic, that does not support gender equality, and that believes men are superior because of a creation story.*

Religion is hegemonic in that the institution itself creates a group of people, both men and women, that adhere to its values. It is also hegemonic in the beliefs and practices it upholds. And the beliefs that most religions hold tend to favor men, furthering the toxic narrative of masculinity. When beliefs turn into a way of thinking that victimizes others, and when values turn someone into believing that another person is subordinate to them, it becomes toxic.

Hegemony can easily and quickly give way to toxic. There are some forms of hegemony that are toxic, like patriarchy. Even though they are different, there is a sense in which they can overlap and become toxic hegemony. What makes masculinity toxic is the way in which society systematically upholds the most extreme versions of men and praises them for it. Oppression is an all too common outcome of the systems that make masculinity toxic.

**Family**

A large part of our belief systems, such as they are, can be traced back to our families. Whether we keep our families' beliefs, traditions, faiths, or lifestyles, or not, the paths we choose to take are set, either directly or indirectly, by our families. Whether we like it or not, I am of the mind that owes a lot of credit to the power of family beliefs.

Beliefs are passed down from generation to generation. These beliefs can be about anything: money, faith, divorce, alcohol, but closer to our conversation, masculinity. What is means to be a man and how a man ought to be is first leaned in our families. Yes, we receive other influences when we gain friends and consume media. But the very first instance of a learned gender, or masculinity, is from our parents and families.

A prominent and early family theorist, Murray Bowen, called the process of beliefs being passed down from generation-to-generation *multigenerational trans-mission*[1] (Kerr & Bowen, 1988). A part of this theory contends how each generation will further their beliefs (or values, faith, lifestyles, or money habits) by espousing them, solidifying the beliefs a little bit more by each generation. For example, the family who keeps their father's first and last name. In the second generation the son is a junior, the next generation a third, and so on. The same can be said for masculinity. If one generation keeps the belief alive that men are supposed to be *macho*, and all the things that come with maschismo, then the next generation will solidify it a little bit more. And if the next generation doesn't change those beliefs, it will become solidified a little bit more, and so on.

Let's specifically use the idea of toxic masculinity. For example, we have a family in which both gender roles of a man and a woman are led by toxic masculinity, where the man is domineering, maybe even violent, verbally abusive, and treats his wife as less than him in front of his children. Yes, this is an extreme example, but it's only an example. Let's also assume the father raises his children in the same gendered beliefs they live in; men are hard, aggressive, and women are to be looked down on. If the son grows up in this belief and ideals and does not change them, then he will more than likely solidify those a little bit more than the previous generation. Therefore, the son might be a little bit more aggressive, domineering, misogynist, sexist, or any other harmful masculine trait than his father. And if he has children, and doesn't change those gendered beliefs while raising children, then his boys are at risk of solidifying those ideals even more than him. You see where this goes.

Kerr and Bowen (1988) refer to this as a continuum of functioning, where each generation functions a little bit better or a little bit worse than the previous one. If we're asking what keeps toxic masculinity alive, what keeps it as a popular "belief" in which people live by, then this family theory helps us with an answer. If take this portion of Kerr and Bowen's family theory, where generations trend in functioning and apply this to larger societies, we need to ask the question about generational societal functioning. In what way do societies trend in their functioning, or, in what direction to societies trend in functioning?

To mention toxic masculinity, we need to theorize about the way in which destructive masculinity has trended in the previous generations within societies.[2] If we think about the amount of violence over the past 100 years, Steven Pinker (2022) argues how these rates have gone down, along with rates of burglary, rape, and other violent crimes. If that's the case, why is toxic masculinity still such a dominate topic of conversation to describe men?

To reference violent crimes is to also associate toxic masculinity with violence, as is commonly done. At the same time, violence is only one trait frequently associated with toxic masculinity. There are others beyond violent crimes: domineering, verbal aggression, and the overall mindset of seeing others as inferior, especially women, because they are not as "strong" as a man is.

As we will see in the next chapter, toxic masculinity is not only about "things" men do, but also about the way in which these "things" are spread, and how the larger part of societies adopt these traits. Therefore, if we're asking the question of societal generational trending, we don't necessarily have to ask questions about crimes and violence, we need to ask questions about the overall mindset of masculinity, and how people believe in these harmful traits. This is more difficult to determine as compared to crime rates. Even though they might have been on the decline over the past 100 years, the decline does not speak to how we view masculinity, and how we adopt these toxic traits in men; more importantly, how acceptable these traits are. Therefore, the question we need to be asking as far as societal trends go is: how has the acceptance of harmful masculine traits trended in the last 100 years? I use 100 years only as a generic timeline for reference.

Again, this is difficult to determine. Acceptance, or lack of acceptance, does not mean the norm. For example, in the 1950s where the nuclear family consisted of more stereotypical gender norms: the husband worked, the wife stayed home and cooked, and she raised the kids. There may have been some dangerous, masculine beliefs during this time in American history, like the belief that women were not "able" to work, or they weren't strong enough to work like a man, planting the gender inequality seed in society. Even though this was the "norm," it does not show acceptance – maybe women hated being stay-at-home moms and not being able to work. Or maybe they loved it.

Which is why we have had movements like the feminist movement and women's rights movements. At some point, women were tired of being treated as unequal, and they fought back. The movements showed the overall mindset toward the harmful aspects of masculinity: the degrading, the inequality, and the overall belief of being superior to women. Which also gave rise to the men's rights movement. Even though it's not called this, in the 1970s and 1980s, there was a small battle over whose rights were more important. Again, this shows the overall attitude and mindset behind masculinity. After women started the feminist movement, men responded, or reacted, with the men's movement, trying to protect their masculinity. Some scholars even refer to the men's rights movement as overt misogyny (Dragiewicz, 2011).

Even though women's movements like Women's rights and the feminist movement were a step in the right direction in terms of equality, and therefore the overall effort to diminish male dominance over women, harmful aspects of masculinity have still survived. For example, if we fast forward to today, men are still paid more than women, still are physically assaulting them, and the overall mindset of being superior to women is still active, maybe even thriving. We see this in examples like Harvey Weinstein and Sean Combs, who use their status and power to assault women.

Returning to the generational trend of society, I believe Western societies, specifically the United States, have trended in the wrong direction. Even though there have been efforts to reclaim gender equality, specifically with the Millennial and Gen Z generations, we have been on a downward trend for some time now. One generation may make progress, but the undoing of the decades before is a big task. Hence a book like this, and a conversation to deconstruct the harmful aspects of masculinity that have plagued our societies for generations.

**Critical Race Theory**

Critical race theory has received a lot of attention in the past few decades. There has even been a backlash in certain western universities where professors are not allowed to teach the theory. It has been banned from classrooms and has been used to further some policy. In 2021, the state of Texas signed a bill that permitted critical race theory to be discussed in public classrooms. In 2020, President Trump banned federal employees from training that discusses critical race theory or white privilege. For our purposes, there are some components of critical race theory that speak to toxic masculinity and privilege. Both can be examples of how toxic masculinity is fed in our societies. Even though not directly tied to toxic masculinity, critical race theory does offer certain areas that keep harmful aspects of masculinity alive.

Critical race theory as a social theory focuses on issues and components of race, ethnicity, policy, and other social aspects like media and religion. Because there are several areas to the theory, most scholars see an interaction among them, making a systemic web of parts that make up one's experiences. In particular, critical race theory believes issues of racism and prejudice are intermixed and systemically derived from the working parts of these different components (Christian et al., 2019).

A way of conceptualizing the different components of critical race theory is also known as intersectionality, which is one of its key tenets. Intersectionality is the different social mechanisms that form inequality by the interconnections of race, gender, class, and disability (Gillborn, 2015). For example, the experience of a middle-aged, middle-class, black woman will be different from that of a middle-aged, upper-class, white male. Because one experiences certain components of society differently (race, gender, class), they tend to experience forms of racism and prejudice. Critical race theory focuses on each one of these components of an individual's experience. Also seen as a feminist approach, intersectionality describes the experience of women in relationship to men. Since women have traditionally experienced race, class, and gender as areas of oppression, it is men's social components that have "intersectionally" benefited them (Crenshaw, 1991). These axes (race, gender, class) in men's experiences have given rise to the harmful traits of masculinity. These traits become toxic when they manifest themselves into intersecting areas to make a man's experiences.

For example, let's use one harmful masculine trait: superiority. At one point, it was more common for the white man to be "superior" to others, which arguably dates to slavery. In such cases, race and class may have separated men in how they were superior to other men and women. It's safer to say how today, race and class do not necessarily separate men who may harbor a sense of superiority (even though to some it might). But because one is a man, regardless of class or race, a sense of superiority may still exist in them because of how the trait has infiltrated the male narrative.

From a feminist perspective, intersectionality tells us how different components of one's social world can lead to oppression. However, the same is true for the other side of that equation, where multiple axes (gender, race, class) can lead to harmfulness. At one point, only one axis may have been the culprit for harmful masculinities.

*Toxicity exists when harmful traits are normalized across multiple axes of intersectionality.*

According to our definitions of toxic from the previous chapter, there is an amount of infestation, harmfulness, or unhealthiness which makes something toxic. The fact that harmful masculine traits seem to know no boundaries and overtake all intersecting aspects that make the masculine narrative is a central component to feminist thought, and what leads to toxic masculinity.

What is important to our conversation is the specific intersectional component of gender. Critical race theory believes how race is largely a social construction and not a biological inherited trait. Even though there are some physical differences to everyone's appearance, the way in which society has been structured around these physical differences furthers how different people are treated unfairly. *When people in power create laws for a structured society, and when those in power all look the same, they create a system of oppression and a lack of tolerance toward people who are different from the majority.* This includes gender.

The masculine side of gender has been molded into a common form, and therefore the expectation of how a man ought to be. The intersectionality of a young, black, transgender man is going to create a different experience for a straight, middle-aged, white man. The fact that one inherently has "power" over the other is where toxicity lies. In one sense, one of these men may (or may not) know their privileged state. The other man knows (or doesn't) that they lack the same privilege. It is when the man with the "power" happens to fit into the mold of harmful masculine traits (aggression, violence, domineering, hypermasculine), and when those traits are inflicted on others, especially onto the man with the less privileged position, where toxicity comes to life.

Gender, and the differences they carry, is an outcome of the socially constructed system of society we have today. Western society has created a large difference between men and women. For a long time, in the United States, women were not allowed to vote, hold a checking account, or use a credit card without their husband's permission. And, as is well known, for a long time in America's history, Black men and women were owned by White families, where the "head of the house" was a White man. The structure of the White man, the man who "owns," is still a part of our society, be it a business, a CEO, or someone else important and in charge. The systems that existed in times of American slavery are not far removed from our society today. No, we do not own other people as slaves, but the mindset, the hierarchy, and the power of the White man has not changed much, if at all, since then.

What is the "White man," then?

## Epistemic Bubble

The question poses a lot of difficulty, as well as potential harmful biases that could easily offend. The purpose of the question is not to raise racist, homophobic, or superiority blaming. The purpose of this question is to challenge what we think we know of the metaphorical and literal image of the white man, the metaphor that is arguably at the center of critical race theory, slavery, sexism, and some of the characteristics of harmful masculinity. The metaphor for the white man is more than one person; it's a way of thought, it's a belief, and it's a system of labels, traditions, attitudes, rhetoric, narratives, and people who have espoused such beliefs. And the more people who espouse it, the more solidified the image becomes.

This is not a critique of one race, this is a deeply philosophical intertwining of peoples who have lived in a way where their beliefs have been skewed without ever recognizing it. Our lack of questioning the beliefs and truths that surround us has devolved into being stuck in an epistemic state. I use the phrase epistemic because of its implications on belief and knowledge. What we know to be true, and what we think truth is and where it comes from, is at the core of epistemology – the study of knowledge. How we know what we know about privilege and masculinity is a deep question we ought to be asking ourselves.

Epistemology asks what knowledge is, how we gain knowledge, and what it is we think we know; how we know what we know (Perez, 2021; Steup & Neta, 2024; Greco, 2017). The knowledge we carry, or the knowledge we think we come to carry, is rarely reflected on. How is it that we know what blue is? How do we know an apple is an apple? To get to our conversation, how is it we know what masculine is? Where does the definition of masculine come from? Who made the definition of masculine? How did that image become so universally accepted?

This is interesting because today's masculine is not the same as 17th-century masculine, or before that. At one point, during the 18th century, Napolean Bonaparte wore tights, red slippers with heals to make himself taller. Some men during the French revolution even wore wigs. Napolean himself was also not a tall man, standing at 5 feet 6 inches. Today, masculine looks different, where men stand over 6 feet tall and show off their strong physiques.

The way we gather knowledge is important to privilege and masculinity. The social aspect of epistemology (more on social construction and privilege next) creates what Nguyen (2020) calls epistemic bubbles:

> An epistemic bubble is a social epistemic structure in which some relevant voices have been excluded through omission. Epistemic bubbles can form

with no ill intent, through ordinary processes of social selection and community formation. We seek to stay in touch with our friends, who also tend to have similar political views. But when we also use those same social networks as sources of news, then we impose ourselves a narrowed and self-reinforcing epistemic filter, which leaves out contrary views and illegitimately inflates our epistemic self-confidence.

(p. 2)

An epistemic bubble is different from an echo chamber. In an echo chamber, someone chooses to distrust those outside their chamber, actively distrusting the source of information (Jamieson & Cappella, 2008). We see both instances play out, particularly in politics today. The extremes of the right and the left have become so polarized because of one's intention behind excluding the other's point of view, beliefs, or overall stance. There is an overt effort to not believe the opposing's view – echo chamber – choosing to stay within their political thought.

An epistemic bubble, though, is not intentional, as in the case of purposefully rejecting information we disagree with. Epistemic bubbles happen when we surround ourselves with and filter our information based off things around us: Facebook, our personal friends, what we read, and our overall social media algorithm. We keep coming back to the same sources of information, creating a knowledge bubble around us. There is some intention behind the creation of our bubble, but it is different than overtly rejecting other sources of knowledge.

*What is dangerous about an epistemic bubble is how they tend to influence what we think is real, "true," and factual.*

Epistemic bubbles tend to offer us inadequate coverage of information through a process of exclusion by omission (Nguyen, 2020, p. 5). Be it our algorithms or our choice of friends, there is a process of leaving out other relevant sources of information through "selective exposure" (Nelson & Webster, 2017), meaning we select what we surround ourselves with, and therefore things are decided for us through our social filters.

If we think about our definition of the white man, the definition itself can largely be a result of our epistemic bubble. The sources of information we surround ourselves with, the people we choose to be with, and even the links we click on in our social media apps, they will all portray the image of the white man in a certain way. Through privilege, class, or elitism, the people and things we surround ourselves with will offer us an epistemic picture of the white man, and therefore privilege, racism, sexism, and the components of critical race theory.

I live in Texas where critical race theory is not allowed to be taught in major public universities. If I were "a part of the system," the choice to teach critical race theory would be decided for me, therefore making my selection of knowledge for me, my epistemic bubble.

The same is especially true for masculinity. If we surround ourselves with the right people, our picture of what masculine is will be offered to us as epistemic knowledge; the "ideal" picture of masculine. If I surround myself with people who believe in the non-binary view of gender, or other postmodern thinkers, then my knowledge of masculine will be different than if I were to surround myself with people who don't believe in critical race theory.

What is especially dangerous about epistemic bubbles is how they can also feed toxic masculinity, even enhance it. Being constantly exposed to harmful masculine traits, so much so it becomes our knowledge of what masculine is, is breeding grounds for spreading such ideals. The spread of harmful masculine traits, with the amplification of an epistemic bubble, is one of the most toxic things to live in.

### Online Epistemic Bubble

For example, Cody Turner (2023) explains the process of being immersed in an online epistemic bubble, where one's interaction with their online environment runs the risk of lowering their cultivation of open-mindedness. This can exist on a small and large scale. Individually, we can be swept up in our social media, spending hours on our devices. As noted above, this creates an epistemic bubble around us, keeping our own ideas and beliefs in a continuous loop. Sites like Facebook and X are excellent at providing this for us, filtering our ads while we choose our friends, who are like us.

On a larger scale, this online epistemic bubble is arguably manufactured for us as well. The algorithmic effect of digital creators forming a theory of who we are, what we will search next, and what keep us scrolling is a filter that is made for us, a filter that purposely feeds our social media to create our epistemic bubble (Pariser, 2011). Turner (2023) also argues how epistemic bubbles, and echo chambers, have the potential to create cult-like indoctrination, where the members of the cult (or the epistemic bubble) become intellectually isolated from the rest of the world. Elzinga (2022) goes even further to say these sorts of echo chambers and epistemic bubbles create a sense of trust and distrust within the communities – trust of the information shared within the bubble, and distrust of things outside the echo chamber.

The danger in this, as it pertains to masculinity, is the potential continuous exposure to harmful masculine traits, and the trust and distrust of each. Being so engrossed in our online environment can lead us to believe and trust sources promoting harmful traits of masculinity, and therefore distrusting other forms that may be healthy. For example, filling our online environment with people like Andrew Tate, or Jordan Peterson, our knowledge (epistemology) of masculine is going to start looking a certain way, and we will then start behaving in that certain way. We will begin to trust their example or projection of masculinity and distrusting other men who could be a different form of masculine.

The scary part of online epistemic bubbles is the larger scale of it; this is a worldwide phenomenon. All over the world, there are men and women who are living within their epistemic bubbles, being fed information that might be supporting harmful traits of masculinity. This is toxic because of the spread that happens within each bubble, by way of how each bubble is manufactured. *Our algorithms are created because of us, and more are created outside our bubbles because of people like us. Imagine how many people are constantly being fed images and messages of harmful masculinity. In this case, epistemic bubbles do not allow us to choose for ourselves the type of masculine we want to live. By creating our own*

*bubble of masculine information, we are limiting our view and therefore choice in*
*masculine, robbing us of our ability to make an open-minded decision.*

Online epistemic bubbles are also how privilege is kept privileged. This is done in a few ways. First, epistemic bubbles have the power to normalize privilege itself. These bubbles can potentially make it difficult for someone inside to critically see their place of social status, or to see someone else's status (or lack thereof) outside their bubble.

Second, issues of oppression are commonly not seen withing epistemic bubbles. For example, issues of racism, sexism, or inequality between genders; those inside the bubble are not faced with the realities of inequality, leaving their place of privilege unchallenged. This relates to Miranda Fricker's (2018) concept of hermeneutical injustice, meaning marginalized groups lack the means and platforms to voice their injustice, furthering privilege. When it comes to those who have bad experiences with toxic masculinity, epistemic bubbles have the potential to keep the dominate ideas of masculine in a place of privilege, and those who have been harmed by it marginalized. The online platform itself is arguably the means and resources that those who are marginalized lack.

Similarly, epistemic bubbles also can exclude alternative perspectives, not only marginalized voices, which by default reinforces certain stereotypes of privilege. The information found inside an epistemic bubble naturally causes a narrow worldview, often biased. When our social media becomes flooded with images of lower-income people of color, they are painted in a certain light. Because of this, the stereotypes of classes, on both sides of the bubble, become reinforced. This again becomes especially true when it comes to masculinity. The stereotypes on both sides of an epistemic bubble become reinforced by the bubble itself, and therefore silencing any external voice outside the bubble. The effect of this keeps marginalized forms of masculinity marginalized, and privileged forms of masculinity privileged, infecting our societies.

Turner (2023) points to the lack of open-mindedness within epistemic bubbles, where the phenomenon of the bubble itself reduces our intake of other information, driving us to not confide in outside sources. I will take it one step further; I will call it ignorance. *It is ignorance created by privilege, created by an epistemic bubble, where those in privilege remain unchallenged in their dominance. The result keeps the status quo and furthers any sort of gap between those in the bubble and those out of it.*

Ignorance, with the help of epistemic bubbles, may be a key component in toxic masculinity. This is the sort of ignorance that has gone unchallenged, and at the same time not allowing other resources to other marginalized forms of masculine. The masculine staying in the dominant position, the one which tends to be harmful, is the one living inside the largest epistemic bubble. Because both men and women are living in that bubble, they can avoid confronting their own roles in perpetuating the toxicity of masculinity, with no pressure to self-reflect or have empathy for those outside the bubble.

## Toxic Tribalism

Like epistemic bubbles, toxic tribalism refers to the group mindset behind the beliefs holding that group together. One of the dangers of toxic masculinity is the in-group/out-group functioning supporting the group. Tribalism usually involves an "us vs. them" mentality, which tends to create polarization between groups. It's "my tribe," against "them."

Along with the polarization, a result of tribalism (toxic) is the demonization of other groups. This is more than mere opposition; this is a mindset of superiority over the other groups. This is what Michale Morris (2024) calls tribalism toxicity, when it creates a sense of justification in someone's attitudes that can demean someone else in the out-group. This can even go as far as creating hate and disgust within the in-group toward the out-group.

If we think about toxic masculine examples like homophobia, this sort of tribalism is very evident. We can name other toxic masculine phenomena: politics, patriarchy, and religion. They all can possess a certain amount of tribalism, and they all have the potential to demonize those in the out-group, creating a sense of disgust toward those not involved in the "right" political party, religion, or masculinity. This disgust can also lead to emotional manipulation, creating anger to motivate people to act in the way the in-group thinks they ought to, and to join in the negative sentiment against those in the out-group, "if you're not with us, then you're with them."

*Tribalism becomes toxic when the in-group tries to indoctrinate others who are not a part of the group, when they try to "baptize" them into believing what they believe in.*

Toxic tribalism also creates its own echo chamber. The tribe intentionally creates its own way of filtering out information and beliefs that don't conform to their own, intentionally rejecting outside information and dismissing it as "false." Furthering the belief of "false" knowledge creates the epistemic dynamic to the group: "this is what we believe in, this is what's true."

When it comes to toxic masculinity, this is especially dangerous. Tribes tend to create their own truth about what masculine is and isn't, and they try to indoctrinate others into joining their tribe. This is done with similar toxic tactics of instilling anger and hatred toward the other group. Unfortunately, the hatred toward other groups tends to be things like homophobia and superiority over women.

The group aspect of belief, when it comes to not only masculinity, but anything, is a key component of how harmful masculinity spreads. The spread of knowledge and how we begin to believe what is "true" is one of the roots of toxic masculinity.

## Socially Constructed

This leads us to the idea of our knowledge being socially constructed. Like epistemic bubbles, there is a social process by which we acquire knowledge. The way we acquire knowledge of masculinity is just as important as any other knowledge we gather.

Social constructionism was given rise to the field of sociology. Perter L. Berger and T. Luckmann (1966) wrote one of the first works titled *The Social Construction of Reality*. What social constructionism then highlighted was the social nature of knowledge. In more recent decades, social constructionism has grown to other social sciences, including therapy and qualitative research (Perez, 2021). Other social constructions scholars include Kenneth Gergen (1985, 1994), John Shotter (1993, 1994), and Rom Harré (1986) to name a few. Consider the following definition put forth by Kenneth Gergen (1985): social constructionist inquiry is the process by which people come to describe, explain, or:

> otherwise account for the world (including themselves) in which they live… What we take to be experiences of the world does not itself dictate the terms by which the world is understood. What we take to be knowledge of the world is not a product of induction, or of the building and testing of general hypotheses… The terms in which the world is understood are the social artifacts, products of historically situated *interchanges among people.*
>
> (pp. 226–227)

Given Gergen's definition, the relational aspect of knowledge is key to understanding the social nature of knowledge. The meaning of language and the special attention we give certain aspects of our lives, the way "problems" are descried, and what we deem as important to each respective process and area of our lives, are all the result of relationships in which interactions and dialogue occur. Knowledge, then, in whichever form it may come, requires interaction for it to be knowledge (Perez, 2021). When it comes to what we know about masculinity, including the toxic aspect of it, are all the results and outcomes of interactions we've had through multiple relationships; be it our family, friends, social media, or any other source of information we consume.

The interesting part about social constructionism, which is seldom mentioned, is the interactions between what is constructed and how it is accepted. On the one hand, social constructionists believe in objective truth that is subjectively experienced by numbers: if enough people believe in on thing, it is their objective truth. If the masses believe in Jesus Christ, then the truth of the story of Jesus becomes that much more real. Truth, according to the social constructionist, can grow if enough people support or accept the truth collectively believed in.

The White man, then, has been socially constructed, and he has been for decades. For those decades, more and more people, both men and women, have been "feeding" into the belief of the White man. From slave owners to the "nuclear" family, to the Men's Rights movement, to politicians who are for the large part White men, men have been socially constructed to have power. Even today, men (again, for the most part White men) make decisions over a woman's body in Western America. This leaks into the gender of men as well.

Because the White man has been constructed to have power over men and women, this has tended to be generalized to men overall. Which presents the danger of using the phrase to being with – toxic masculinity. This tends to tie into the physicality of a man; being stronger than women, taller, more dominating, and sometimes physically violent. These traits have all been constructed to exemplify masculinity. And for the large part, these traits are supported by, or "fed into" by both men and women – both tend to believe in the physical strength of the man to determine his masculinity. These physical traits also tend to be tied to the harmful characteristics of a man and masculinity.

It is these traits which have been believed in, and because they have been associated with men, specifically the White man, they have also been associated with harm. According to this school of thought, social phenomena, including the White man, are:

> largely constructed through social means: symbols, language, relationships, socially available understandings of reality and what those realities mean… social information is the process through which we give meaning to our realities. This process of social information is only made through interaction. What our lives mean to us, what we perceive as truth, our knowledge, they all exist and are made through interactions.
>
> (Perez, 2021 p. 26)

Social interactions, or social information, supports said beliefs. The way men and women interact with each other, the way they believe men are "superior" and women are "subordinate," keeps the construction of the White man, the man having power and privilege over other men and women. In the same regard, social construction keeps alive the harmful aspects of the power dynamic.

This becomes more complicated when the socially constructed White man's norms further racial and gender oppressions. This is also how toxic masculinity is kept alive, how it becomes toxic: when there are enough people who believe in the narrative norms of the White man (or any man of power and privilege), which vicariously promotes the spread of such beliefs and supports such behaviors.

*Through politics, policy, or simply relationship norms where men are dominate over women and other men, when we promote these behaviors, we socially construct toxic masculinity.*

Westen society is structured in a way that keeps men in power, more specifically, White men. That narrative is slowly changing; there are more women in positions of power, the pay gap is slowly closing (we still have a way to go, however), and we have elected officials of minority status. The majority, though, still lies in White men. The expectations held by people in power, specifically expectations that further oppression based on race or gender, are also what keep masculinity toxic.

## Constructed Hegemony

Gender is socially constructed. The assumptions, expectations, and stereotypes each gender holds are arguably something constructed; we've learned along the way how to "do" our gender. For men, we've been constructed to be strong and tough, not show emotions (in fact, not showing emotions is strong), to be providers, "man of the house," domineering, and even violent.

These expectations are constructed. At some point, the consensus for what being a man is and does was accepted by the majority. Therefore, the traits and characteristics of a man that can potentially be harmful, like bullying, even withholding emotion, have all been constructed and accepted by the majority. The sullen hero, the stoic, the strong warrior. They are all portrayed as stereotypes, and most often the expectation. The social aspect of expectations needs to be considered when studying gender; the evolution, or devolution, of gender happens because of majority/minority consensus.

There are several gender theories that explain the evolution, performance, and social construction of gender, specifically masculinity. One theory, mentioned before, is a systematic way of looking at gender presented by Connell (1987). His work on *Gender and Power* is one of the most cited works on hegemonic masculinity, and there too, femininity. Even though not a direct social constructionist argument, Connell presents how gender and power are both socially constructed.

Gender is related to power, and therefore the social construction of power. The way masculine and feminine even exist is based on the structural phenomenon of gender; that structure being the dominance of men over women (Connell, 1987). Although dated in his theory, the sentiment of the assumption still holds true today: there is a global structure that caters to the subordination of women and the interests of men. Connell refers to this as "emphasized femininity" (p. 183). There is a social construction happening within this interchange and exchange of masculine/ feminine relationship. The fact that gender, according to his social theory, is in some form of subordination to the other, and the fact that there are several societies that comply with it, makes gendered power that much more constructed.

*When people interact in a way that furthers gendered power, the social interaction itself is the core of social construction.*

The entire concept behind Hegemonic Masculinity is also a social construction. The term itself, hegemony, according to Connell (1987) is the "social ascendency achieved in a play of social forces that extends beyond the contests of brute power into the organization of a private life and cultural process" (p. 184). There is a clear social aspect of this ascendancy. Be it religion, media, policy, class, or the workforce which emphasizes gendered pay gaps, the social component of masculine dominate is clear, and the global structures that uphold this today, either willingly or not, make the power of gender socially constructed – specifically the masculine gender.

This is different from domineering. If gender power is to be achieved by force, it would not be considered hegemonic, nor would it be considered socially constructed. For information to be socially constructed, there is a requirement for social interaction. Information is given, information is received, and then it becomes internalized truth. For men to be the dominate gender, there needs to be other genders, even marginalized masculinities, that interact with the power of masculine, hence emphasized femininity. Femininity is emphasized as one of the structured supports for upholding a dominating form of masculine.

Just like hegemonic masculinity is a social construction, so too is emphasized femininity. Hegemonic masculinity prevents other forms of masculinity from becoming the ascendant form of masculinity. The same is true for other forms of femininity, even those that try to break from the role of being "emphasized." Even though some other forms of masculinity and femininity exist, the construction behind hegemonic and emphasized is a global phenomenon.

*Masculine*

The idea of masculine, then, is also arguably socially constructed. The physical characteristics, the expectation of being strong, sullen, and "macho" are all acceptable and accepted by the large part of our society, both men and women. The way in which Western America glorifies American football for example, encourages physical violence in men and young boys. "The stronger you are, the better you are at football" is a common narrative, which upholds certain aspects of masculinity. The obsession with guns, the gender tradition of bodybuilding,[3] and the way in which we expect boys not to cry are all ways we socially uphold the expectations of what it is to be masculine.

Even more so, we expect specific biological sexes to live within the boundaries of the masculine construction. Both men and women are expected to stay within their lanes of gender, masculine and feminine. When genders blur, so do the terms for which we refer to each individual in that role. For example, if two women are in a homosexual relationship, one is usually going to be the masculine one, and the other the feminine. The same is true with two men being in a homosexual relationship.

*Not only is the idea of what masculine a social construction, but the expectation of who is also constructed.*

## Implicit Bias

Where social constructionism tells us how we come to form knowledge and truth, and therefore how we come to view masculinity and how it's socially constructed, implicit bias describes this process in a slightly more intimate, individualized way. Implicit bias explains our unconscious attitudes, beliefs, and stereotypes playing into our everyday lives, influencing our decisions and behaviors toward other people, events, and beliefs. Implicit bias gives us a closer look at toxic masculinity and how harmful behaviors are accepted and even spread throughout and between groups.

When it comes to gender, its social construction is hard to ignore. If we think about this on a deeper level, the way we react to gender is hardwired in us, so much so that we sometimes don't know it. Greenwald and Banaji (1995), in one of the key works done on implicit bias in gender, explain gender-based biases. How we treat all genders, when it comes to aspects like aggression, attraction, height, even what individuals are named, are all socially constructed, but how we respond to these socially constructed aspects of gender is implicitly biased.

One of the biggest limits to social constructionism is the outcome of bias. This is not a limit in the sense of it being a shortcoming or something we cannot achieve. This is an internal, psychological limit. Because gender is so strongly constructed, how we respond to gender is also so strongly and automatically rooted in us. When describing something like toxic masculinity, the social construction of it is unmistakable, and the way we respond to it is just as much so.

How do you respond to toxic masculinity? How do you "view" it? What are your stereotypes toward toxic masculinity?

A study conducted by Rudman and Glick (1999) showed implicit gender bias in job hiring between men and women. What was fascinating about this study was the bias toward masculine traits when being hired for a job. The bias comes in when expecting job applicants to possess a certain number of agentic traits, like competition and a sense of dominant strength. This bias was the same for both men and women. When women showed up to job interviews with too much agentic traits, they weren't hirable. At the same time, the study showed how women were expected to display some agentic, masculine traits. This, in a way, puts women in a lose-lose situation when it comes to "competing" with men to for work. Therefore, when women deviate from their normalized gender roles, they need to (to a certain extent) do so to be competitive in the job markets.

Men, though, when being hired for a job, have the same expectations placed on them. They were expected to show a certain number of masculine traits as well. However, when men didn't show them enough, they were discriminated against. The study also showed how men who didn't show the right amount of agent traits tended to be better suited for feminized jobs, jobs showing more feminine characteristics in their job descriptions. The same was true for their women counterparts.

The implicit bias found here shows us how we view and treat men and women who carry masculine characteristics, and those who don't. If women show too much masculinity, it goes against the grain of our implicit bias toward them, "women shouldn't be that masculine." But they are expected to have only a certain amount, just enough to where it doesn't hurt them. In the context of being hired for a job, women can't intimidate their male employers, or else they're discriminated again.

For men, if they show fewer masculine traits than they "ought" to show, they're also discriminated against. The implicit bias in how we see men runs deep, where if a man shows less than what's expected of him in terms of masculinity, he's also marginalized.

If we go back to Connell's (2005) work, his idea on hegemonic masculinity speaks to implicit bias. Hegemonic masculinity itself shows us the very fact of how biases are reinforced through toxic masculinity, elevating and upholding certain traits that intentionally suppress others. For example, strength and aggression. The very definition of hegemony is dominance, especially in group settings. These hegemonic traits have long been held as expectations for men. Because these traits are so expected, other areas of masculinity like gentleness and emotional awareness and expression are shunned (Kimmel, 2008). Therefore, bias works in two ways: first, to expect strength, aggression, and violence as a part of masculinity, and second, treating other things like emotionality as something not masculine. The scary part of these biases is how deep they run not only in men and women (and that's scary enough) but collectively as a society.

Phrases like "boys will be boys, are another deep implicit bias when it comes to toxic masculinity. This phrase puts the expectation of identity on young boys, excusing them to act a certain way, aligning them with the violent and aggression stereotypes. When the phrase is used, there is unconscious pressure put on boys to act that way and to give them a free pass for it. If we remember our Freudian concept of protective identification, we tend to project our unconscious ways of thinking about people onto them, and those whom we project onto tend to follow suite. If we believe the phrase "boys will be boys," and if we treat boys just as such, and if the Freudian concepts hold any merit, then boys will follow suit. Given how boys tend to grow up with these expectations placed on them, and how much they grow up showing forms of violence and aggressions, it's safe to say the identity projected onto them does play out in the way Freud imagined.

**Belief and Trust**

Yuval Noah Harari (2014) in his monumental work, Sapiens: A Brief History of Humankind, presents idea theory that supports the construction of gender. Even though he may not call his theory a social constructionism, his historical overview of how humanity has created and come to use money and currency is like our construction of gender. Harari argues how money is a "universal medium of exchange that enables people to convert almost anything into almost anything else" (p. 185). Without money, societies wouldn't be societies. Because of how people and cities have grown, the exchanging of money for recourses has become critical to survival.

However, as Harari believes, money has no inherent worth. A paper dollar is merely a paper dollar. Even then, in today's markets, most money exists behind a computer, a digital measure of how much money one has. Paper money and coins are also becoming slowly obsolete, where we don't see in front of us the money we have; it's not tangible.

Money, then, is a psychological construct. It's something believed in, something the masses have all agreed on. *When speaking of social constructionism, and the lack of objectivity because one's own social means of information, when enough people believe in one thing it becomes more and more objective by degrees.* Money is one good example of a social construction becoming objective truth. People who don't pay their taxes are considered criminals by the federal government, and if you don't "pay your bills," you get chased by a bill's collector. Our entire system of class is based off how well you manage your money; credit scores reflect this. If you don't have good credit, then you are not good with your money, the very thing which is made up in our society that everyone believes in.

Intrinsically, money does not have real value. The green paper dollar used in the United States of America, with the value of $5 or $100, does not mean anything unless the meaning which it's given is agreed upon. Therefore, since we all believe a green piece of paper that reads $20 is equal to 20 dollars of currency, and that 20 dollars can allow me to purchase certain things. The value of money is also socially constructed.

Something interesting Harari points out about the psychological construct of money is how the masses trust in it. "Money is accordingly a system of mutual trust, and not just any system of mutual trust: money is the most universal and more efficient system of mutual trust ever devised" (p. 186). Everyone, literally, agrees on, believes in, and trusts the money system.

The same is true for gender. If money is the most efficient system of trust ever created, I would argue that gender is a close second.

Just like money, we have made our entire world based off gender: how we look, how we dress, how we behave, and those are "supposed" to be whether you're a man or a woman. At one point in time, everyone agreed on what it was to be a man and a woman, gender was more binary than it is now. Things were tabooer at one point, where men would visit brothels to be with either other men or women who didn't fit the societal mold of being a woman.

Just like money has no inherent value, *how* we do our gender has no tie to any mold of gender or biological sex. But just like everyone believes money is worth something, everyone also believes a man ought to be a certain way. If you don't behave in the "right" way, you're considered odd, an outcast, just as if you weren't good with money and were chased by a bill's collector.

At some point in time, societies have placed some form of trust in gender. This trust means we base our expectations on a person based off how they look. If someone looks like a cis gender man, then I expect and trust they would act accordingly. We've misplaced our gender expectations for so long, societies are not keeping up with the changing evolution of the open mindedness of gender. When we do so, we set up people to fail according to society's misplaced expectations, leaving those who don't fit the binary mold of gender on the margins of gender acceptance. This, too, is how masculine becomes toxic.

What if "toxic" like money, is also constructed? The term itself, toxic masculinity, is a fairly recent term only a few decades old. Its use has been somewhat mixed between secular journalism and academic writings. However, even in the mix of its usages, there is still a consensus of what it describes. Toxic masculine, in all the existing literature, rarely describes an all-encompassing person, or a man. It is only a description of certain characteristics.

*I believe we are seeing toxic masculinity being socially constructed in today's world; the box it puts men in, and the expectations it misplaces on men, it's a way we're constructing men to be, which isn't fair.*

## Privilege

There are two components of privilege pertaining to our conversation: privilege of those kept in power, and the privilege to label something as toxic.

For those who are kept in power, privilege becomes an outcome of social construction. The language and rhetoric used to describe those in power is a means to construct power itself. "President," "leader," and more recently, "old white man," all keep the narrative of power alive. When the masses continue to adopt that language, the truth of the construction becomes more and more solidified.

Race is socially constructed. The hierarchies of race within society, and the intersectionality of race, class, and gender are also all socially constructed. Some races are constructed to have more power and authority over other races, which is a crucial part of racism according to critical race theory. Which also results in the privilege found in the race being socially upheld and constructed to have power.

At the same time, I recognize the privilege in simply being able to write about toxic masculinity, critical race theory, and privilege itself. *It is a privilege to write about privilege.* The fact that I have the means and resources; the fact that I come from an academic background where I can study masculinity, critical race theory, and privilege; and the fact that I can analyze patterns, behaviors, and society at large, these are all privileges I carry.

Am I of a privileged race? According to most literature and history, no. Hispanics, Latines, or Mexican Americans are not traditionally privileged. However, being an educated male, my intersectionality does bring about mixed messages of privilege, and there too the way I conceptualize masculinity. The fact that so many other people can learn about the phrase toxic masculinity, and because it has been in popular culture, speaks to how much of a privileged term it has become.

The danger of conceptualizing toxic masculinity in terms of privilege is the fact that it furthers the divide between those who are privileged and those who are not. "I, in my ivory tower of academia, can study and point out how other people are toxic. Therefore, I can rightfully try to change the narrative, from my place of power." My antidote to this is deconstruction; it approaches the conversation differently because we intentionally do not have a negative bias in deconstructing. If we do, then we miss the point. And by deconstructing, we intentionally leave ourselves open to the possibilities of the exploration found in the process.

Privilege is also a section of intersectionality, one of which has been directly associated with oppression. Feminist scholars have argued how privilege, specifically male privilege, has kept men in power, and as a result, women in a place of oppression. This can be tied back to toxicity since male power has tended to include traits such as violence, superiority, abuse, and other forms of inequality like pay gaps and career opportunities.

Even though the idea of male power is not organically "toxic," it is one of the social components of intersectionality that can give way to toxic behaviors; it has the potential to give space to harmful, masculine traits. The amount of discernment and wisdom, or lack thereof, gone into power is frightening. Feminist movements have attempted to dismantle the quality and quantity of power that has created inequality between genders. There is still a long way to go.

### Memo # 2 On Critical Race Theory

What if there is a connection between Critical Race Theory, hegemonic masculinity, and therefore toxic masculinity?

If CRT tells us that power, structure, and society at large are all made through the lens of race, primarily White, and the biases in all of that…then can the same be said about gender? The vast majority of laws, for example, most are overwhelmingly made by white men (I'm thinking specifically about Western America). It's only in 2024 that the Western Country of Mexico elected a women president. And these laws, made by men, also determine the lives and rights of women.

Take abortion. It's been very recent that Rowe v. Wade was overturned, making it very difficult for women to have an abortion in the United States. And guess who is making these laws in states that make it difficult…men.

So, CRT might be telling us that there is racial bias in the structures of our socie-ties. But the ones behind those structures for the large part are men. What if CRT is also a theory of gender?

This gives way to hegemonic masculinity; a masculinity that is dominating, controlling, and even radicalized by its dominance. We see this in our laws, politi-cal landscape, and positions of power. We see it in religions whose positions of authority are given to men. When was the last time, we saw a woman pope? I think it's safe to say: the bias in structure, in power, and in our societal landscape lends itself toward men.

We can talk about wage gaps, women's rights (who were allowed to vote way after men, and even later in Mexico), even research in car buying that says men are more likely to get a "good deal" than a woman is. We can also talk about parent-ing, where assumptions are made toward parental figures, sometimes (maybe most times) the lesser assumption is made toward the woman, the "homemaker," the nurturer, or the one who "stays home with the kids."

Yes, some women choose that. It's exactly this choice that makes masculinity hegemonic. If it works for some, then great, more "power" to you. But if we have people filling and living both roles of dominate and non-dominate (subordinate if you want to call it that), then we will always have the bias toward both. Hence, hegemonic.

This starts to lend itself to toxic, in my opinion. CRT, which focuses solely on the bias of race, and hegemonic, which focuses solely on the bias of gender, create a landscape that very easily makes it possible for masculinity to become toxic. Give someone power and it has the possibility to make them jerks. Give someone power with the sway of bias in their favor and the potential to be destructive emerges. And you don't need another role filled to be that, like you do to be hegemonic. There is not systemic reciprocity in toxic like there is in hegemony.

Taken to the next area of thought; CRT gives way to hegemony; hegemony makes toxic possible.

CRT-Hegemony-Toxic

## Notes

1 For more on generational functioning, see Appendix 6.
2 This is not meant to be an exhaustive or historical overview of masculinity. For a broader view of masculinities, see Ivan Jablonka's *A History of Masculinity: From Patriarchy to Gender Justice,* or, Stefan Dudink's *The Trouble with Men: Problems in the History of 'Masculinity.,'* or, R. W. Connel's *Masculinities,* or Michael Kimmel's *Manhood in America, A Culture History,* and *Gyland: The Perilous World Where Boys Become Men.* What this chapter aims to do is only to theorize about phenomena keeping masculinity alive, and how we have trended in the wrong direction when it comes to masculinity.
3 Even though women are becoming much more active in this sport, the tradition of body-building has typically been inhabited by men. And to this day, the women that do par-ticipate in the sport are not as extreme as men. Men still dominate the sport in their size and strength.

## References

Baetson, G. (1976). *Steps to an ecology of mind: A revolutionary approach to man's understanding of himself.* Ballantine Books.

Berger, P. L., & Luckmann, T. (1966). *The social construction of reality: a treatise in the sociology of knowledge.* [1st ed.] Doubleday.

Butler, J. (199). *Gender trouble: Feminism and the subversion of identity* (10th anniversary ed.). Routledge.

Christian, M., Seamster, L., & Ray, V. (2019). New directions in critical race theory and sociology: Racism, white supremacy, and resistance. *American Behavioral Scientist, 63*(13), 1731–1740. https://doi.org/10.1177/0002764219842623

Connell, R. W. (1987). *Gender and power: Society, the person and sexual politics.* Stanford University Press.

Connell, R. W. (1995). *Masculinities.* Polity Press.

Connell, R. W. (2005). Globalization, imperialism, and masculinities. In M. S. Kimmel, J. Hearn & R. W. Connell (Eds.), *Handbook of studies on men& masculinities* (71–89). Sage.

Crenshaw, K. (1991). Mapping the margins: Intersectionality, identity politics, and violence against women of color. *Stanford Law Review, 43*(6), 1241–1299. https://doi.org/10.2307/1229039

Derrida, J. (1977). Structure, sign, and play in the discourse of the human sciences. In R. Macksey & E. Donato (Eds.), *The structuralist controversy: The languages of criticism and the sciences of man* (pp. 247–272). Johns Hopkins University Press. (Original work presented 1966)

Dragiewicz, M. (2011). *Equality with a vengeance: Men's rights groups, battered women, and antifeminist backlash.* Northeaster University Press.

Elzinga, B. (2022) Echo chambers and audio signal processing. *Episteme 19*(3), 373–393. https://doi.org/10.1017/epi.2020.33

Faber, T., & Coulter, N. (2023). "Let's go make some videos!": Post-Feminist digital media on tween-coms. *Television & New Media, 24*(7), 825–841. https://doi.org/10.1177/15274764221150162

Foucault, M. (1977). *Discipline and punish: The birth of the prison* (A. Sheridan, Trans.). Pantheon Books. (Original work published 1975)

Fricker, M. (2018). Epistemic injustice and recognition theory: A new conversation—afterword. *Feminist Philosophy Quarterly, 4*(4), 1–5. https://doi.org/10.5206/fpq/2018.4.6235

Gergen, K. J. (1985). The social constructionist movement in modern psychology. *American Psychologist, 40*(3), 266–275. https://doi.org/10.1037/0003-066X.40.3.266

Gergen, K. J. (1994). Exploring the postmodern: Perils or potentials? *American Psychologist, 49*(5), 412–416. https://doi.org/10.1037/0003-066X.49.5.412

Gillborn, D. (2015). Intersectionality, critical race theory, and the primacy of racism: Race, class, gender, and disability in education. *Qualitative Inquiry, 21*(3), 277–287. https://doi.org/10.1177/1077800414557827

Greco, J. (2017). Introduction: What is epistemology? In J. Greco & E. Sosa (Eds.), *The Blackwell guide to epistemology* (pp. 1–24). Wiley Online Library.

Greenwald, A. G., & Banaji, M. R. (1995). Implicit social cognition: Attitudes, self-esteem, and stereotypes. *Psychological Review, 102*(1), 4–27. https://doi.org/10.1037/0033-295X.102.1.4

Harari, Y. N. (2014). *Sapiens: A brief history of humankind.* Harper.

Harré, R. (1986) *The social construction of emotions*. Blackwell

hooks, b. (2004). *The will to change: Men, masculinity, and love*. Washington Square Press.

Jamieson, K. H., & Cappella, J. N. (2008). *Echo chamber: Rush Limbaugh and the conservative media establishment*. Oxford University Press.

Kerr, M., and Bowen, M. (1988). *Family Evaluation: An Approach Based on Bowen Theory*. Norton.

Kimmel, M. (2008). *Guyland: The perilous world where boys become men*. HarperCollins.

Klein, M. (1946). Notes on some schizoid mechanisms. *The International Journal of Psychoanalysis, 27*, 99–110. https://pmc.ncbi.nlm.nih.gov/articles/PMC3330415/#_pon93_

Mahalik, J. R., Burns, S. M., & Syzdek, M. (2007). Masculinity and perceived normative health behaviors as predictors of men's health behaviors. *Social Science & Medicine, 64*(11), 2201–2209. https://doi.org/10.1016/j.socscimed.2007.02.035

Morris, M. (2024). *Tribal: How the cultural instincts that divide us can help bring us together*. Thesis.

Nelson, J. L., & Webster, J. G. (2017). The myth of partisan selective exposure: A portrait of the online political news audience. *Social Media + Society, 3*(3), 1–34. https://doi.org/10.1177/2056305117729314

Nguyen, C. T. (2020). *Echo chambers and epistemic bubbles. Episteme, 17*(2), 141–161. https://doi.org/10.1017/epi.2018.32

Pariser, E. (2011). *The filter bubble: What the internet is hiding from you*. Penguin Press.

Perez, C. (2021). *Integrating postmodern therapy and qualitative research: Guiding theory and practice*. Routledge.

Rudman, L. A., & Glick, P. (1999). Feminized management and backlash toward agentic women: The hidden costs to women of a kinder, gentler image of middle managers. *Journal of Personality and Social Psychology, 77*(5), 1004–1010. https://doi.org/10.1037/0022-3514.77.5.1004

Shotter, J. (1993). *Cultural politics of everyday life: Social constructionism, rhetoric and knowing of the third kind*. University of Toronto Press.

Shotter, J. (1994). *Conversational realities: Constructing life through language*. Sage.

Steup, M., & Neta, R. (2024). Epistemology. In E. N. Zalta & U. Nodelman (Eds.), *The stanford encyclopedia of philosophy* (Winter 2024 Edition). Stanford University. Retrieved from https://plato.stanford.edu/entries/epistemology/

Turner, C. (2023). Online echo chambers, online epistemic bubbles, and open-mindedness. *Episteme, 21*, 1–26. https://doi.org/10.1017/epi.2023.52

# 3  Deconstructing Toxic Masculinity

Secular uses of the term deconstruction have caused the term, and therefore the philosophical practice, to lose its original meaning. There is even some scholarship that misuses the term to communicate critical thought, examination, or even to "tear down" to rebuild. Even though by definition this is what the term may imply, it's not the original intent as proposed by Derrida. Here, we will go back to the inception of deconstruction, offer a brief history of its practice, and present how this timeless philosophy can aid our understanding of toxic masculinity. To say deconstruction is critical thought is only one part of the equation. To say it's "rebuilding" something anew is to go two rings outside the bullseye. To use it to describe modern home decor, clothes, or even automobiles is to miss the original intent entirely.

To deconstruct toxic masculinity, we need to deconstruct several things. Toxic masculinity involves masculinity, femininity, gender, toxicity, and then toxic masculinity. It becomes even more complicated when we assign specific genders to masculinity and therefore toxic masculinity. All of which we will define here.

### Masculine and Gender

Before we enter the deconstruction process, we need to establish what we are deconstructing, of which toxic masculinity presents an interesting challenge. It is not sufficient to deconstruct toxic masculinity, there are other deconstructions within this phrase necessary to our process. We must first start with masculinity. This is difficult because we also need to venture into the gender conversation – just like toxic masculinity, when it comes to masculinity, both women and men can be masculine according to societal norms. Once we deconstruct masculinity,[1] we can venture into the process of deconstructing toxic, and then the combination of toxic masculine.

To deconstruct a phenomenon like toxic masculinity, we first need to clarify (or at the very least have some groundwork from which we can build on) the conversation around gender, as this is also a part of the larger topic at hand. Masculinity does not necessarily have to include only men, and by default exclude all women. The fluidity of masculinity is a key component in deconstructing its potential toxicities. Yes, the biological male is traditionally seen as masculine. But that line has been

DOI: 10.4324/9781003464228-3

blurred in recent decades; female bodybuilding, transgender males and females, and even the feminist movement have supported all biological sexes, adhering to all identities and possibilities of gender.

There is a difference between sex and gender. Sex refers to the biological makeup of being male and female, chromosomes, genitalia, and sex character-istics. Gender refers to the psychological, social, and cultural experiences one has surrounding their life as either sex (APA, 2018). Each sex comes with its own assumptions and expectations, social norms, and stereotypes (Thompson & Pleck, 1995). When it comes to the gender of being a man, there are specific expectations and assumptions one inherits. Some of those expectations include being masculine.

What does it mean to be masculine, though? What does it look like? Who owns what masculine looks like and who can wear it? More importantly, who is to decide what masculine is and who can be masculine? These are not easy questions to answer because I believe they will never be answered in full. There will always be an evolution and blurred lines of gender, especially when it comes to the biologi-cal ownership of masculine. However, we do have general definitions which will provide us with a starting point.

The Merriam-Webster Dictionary defines masculine as: marked or having quali-ties, features, etc. traditionally associated with men. According to Levant and Rich-mond (2007), masculinity ideology, or the principles of being a man, are sets of descriptions and prescriptions of what being a man entails. There have been many different masculine ideologies and beliefs, but there are common factors between these beliefs that hold true for most theorists. These common ideologies include anti-femininity, achievement (particularly those that display physical strength), not appearing to be weak, high risk, and violence. These characteristics are known as traditional masculinity ideologies (Levant & Richmond, 2007).

There are several traditional, and stereotypical features associated with mas-culinity: tall, muscular, strong, facial hair, or a deep burly voice. Men tend to be associated with sports, such as American football, basketball, golf, and American soccer. Sports populated by men also tend to be more aggressively driven; the stronger you are, the harder you hit, the better you are at the sport. Even though the women's equivalent exists for most sports, save American football, the pairing with physical strength is held in high esteem, even preferred.

Aside from literature and dictionaries, this project also sought the voice of indi-viduals, both men and women, on what masculinity is. When surveying the ques-tion, "What is your definition of masculinity," this is what a few participants had to share:

— *Associated with traits such as severity, pride, and toughness.*
— *Physical and behavioral attributes socially associated with men.*
— *Self-disciplined, brave, confident, good leader, takes charge, focused, physically fit.*
— *In my opinion, it's everything that is traditionally characterized as masculine. For example, through social behavior, physical traits or qualities generally attributed to men such as strength or protection.*

- *I think of masculinity as a set of traits that are ascribed to men or masculine presenting people. In a patriarchal society like ours these traits are not only associated with men, but it's socially expected for men to demonstrate some of these traits, such as being very confident, being dominant, being chivalrous, being powerful, and suppressing emotions that aren't tied to anger.*
- *The essence of being a man.*
- *Physically strong, engages in hobbies and sports traditionally associated with men (e.g., hunting, fishing, combat sports).*

One of the more common responses to this question, according to participant surveys, tends to lead to both physical characteristics of being physically strong. Some answers refer to the qualities of masculine, like being a leader and a provider. More on these answers in Chapter 4 where these are further analyzed.

Gender, though, is a little less straightforward. The Oxford Language dictionary defines gender as such: the male sex or the female sex, especially when considered with reference to social and cultural differences rather than biological ones, or one of a range of other identities that do not correspond to established ideas of male and female; the fact or condition of belonging to or identifying as having a particular gender.

There is a strong social, cultural, and individual component to gender. What gives this another dimension of complexity is the fact that gender tends to be seen on a spectrum: there is no "one" gender, but an array of choices one chooses to live in. Call it gender choice, non-binary, or fluidity, we cannot put gender into a binary for the sake of deconstructing, and for the sake of those choosing to live as gender fluid.

One of the stronger arguments about the fluidity of gender, and the fact that gender is not as straightforward as it has been argued to be, is how gender is performative. Judith Butler (1988) supports the philosophy that frames gender in terms of acts, where gender is communicated through behaviors or performances. It is because of and through these performances that different genders can be interpreted:

Further, gender is instituted through the stylization of the body and, hence, must be under – stood as the mundane way in which bodily gestures, movements, and enactments of various kinds constitute the illusion of an abiding gendered self. This formulation moves the conception of gender off the ground of a substantial model of identity to one that requires a conception of a constituted social temporality. Significantly, if gender is instituted through acts which are internally discontinuous, then the appearance of substance is precisely that, a constructed identity, a performative accomplishment which the mundane social audience, including the actors themselves, come to believe and to perform in the mode of belief. If the ground of gender identity is the stylized repetition of acts through time, and not a seemingly seamless identity, then the possibilities of gender transformation are to be found in the arbitrary relation between such acts, in the possibility of a different sort of repeating, in the breaking or subversive repetition of that style.

(pp. 520–521)

The more we act in a certain way, the more we begin to believe that about our-selves, about the way in which we are acting. For example, if a young boy flexes in the mirror to show his muscles, and if that act or behavior is continuously repeated, then his relationship to that aspect of the gender's performance will be more and more believed. In this example, we will call that aspect of gender masculine since physical strength is commonly associated with masculinity.

The same can be said for a young woman who repeatedly plays with dolls (I'm using the traditional stereotype only to make a point). The more she continuously behaves in that way, the stronger and more solidified her belief will be in relation to that aspect of gender – feminine.

Of course, gender is not biologically limited. In either one of these examples, we can flip the person behind them and still make the same argument: the more a young boy plays with dolls, the stronger his belief will be in that aspect of feminin-ity. And the more the young girl flexes her muscles in the mirror, the stronger her relationship will be to that belief of masculine.

Butler helps us further prove our thesis regarding the gender behind toxic mas-culine: both men and women can be considered toxic masculine.

### Structuralism/Poststructuralism and Gender

There are two movements that need review before we enter the conversation of deconstruction. First, structuralism, which its critiques later gave way to decon-struction. Led by Lacan (Corvez, 1971), structuralism believes in the objectivity of language, where language is the means to several realities: identity, subjective thought, the self, and self-consciousness. Since we can speak things, and put things into language, we can therefore speak things into existence; subjects don't exist without language. We also come to define things through language, we put defini-tions on words themselves, therefore making a word have meaning.

For example, to our current conversation: gender. We have the language to place attributes as male and female, we have words for each and their respective roles and experiences – what it means to be a man or a woman. But there is an inherent problem with this philosophy. *If we reduce one's experience to words, we also limit the possibilities of their experience.* If we place certain language on what it means to be a man, we also leave out any other possibility of being a man that might not exist in that set of language and words that describe what it is to be a man.

Structuralism, and so too certain structuralist thinkers, believed in the objectiv-ity of language. But poststructuralism believed and argued for the possibilities that lie beyond language. This was a new way of conceptualizing language altogether. Many today still believe deconstructionism to be a part of poststructuralism, but Derrida would disagree with that – more on this in what follows. Poststructural-ism made efforts to not view language as objective, but to describe things beyond language, all while using language to still conceptualize what might lie beyond it. This was where many believed poststructuralism to have its limits. How can we describe things that lie beyond language if we need to use language to do so?

Many post-structuralists believed in the realities of oppositions, where we come to know things by placing them in their relationship to their counter-opposites. I know I am alive because I am not dead. I know I am not dead because I am alive. I know I am a man because I am not a woman; this, too, comes with language used to describe each place of the opposites. The language we choose in these binary oppositions, and the language to describe what is beyond an objective reality (with the help of language), is where Derrida and deconstruction comes in.

## Binary Oppositions

Deconstruction offers us a certain strategy. This strategy begins with, helps us engage with, and makes sense of the tension we have in binary oppositions. Therefore, we must first define and identify key binary oppositions in deconstruction. According to other major philosophers like Nietzsche, Hegel, and Aristotle, the fundamental aspect of metaphysics is the belief in binary oppositions. It's difficult to imagine a world without binary oppositions. We naturally use binary language everyday: either this or that, exercise or not, go to bed early or late, follow our new year's resolution to the end or not. It's rare when we use language that encapsulates any sort of in between. For example: gender. It's only recently (the last 20 years or so) that the option to be more than one gender has gained mainstream attention. Before this new wave of identity, one was either a male or female – binary. Anything between those two options created some form of dysphoria, gender dissociation, or even disorder. But again, this still creates a binary; either one was in the "normal" binary of male/female, or you were not, therefore disordered. This opposition created, and still to this day, a very common binary of normal versus not normal (disorder).

But the rise of poststructuralism and, there too postmodernism, gave way to challenging conventional norms, even gendered norms. Postmodernism asked: What if there was more than one way of gaining knowledge outside the scientific method? What if there is no such thing as Truth, but that which one creates and experiences instead? As it relates to gender: what if there was more than just the male/female experience of gender? What if gender was a continuum? This challenge supported(s) the non-binary gendered experience, which is still met by some opposition in most places of western societies.

However, with the evolution of gender identities, and the option to identify as non-binary, we still create an opposition; you are either binary (male/female) or non-binary (binary versus non-binary, which still creates a binary). It's difficult to escape the world of binaries, which makes deconstruction more important to our conversation. According to Derrida (1997) and deconstructionism, with binary opposites comes inherent power. By deconstructing toxic masculinity, we have several important binary opposites to consider: the opposite of toxic masculine, masculine, and toxic. Each set of opposites comes with their own inherent power.

### *Positions of Power*

The order in which we place binary opposites is a key factor in determining the deconstruction strategy. In everyday language, we tend to place the order of opposites in positions of power. For example: good/bad, right/wrong, and healthy/unhealthy. We tend to give a more positive sentiment to the first term in binary order. This has traditionally been true for the male/female binary. As a western society still relatively young in its feminist beliefs, the order in which we place Males ahead in binary has created a hierarchy of genders. By way of the nature of opposites, and the way in which we've traditionally placed the order of male/female, the position and gender of male have historically been given more dominance.

What has resulted from such dominance has spilled over into the experience of men and women. Because western societies have placed the dominance on the male gender, by nature of the binary, the gender of women has suffered, been oppressed, been subjugated, and has been treated as the "lesser" gender. Other feminist scholars have contributed so the development of women oppression and their gender (Beauvoir, 1951; hooks, 1981; Davis, 1981; Butler, 1990).

A primary strategy in deconstruction is to recognize the power binary opposites place on that which they are comparing. When considering toxic masculinity, there are a few binary opposites we can consider. What is the binary opposite of toxic? Masculinity? Toxic masculinity? We must also consider the gender spectrum, not only the opposite of masculine, but the opposite of man and gender altogether. The feminine portion of the opposite of masculine is crucial in the deconstruction process. This becomes more than a simple one set of opposition. Let's review these.

### Gender[2]

Of the terms to be defined, gender might be the most challenging because of its wide-ranging definitions. Even though there are "simple" definitions to gender, there are other implications to its lived experience. For example, the Oxford Language dictionary defines gender as:

> the male sex or the female sex, especially when considered with reference to social and cultural differences rather than biological ones, or one of a range of other identities that do not correspond to established ideas of male and female.

Simple in terms; it's quite quick to conceptualize gender as a social and cultural difference, and how biological make up refers to our sex. However, since gender does not necessarily correspond to our biological sex, the possibilities of gender become a moving target, which makes deconstruction that much more challenging. On the one hand, the opposite of male is female, and the binary opposite of female is male. Easy enough. That is only one binary aspect of gender. What about gender overall?

As mentioned before, the binary opposite of a binary gender is a non-binary gender, where gender is a spectrum. However, that still leaves us with a gendered binary: gender binary versus gender non-binary. The opposite of gender overall, not including any aspect of male/female, but encompassing all possibilities, is much more difficult to comprehend.

What is the binary opposite of gender (a gender that is all inclusive and non-inclusive at the same time)? Non-gender? *Can there be such a thing as no such thing as gender?* If so, then the binary opposite of gender would be non-gender, without gender, genderless. Let us entertain such a thought.

If there is such a thing as genderless,[3] then we cannot derive a binary opposite, we end up right back to the original binary; the binary opposite of genderless, then, would be gender. That brings us back to the binary/non-binary dilemma. In addition to the genderless option, the overarching and expanding view of gender limits the possibility of any sort of opposite. For the sake of not ending up with endless options of gender, we would need to narrow the definition back down to binary versus non-binary. What helps us deconstruct gender, or at the very least conceptualize it in a deconstructing way, is both the social construction of gender and the expectations cultures have placed on gender. In our case, this refers to the conversation of masculine.

We can more easily study the performance of gender (Butler, 1990), or the social and cultural norms of gender (Simons et al., 1979) to understand the binary opposites of certain aspects of gender. For example, if being feminine means X, then the opposite of X must mean masculine.

### Masculine

The Oxford English Dictionary defines masculinity as: the state or fact of being masculine; the assemblage of qualities regarded as characteristic of men; maleness, manliness. The Merriam-Webster Dictionary defines masculinity as: the quality or nature of the male sex: the quality, state, or degree of being masculine, or manly.

The binary opposite of masculine, then, would be feminine. The Oxford Dictionary defines feminine as: having qualities or an appearance traditionally associated with women or girls. The Merriam-Webster Dictionary defines feminine as: considered to be characteristic of a woman; marked by having qualities, features, etc., traditionally associated with a woman.

As noted above, the order in which we place binary opposites is a distinction of power, or the order in which we place the opposition holds more power over the other. I am guilty of ordering gender as male/female, binary/non-binary, and our made-up word of gender/genderless. The fact that we place males first in most masculine/feminine oppositions insinuates something about the power that lies within each, or the lack of power. As Derrida (1981) describes it, this also has the power to represent a "violent" hierarchy. Which then translates to the way in which our society espouses and lives gender. More on the order of gender later in this chapter.

It becomes further complicated with we assign biological sex to each gender, where biological men are masculine, and biological women are feminine. We know the gender spectrum changes that, and we know everyone has the right to choose their own gender. *It is when we hold too tightly to the expectations of who ought to be which gender, we create the violent hierarchy of binary opposites.*

It is becoming more common for a spectrum of gender characteristics to be more fluid between identified genders. Therefore, one gender does not "own" one characteristic – it's becoming more socially acceptable for women to have large muscles, and for men to wear facial makeup. This is more than a spectrum. A spectrum can and does include all the possibilities that lie between each opposite end. But the difficulty, again, lies in the inescapability of binary opposites. We say the opposite of masculine is feminine, but then the options on a spectrum present to us the non-binary choice; non-binary (all the options) versus binary (only two choices). It becomes slightly more complicated when we tie in toxic to the equation.

### Toxic

The Oxford Dictionary defines toxic as: containing poison; poisonous. The Merriam-Webster Dictionary defines toxic as: containing or being poisonous material especially when capable of causing death or serious debilitation; containing or being poisonous material especially when capable of causing death or serious debilitation; extremely harsh, malicious, or harmful. In financial terms, it's defined as: relating to or being an asset that has lost so much value that it cannot be sold on the market.

The binary opposite of toxic, in everyday language, would be "non-toxic." However, non-toxic would be non-poisonous. There are other options, though. The opposite of toxic can also be healthy. It can also be nurturing, which communicates an environment that allows growth, life, and well-being. As opposed to toxic that communicates something unhealthy, and dangerous to our health.

The problem with nurturing being the opposite of toxic is the gender it implies, a stereotypically feminine quality. It is usually women who are nurturing, motherly, or gentle, the "nurturers." This also automatically puts men in the opposite category of nurturing. Placing gendered assumptions on each label is problematic. In the case of men being not nurturing, we do not usually assume toxic, only not nurturing. But we do place men into that category of not being nurturing. What makes something toxic, then?

What constitutes poisonous? It can be easily understood that drinking Clorox bleach is poisonous to our body – it could kill us. If your appendix bursts inside of you, your blood becomes toxic, and over a period could also kill you. Alcohol poisoning is when our consumption of alcohol becomes too much for our bodies to handle, also becoming toxic, and can also kill you.

What is it about masculinity that makes it toxic? If a poisonous material like Clorox is toxic to our bodies, what is the equivalent of masculinity? How are certain characteristics of masculinity poisonous to us? And in what quality are they dangerous to us, relationships, and society? How can masculinity be poisonous to us like Clorox is to our bodies?

To begin to answer this question, survey data from both men and women will help us. Responses to the question, "How, if at all, can masculinity be problematic or toxic?" were shared. Here is what some participants had to say:

– *Masculinity is and of itself is not problematic/toxic, a caricature of masculinity can be. A lack of balance is the problem, just like a lack of balance in femininity can be a problem too. For example, the masculine trait of courageousness, if overdone just leads to stupid and reckless behavior. That's toxic. Overconfidence as well, not knowing one's limits. Being a good leader turns toxic if you're just overpowering everyone else not respecting anyone else's say, etc. Caring too much about physical fitness leads to being a shallow meathead. Too much self-discipline and you become repressed. When taking action becomes over aggression. And so on and so on.*

- *Making masculinity the primary aspect of your character is a sure way to never be "enough."*
- *It can be used to condescend to people.*
- *Sexism, pretend incompetence and pretend stupidity regarding human rights and interpersonal respect, rape culture, controlling female right, low emotional intellect, violent dominance through covert aggression, overt aggression.*
- *When it opposes or rather imposes femininity or womanhood. In my opinion, there should be no superior identity that should rule over one or the other or that is more important than the other. Just mutual respect.*
- *I think masculinity can become toxic when the societal expectations for men to act or to be a certain way pressures someone to change who they are. For example, expectations around men suppressing their emotions (aside from rage, which is societally acceptable for men) can lead men towards not being able to process or communicate their emotions in a healthy way. In a similar way if someone feels that society will value them more if they perform what they perceive to be more masculine in the form of being hyperconfident, aspiring for material wealth, being dominant, etc. It's easy for men who don't have a strong internal sense of value or belonging to change themselves to fit those ideals, sometimes hurting themselves or others along the way.*

### Toxic Masculine

The binary opposite of toxic masculine is also not straightforward. The opposite of toxic masculinity is not feminine. That answer itself presents several problems and assumptions. It assumes gender to be the opposite of toxic given the general assumptions of each: man = toxic, therefore woman = feminine and healthy. This is limiting, gender assuming, and problematizes both genders. If feminine (woman) is the antidote to being toxic (man), then the answer is for all of us to be women, which leaves no room for a man and masculine. One option as a binary opposite, then, would be non-toxic. That is too vague, however. For our purposes, let us assume the opposite of poisonous to be healthy (something that is not harmful to our bodies). Therefore, healthy masculinity would be the binary opposite of toxic masculinity.

This is similar to what surveyed participants shared when asked "what is the opposite of toxic masculine." Consider these responses:

- *Interpersonal relationships and socialization without ulterior motives.*
- *Balanced, healthy masculinity.*

- *Letting go of self-judgment as to whether you are masculine enough.*
- *To me the opposite of toxic masculinity is intersections feminism. Feminism in the sense of fighting to dismantle sexism. In other words, dismantling patriarchy would not only help women/nonbinary folks but men as well, by helping to free men of the societal expectations of masculinity and manhood, allowing people to explore masculinity in a more healthy context.*
- *Healthy masculinity? Where the individual does not feel attacked by everything that is different from the identity he has chosen.*
- *Healthy masculinity would put aside fears of stigma and confidently embrace empathic relationships with oneself and one's surroundings.*
- *Toxic masculinity is opposed by wholesome masculinity.*
- *Being supportive of other people regardless of how they present and not trying to control women's bodies and being in their own lane.*
- *Natural masculinity, like doing things because you want to and not to impress, true confidence not arrogance, strength in understanding and procession emotions rather than blind repression and projection/perpetuation, inclusivity rather than bullying.*

A common theme in these responses was the idea of letting go and being comfortable with who you [men] are in their own quality of masculine. Be it empathetic relationships or how they dress, these seem to oppose toxic.

*Healthy Masculinity*

If healthy masculine is the opposite (by working definition) of toxic masculine, or if healthy is the opposite of toxic, what then is healthy masculinity? We have visited the academic literature covering the definitions of toxic masculine; there is some literature that addresses its opposite.

Like toxic masculinity, healthy masculinity is not widely accepted in academic literature. It is even more sparce in secular literature. The closest we get to "healthy masculinity" are the rebuttals and corrections to toxic masculinity. Even though this is a start, there is more to healthy masculinity than only changing toxic ways.

One aspect of healthy masculinity is to honor, respect, and own in a responsible way one's masculinity, by both boys and men. This is arguably a feminist argument (Berggren, 2014), where men are conscious of their own power, how traditional powers of masculinity have oppressed women, and to overtly reject the narratives and rhetoric of masculine dominance. According to Seidler (1991), this notion calls for and puts the onus on men to take responsibility for their masculinity. This responsibility primarily includes taking ownership for any form of toxic behaviors, and intentionally changing them.

There is some disagreement with this thought because the argument also suggests boys and men view their masculinity as a "gift." A gift in which they are responsible for treating responsibly. This is a controversial notion because this implies that masculinity, of which only men arguably possess, is only for them, which leaves women without the "gift" of masculine. On the one hand, I agree with men taking responsibility for any form of toxicity. If there is going to be a change, it is men who need to initiate it. On the other hand, I would not go so far as to call masculinity a gift. It is something to live responsibility with, just as is femininity. *If masculinity is a gift, then femininity ought to be a miracle.*

Healthy masculinity also encourages boys and men to be more engaged with their emotions, specifically when it comes to their relationships with women. It also calls for an intimate, emotional connection with other men (Nagayama Hall, 2017). These aspects of healthy masculinity are all in hopes and efforts to reverse gender inequality. By treating masculinity differently, by taking responsibility for its past oppressions, the hope is to change the way men live in relationship to their own selves and with other women.

However, in addition to the small literature on healthy masculinity, there is also very little consensus as to what it means exactly. Even though there might be some aspects of what a healthy, emotionally functioning man might look like, there are still vague aspects of what that might mean for all men. Class, gender identity, marginalization, and race can all complicate what a healthy masculinity might look like (Waling, 2019). This also runs the risk of dismissing traditional masculine traits, such as physical strength, for toxic. Not all masculine traits are toxic. The binary of healthy versus toxic does tend to imply such.

What also may be problematic is the essentializing of experiences by using both toxic and healthy. As we have stated numerous times, no one gender is limited to anything toxic, and for the sake of argument: healthy. Both men and women can show and live characteristics that are toxic masculine, and healthy masculine. What becomes somewhat confusing is the gendered expectations of the two. Traditionally, it has been the expectation that only men are toxic masculine, and therefore, "healthy masculine" has been commonly paired with femininity. The term healthy masculine, in my opinion, can be a little more problematic than toxic masculine. Since all genders can be healthy masculine, and since a healthy show of emotions, display of gentle masculine, and exercising equal relationships between genders is a good thing that everyone should strive for, limiting those to only "healthy masculine" is exclusive by description.

The only argument for healthy masculine that can be directed at a specific gender would be the fact that men practice ownership and repentance for their oppressive masculinity. Even so, that oppression is not limited to only women. Men are also victims of toxic masculine. Aside from this one facet of healthy masculine, I argue that everyone should practice these traits, and it should only be called healthy – no need to limit good relationship practices to only men or women, it is something we ought to all strive for.

*Positive Masculinity*

Like healthy masculinity, positive masculinity is another option when defining the opposite of toxic masculine. The next chapter will present data on what others believe the opposite of toxic masculinity is, of which a common response is positive masculinity.

Positive masculinity is also widely defined in literature. It can range from behaviors and characteristics that may represent positive masculine role norms (McDermott et al., 2020), like problem solvers, providers, and courage in the face of obstacles. These attributes can also be represented by a sense of duty, responsibility, perseverance, or loyalty (Englar-Carlson & Kiselica, 2013; Roberts-Douglass & Curtis-Boles, 2013). Other researchers have even created a positive masculinity checklist (O'Neil & Luján, 2009), listing 60 positive masculine attributes.

Positive masculinity is defined as a masculine perspective, or a view of masculinity, that accentuates the strengths and beneficial aspects of a masculine identity (Aspinwall & Staudinger, 2003; Kiselica et al., 2016). There are key aspects of positive masculinity which can stand in opposition to toxic, harmful masculine traits. For example, a central part of positive masculinity is the encouragement for men to be emotionally aware, intelligent, and to be able to express emotions freely.[4] This includes emotional experiences like empathy and compassion, which encourage men to understand each other and engage in emotionally healthy relationships with both women and other men. These healthy relationships especially promote the practice of non-violence, combating aggression and oppression of women.

Another aspect of positive masculinity, which also opposes toxic masculinity, is the respect for gender equality. This specifically challenges traditional, patriarchal norms. Men who embrace positive masculinity intentionally reject sexism and overtly work to advocate for women's rights, which also rejects gender norms. Judith Butler (1990) writes about combating gender norms and advocating for a truly feminist society, challenging the binary views of gender and opening the conversation to different interpretations of masculinity. Positive masculinity follows scholars like Butler in the effort to oppose masculine traits that have furthered the gender binary, also furthering the destructive areas of masculinity which come with it.

However, once again, by defining positive masculinity as the opposite of toxic masculinity, we run into a few challenges. The language itself, positive *masculinity*, does seem limited to men. In the literature I've encountered, positive masculinity does not include women. If women were to be positive masculine, they would arguably be feminine. Like healthy masculine, even though positive masculine gives us good and nonharmful traits of masculinity, we are still stuck in the binary of toxic versus non (positive) masculinity, which will be "resolved" in Chapter 5. And because we are still stuck in the binary, we are also arguably stuck in a continuum of toxic/non (healthy, positive, or whatever else might be on the other end). To define the spectrum is not enough, though. A spectrum does not reach the goal of deconstructing. Instead, we need to explore the different dimensions or areas of the spectrum, which we will begin to do in the Overturning phase of deconstruction.

*Toxic/Infect*

In addition to the binary opposite of toxic masculinity being some form of healthy masculinity, we need to include an additional opposite. The opposite of toxic, by one specific aspect of its definition, is essential to our deconstruction. Toxicity also implies spread, an infection, an infestation, or to *intoxicate*. When put this way, toxic becomes more than only a description of the dangerous masculine men (and women) can *be*. This itself is worth deconstructing, which is the central component to our conversation and definition of toxic masculinity. Yes, toxic masculine can be and is a list of descriptions. At the same time, if we are truly taking all options of the definition of toxic, it is also used to describe a process, something *done* to someone. Just like when our bodies become toxic our appendix bursts inside of us, and one by one our organs start to become infected by our septic state, so too is the connotation for toxic masculine. There is a sense of spreading, intoxicating, a process by which people believe, live, and espouse a set of harmful masculine traits. That process of infecting, becoming toxic itself, is what we need to define in terms of opposites.

The opposite of the intoxicate has a few options for us, depending on how it's used. First, one option for its opposite can mean to detoxify, which seems straightforward. Just like when someone becomes intoxicated by consuming too much alcohol, they would need to stop their consumption for a period to "detox." Which has several implications when it comes to masculinity. One is the intentional ceasing of feeding ourselves something destructive; detox from harmful masculinities. Second, specifically when detoxing from substances, there is a period where the body must find its new homeostasis, cleansing the body of the toxic substances, which is rarely a pleasant process. What does it mean to detox our minds of harmful thoughts?

Another similar opposite of the verb form of toxic can be to purify. The process of becoming infected is the opposite of what we're aiming for with purify. Like detoxify, there is a process of removing harmful substances, and there is also a process of adding something healthy, something that will help cleanse and renew what was poisoned. Again, this is not an easy process. When it comes to masculinity, and the binary opposite of the verb toxic, this means removing the harmful aspects of masculinity, detoxing from them (however it may look for each person), and then replacing it with something healthy.

As we will define in more detail in the next chapter, a secondary and central definition for toxic masculine in this book is masculinity without choice. It's a masculine one either conforms to, which is the traditional form of masculine that tends to be harmful, and if not, you're considered something less than, and marginalized. The choice is to be this, or risk being exiled into other forms of masculine. For this, too, we need to find its binary opposite.

What is the opposite of masculinity without choice? This is also not a straightforward answer, for which we can say plenty. The opposite of masculinity without choice is masculinity with choice, inclusive masculinity, masculinity without judgment, freed masculinity, acceptance of masculinity, diversity of masculinity, we could go on…

To simplify it for ourselves, let's agree on masculinity *with* choice, meaning one has the power and privilege to choose what sort of masculine they want to identify as. There are several factors needed for this. It requires safety, courage, and acceptance from everyone else. However, if we are defining binary opposites, this is where the extremes may lie. More on safety later.

The above definitions of toxic filter together, though, are both the action and process form of the word, the description of masculine traits, and the lack of choice. The harmful aspects of masculinity, like aggression and violence, are traits we learn from others, and are taught to us. The very act of teaching someone how to be masculine, or how not to be, is the verb part of toxic; it's the *intoxicating* part of the process, the infestation, spreading into our beliefs and worldviews about masculine. Once these masculine traits have been believed and espoused, they create a world without choice. Those who do not fit the mold of masculine, the masculine which others have been indoctrinated into, are cast aside, marginalized, and seen as a lesser form of masculine. They don't have a choice in their masculine. If they choose to live their lives as something else, they're labeled as such. This is where xenophobia and homophobia come into the reality of society.

One more aspect to deconstruct, when holding true to the definition of toxic, and when thinking of binary opposites, is the opposite of spreading, infecting, and infiltrating. What is the binary opposite of spreading? It depends on how we define it. For example, the act of spreading can be opposed with containing. However, when speaking of masculinity, the spread of harmful traits is what we're defining as toxic. Therefore, its opposite would be the *containing* of those traits. Or, if we're defining spreading as *contaminating*, then its opposite can be *sterilizing*, which presents a different aspect to masculinity; a "sterilizing" masculinity, or a "sterilized" masculinity. We could go on with definitions and binary opposites, hence the challenge of deconstructing presents.

*There is something powerful about how our world today has shaped the experiences of those living in the gender binary, the gender limited by two choices. Deconstruction helps us organize and transform these binaries into something livable, something that goes beyond the pressure of choice.*

Therefore, our working definition of toxic masculinity, when taken from the above definitions, is as such: when we take the choice away from individuals to experience their form of gender, masculinity, or femininity, when we expect them to conform to the standards set by society, and when those expectations are taught to the masses, the lack of choice spreads. And the spreading of, the infiltration of the lack of choice is what makes masculinity toxic.

## Overturning

After (I say after only because there is a sequence of thoughts, which need to happen in some form of sequential order to accomplish any sort of deconstruction) we have defined our binary oppositions, we then need to turn to a process Derrida calls double science (1981), which consists of two phases, or steps. According to the "strategy" of deconstruction, we must first *overturn*. This is a very important part of the process since Derrida believed binary oppositions to create power, or a violence hierarchy. Overturning is an attempt to reverse the power and hierarchy that comes with the placement of opposites.

The overturning aspect of deconstruction is where we begin to rearrange binary opposites, releasing any power held by one, and at the same time reversing the order of power. As Derrida describes it, "brining the low to high" (Derrida, 1981). As an example, and for the sake of gender, what would it mean to overturn, or reverse the order by which man/woman are placed? If certain structures give way to the hierarchy in which these opposites are placed, what would it mean to reverse those? What would it mean to bring the "low to high" in terms of man/woman?

When we reverse the order of the opposites of man/woman, we uncover a new way of thinking, relating, and being. To imagine a woman in a place of power over a man would be the start of such a reversal. Even today, that might be a difficult concept to grasp. Take for example the 2020 presidential election in the United States. Hilary Clinton was the first woman candidate in the history of the presidential election, after hundreds of years of the election process. And interestingly enough, the presidential candidate for the United States of America is once again a woman (Fall of 2024).

Or perhaps overturning the opposites of man/woman would entail a creation story, like we find in the book of Genesis, where a woman was created first. And she was given dominion over the animals and land. And then a man was created for her, in her image, as a suitable partner. That's a different thought. Imagine a Christianity where their God was a woman, God the Mother. How different would our world be?

Next, we reverse the order, or flip the script, of toxic masculinity. I am guilty of ordering toxic masculinity, and therefore its binary opposite we've identified, like this: toxic masculinity/healthy masculinity. The fact that I tend to place toxic before healthy assumes the order of things, the power I give it, just like man/woman, true/false. Even though there is a seemingly negative intonation to it, sometimes "bad" things are placed first in binary opposites. For example, the classic sign in American Western movies where the outlaw is wanted, "dead or alive." Placing dead first does offer preference – the authorities prefer him dead, but if he's captured, they'll take him alive. The same is true for toxic/healthy.

This also speaks to the amount of attention toxic masculinity has received from our societies. We have written news articles, made documentaries about the harm of raising young boys, and made entire movements in response to the harm masculinity has brought to our society. It is safe to say, toxic masculinity receives most of the attention, therefore placing it before healthy.

What if that was reversed, though? If those binary opposites were reversed to healthy masculinity/toxic masculinity, it would be a different conversation. I wouldn't be writing this book. We cannot overlook this part of deconstruction. As Derrida (1981) puts it, "to overlook this phase of overturning is to forget the conflictual and subordinating structure of opposition" (p. 41). This part of Derrida's double science is so important I have created a small guideline of thought below.

### Philosophical Overturning

There is a philosophical exercise that comes with overturning, a certain stance of empathy where we must put ourselves in those shoes; the shoes of the opposite from where we are in relation to in the hierarchy power structure. This may be a difficult exercise, but it is where deconstruction begins, the mental positioning of the reversal of the power inherent with binary opposites.

This is not as easy as it seems. This part of the deconstruction process, even though little explored in the writings of Derrida, is a key aspect. Within this strategy of overturning, I argue steps within the steps of deconstruction. What does it require of us to overturn? How do we place ourselves in a philosophical stance that will allow us to enter the space of overturning?

*Recognize*

The first thing that is required of us, depending on which side of the overturning you find yourself on, is to recognize your position of hierarchy, or lack thereof. It might be easier for those at the bottom of the hierarchy to recognize their position, and at the same time, there might be those oblivious to it. The same can be said for the top of the hierarchy; it might be easier to recognize one's position of power, simultaneously there might be some who are unaware of their position of power within the hierarchy. When it comes to those in power, it is a conscious decision to recognize the power one holds.

*Acknowledge*

The next step is to acknowledge the oppression that has come with said power. This is also a two-sided coin: the oppression which has come with the hierarchy, and the victimization of it. With our conversation of gender, it is critical in this step to recognize how toxic masculinity has overtly and directly taken both men and women as its victims, and how both men and women are guilty of being toxic masculine. Therefore, the need to acknowledge and recognize their own part in this "violent hierarchy," which Derrida outlines for us.

EMPATHY

There is a large amount of empathy that comes with this process, especially if we are highlighting the victimization that comes with the violent hierarchy. This might be the most difficult part of the overturning process because it requires a large amount of vulnerability. When describing empathy, Brené Brown (2012) describes it as more than simply putting yourself in one's shoes. Vulnerability requires us to feel the emotion someone else is experiencing. All emotions are universal, therefore we can all feel them. To empathize is to investigate our own experiences and tap into the feeling we are trying to empathize with. For example, toxic masculinity. To empathize with it is to see how others have been victimized by it. How have men and women been damaged because of toxic masculinity? They have been bullied, shamed for being sensitive, made to feel less than an inferior, demeaned...I could go on. Now, just because you have not been bullied does not mean you cannot empathize with bullies. People that are bullied are made to feel weak, they are afraid, and they tend to not trust people. When was the last time you were made to feel weak? When was the last time you were afraid of someone? When was the last time you had difficulties trusting someone? If you have experienced those things, then you can empathize with a bully, and you can empathize with being a victim of toxic masculine.

This is challenging because we need to dig into our own selves to access these experiences, which is difficult for a lot of people. It is vulnerable because we must show that we have experienced those things, accessed those hurts, then to relate to someone based on the mutual experience. It is the equivalent of taking off your bullet proof vest and risking being shot. But this is a key part of the overturning process.

*Repentance*

The last step in overturning is repentance. There needs to be an overt change that comes with this form and quality of acknowledging. It is not enough to only recognize one's position in this hierarchy and the damage it's caused. The rest of this philosophical stance is an internal change. If our introspection does not cause us, spur us, nor give us the onus to change the structure of the hierarchy, and therefore the experiences which it causes, then we cannot properly deconstruct toxic masculinity.

Overturning, though, and reversing the order of binary opposites is only one part of the exercise, the double science. To overturn, and to place women in front/over men is merely exerting power and would not be an accurate depiction or practices of deconstruction. Reversing the order of opposites, for the sake of reversing their order, is repeating the problematic hierarchy that deconstruction tries to untangle.

Inherent power and hierarchy, no matter what opposites are across from each other, is a foundational aspect of deconstruction. The metaphysical world in which we live exists in hierarchies. Some of which are problematic. For the example at hand, the gender hierarchy has led to oppression, inequity, even violence. To only reverse the hierarchy would not "solve" our problems that come with the existing order of the opposites. It would only replace the order of opposites, which is arguably the same problem with a different order. Even though flipping the order is the first area of focus, it is only the beginning of the thought exercise.

For example, the argument brought forth by bell hooks (2004), where she claims some feminist sought to only take back power and "win" over oppression. For some feminist efforts, the goal was to not become equal across genders, but to replace the existing power the with ones who were oppressed by such inequalities. To only overturn would be the equivalent of replacing one gender's power over the other, which is just as equally oppressive, only a different gender.

There is an overt intention in overturning. Something we choose when we overturn, and to give precedent to. Something we you choose to internalize, believe, live, and exude. It's more than simply reversing the order of things; it's living the outcome of such a belief.

By reversing a hierarchy, and by exuding that belief, imagining what's beyond mere power of conceptual order, something organic happens. Not as words, but as something we inhabit. It may be a thought, or it may be something we want to achieve. It will always be something we strive for. And that striving is the natural result of the double science: overturn and displace (next), the natural result of deconstruction.

*Deconstruction is not only a fancy philosophy, but it should also be a deep motivation in us to fix a structure that has and continues to cause damage.* Which binary opposites tend to do. When done correctly, deconstruction is more than an exercise, it becomes something more.

## Displacement

Overturning a binary opposition solves half the problem and leaves the rest to a mere change in hierarchy; it creates the same problem in a different order. Even though making the effort to examine the hierarchy in and around binary oppositions is a worthy effort, there is more to the process of the strategy. We also need to examine the space, narratives, and rhetoric between opposites, and then again (even closer) as we overturn them. The question to be asked as we do so is this: what happens to the language of opposites as we overturn them and explore what may be between them as they are overturned. As Derrida (1981) explains it: "we must mark the intervals between inversion, bring low what was high (p. 41)."

The exercise of displacing requires several components to its thought process. Let us use the example at hand: male/female. To overturn its opposite, we would remain with not male/female, but instead, female/male. That positioning may be difficult on its own. However, this is only one aspect. We then need to explore the concepts, ideas, thoughts, and possibilities that emerge from such an overturning. In theory, and if done well, new ideas ought to present themselves to our vocabulary and thought toward each side of the opposite when they're overturned and displaced.

Displacement is more than presenting a continuum, or a reversed continuum for the sake of reversing hierarchy. Even though the exercise of exploring their possibilities between opposites on a continuum is good, that is not deconstruction. Liz Lerman (2014) speaks of "hiking the horizontal," where she conceptualizes the possibility of multiple perspectives toward art (interpreting binary opposition for our purposes) to live. As a dancer and scholar of movement, she describes flipping the hierarchy from top to bottom and laying it flat. Therefore, minimizing the power of what is on top from bottom. She goes on to describe the horizontal continuum as turning it into a circle, connecting both ends; "and if for a moment you take this continuum and bend it into a circle, you will see that the two ends can lie close, like next-door neighbors" (p. xvi).

Now, imagine that circled continuum with a three-dimensional sphere around it. That is where displacement happens, within the exploration of the overturned opposites, and all the dimensions between and around them, along with the rhetoric, language, beliefs, and sentiments that go along with said oppositions.

When displacing, we need to ask the question: what exists within the sphere of possibilities in, between, around, and beyond the realm that exists between opposites? The art of displacement is where deconstruction is "finalized." I use the term finalized loosely because deconstruction has no end. Rather, it is a process that must go on once it is experienced. Therefore, it is more suited to refer to displacement as the final component or step of the strategy of deconstruction, where new ideas present themselves through the exploration of overturning. This exploration during the phase of displacement results in a "new concept," a non-dialectical third term.

Ancient Egypt and their Gods are a good example of displacing, with only a few small details left out (granted, they weren't deconstructing their gods, but the way in which they created and portrayed their gods is similar to deconstruction). Their gods tended to encapsulate more than one living things, human and animal, and created it into something separate, a new concept, or a new god.

Take for example one of the more well-known Egyptian Gods, Anubis. He is the god of mumification, and death and afterlife. He is as a figure of a man with a black jackal head. The reason for his wearing a jackal head was because wild dogs would commonly scrounge shallow graves once the dead were buried. Therefore, to protect the dead from the canines, their god would protect them from such threats.

Or Isis, the goddess of contradictions. She was known for her magical spells, her healing powers, and her ability to inflict grief on others. She is commonly depicted as a woman, sometimes breastfeeding a baby Horus, while wearing cow horns and a solar disc on her head.

Also, the goddess Ma'at. She was known as the goddess of justice and order. She was depicted with a bird tail on her head, and often with bird wings on her arms. There are more: The god Seth, who was shown as with a long tail and the head of a curved animal, like an aardvark; the god Toth, a man with the head of a now extinct ibis; or the goddess Baset, a woman with the head of a cat, and sometimes shown as a whole cat. Each with the characteristics of both humans and animals.

These examples are close forms and good examples of deconstruction and displacement. Notice the binary between different aspects of the gods, usually the binary of human and animal, of which we would consider humankind to be "above" animals in the hierarchy of oppositions. However, this script seems to be flipped with most Egyptian Gods since the animal aspect of the god is usually placed on the top of a human body, literally flipping or overturning the hierarchy. In fact, Ancient Egypt gave so much regard to animals, they were often a part of their depictions of their gods.

The example of displacement and a new concept comes in when the gods and goddesses' names were something which superseded the animal and human opposites. Even though names were given to their gods, with names and language being the barrier to deconstruction, their belief in both humans and animals transcended the language of the binary opposition. Their extensive believe in their afterlife and how both humans and animals were at the same time equally important in how one died shows the deconstruction of humans and animals.

The new ideas that emerge from deconstruction cannot go back; therefore, it is a natural evolution of thought where new ideas must carry old and new ones simultaneously. Displacement ends with both original opposites, and neither of them, as seen with Egyptian Gods. What emerges is a new concept that explores the boundaries of overturning, while keeping where it came from. Displacement is summed up by Gunkel (2021) as follows:

> This "new concept" that is the product of the second phase occupies a position between or in/at the margins of a traditional, conceptual opposition or binary pair. It is simultaneously neither-nor and either-or. It does not resolve into one or the other of the two terms that comprise the conceptual order, not does it constitute a third term that would mediate their difference in a synthetic unity…Consequently, it is positioned in such a way that is both inhabits and operate in excess of conceptual oppositions by which and through which systems of knowledge have been organized and articulated. It is for this reason that the new concept cannot be described or marked in language, except by engaging in what Derrida calls a "bifurcated writing," which compels the traditional philosophemes to articulate, however incompletely and insufficiently, what necessarily resists and displaces all possible modes of articulation.
>
> (p. 61–62)

What's left, the "new concept," is an evolving matter of thought and experience. The challenge with deconstruction and the new concept that emerges from deconstruction is that language itself brings us back to our original problem: binary opposites. Once you put something into language, any thought that is articulated from our minds out into verbal form, we place it into the system that created binary oppositions: language. The limit of language is that we can argue our way around the contradiction of what it is we are speaking about. For example, if I say out loud that the sky is blue, anyone can say something contrary to that; it is celestial or royal blue, or a completely different color like red. Any option we present for the color of the sky can be verbally contradicted because we have the language to do so. Therefore, once we place a thought into words, we put it into a place where it can be opposed.

This is a problem because this is the exact result deconstruction aims to stop: placing ideas into a system that can bring it to a binary opposite. When we put anything into language, we make it vulnerable to its opposite. This is why deconstruction, in practice, doesn't end. Nor is it put into language. The "new concept" that comes from displacement ought not to be a new written word, phrase, or rhetoric. If it is, Derrida called it bifurcated writing (1981b), which tries to dismantle the very system in which it's a part of: writing. Instead, this new concept needs to be something beyond our system of language and understanding, toward the edges of the boundaries of our conceptual knowledge.

How do we achieve this without words, though? This is difficult. Any words we create as a "new concept" are subject to being opposed. Therefore, we must use words in a way that is not conclusive. We must carefully, and systematically, not draw conclusions by choosing what results from the displacement part of deconstruction. Instead, we explore the possibilities of what we can experience when the opposites are reversed, and in the space that exists beyond those possibilities is explored.

There is one aspect to highlight with displacement, one of which is not original to Derrida's approach nor found in his second phase of double gesture. I believe displacement asks the above questions when overturning and marking the intervals between binary opposites. However, even beginning to ask these questions becomes something more individualized and personal. We can conceptualize and ask questions like "what exists when the continuum of binaries is turned into a three-dimensional sphere?" "What are the possibilities between the intervals during the process of overturning?" But by even asking those questions, and by even conceptualizing binary opposites in this way, we must point out the mental exercise required to do this.

Derrida refers to displacement and the new concept as an eruptive emergence (1997). The choice of words to describe this is not just a way to describe displacement, I believe this to mean an action, one requiring something specific. To allow displacement and let a new concept "erupt" and "emerge," we need to be able to hold the space for it. This means to be able to mentally hold two opposites together, on the same playing field. In this playing field, both positions in binary pairs hold no value over each other, and therefore where they are overturned and their intervals marked. This is difficult. For our example at hand, this means to hold space for toxic masculinity, and its opposite, to live on the same playing field, at the same time. Even though they don't stay there forever, it's necessary to be able to do this. Without being able to hold two opposites, despite how much one may be despised, we run the risk of faulty overturning (more on holding opposites in the next chapter).

Even though it is not a Derrida term, "faulty overturning" has the potential to disrupt the eruptive emergence of a new term. When we lack the ability to hold binary opposites on the same playing field so they can be overturned, we also run the risk of allowing our biases to sneak into the deconstruction of double science. When this happens, we cannot properly overturn; it's more like an overturning to suit what we want the outcome to look like. I call this faulty overturning, or biased overturning. The result of faulty overturning is a skewed displacement, which is not displacement at all, nor deconstruction.

*A faulty overturning does not allow us to hold the space in which displacement has the chance to occur, to allow an eruptive emergence of a new concept.*

To displace, then, requires the mental capacity and the emotional wherewithal to allow opposites to live together for the sake of overturning, and for the sake of displacement. When we can suspend our biases and remove our emotional attachments, we hold to what it is we're deconstructing, only then can we allow the eruptive emergence of a new concept.

Figure 3.1 shows the process in which deconstruction happens. From defining binary opposites, reversing their inherent hierarchy, to their displacement and the forming of a new concept.

This figure should only be used for example purposes. There are many stereotypical traits and attributes that come with toxic masculine and healthy masculine.

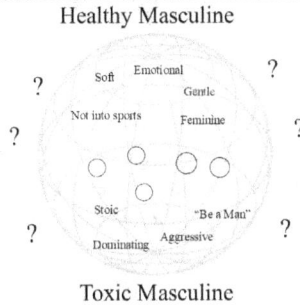

*Figure 3.1* The Process of Overturning and the Exploration within Displacement

Some may be warranted, some may not. The figure is to only show the positioning of Healthy versus Toxic. In this case, Healthy is intentionally placed on top of the sphere because of overturning, reversing the hierarchy. Since that is not the end, the figure also shows how when we reverse the order of opposites, we also need to mark the intervals between. As we "rotate" the positions of opposites, bringing what's high low, we also rotate, or flip, the traits and characteristics that come with each opposite. Intervals are also meant to communicate the possibilities which lie between the extreme opposites. All aspects of the opposites must be present when flipped, therefore marking the intervals between.

As you note, there are empty circles at and between intervals, as well as question marks outside the sphere. This is to communicate the new concept. As we overturn, the very action of "rotating," bringing low to high, brings out this new concept. Or it erupts and emerges. A concept that encompasses our structure of opposites, as we see in the sphere, and a concept that is beyond it, as shown by the question marks.

How do we come up with this new concept, though?

### How to Displace

How do we approach such a conversation? How do we explore concepts that lie beyond the language we possess which describes things in their opposites? How do we explore those places yet to be explored in our limited thought about gender?

I believe we have come a long way in our current conversation of gender. I know a lot of debate still exists around the spectrum of genders, though. Yet, considering how much progress we have made, there is still a long way to go.

### Redefining Toxic Masculinity

My personal favorite definition of toxic masculinity is one provided by a participant: toxic "masculinity is masculinity without choice." Meaning toxicity lies when one is forced to be a certain type of masculine, and any other type is purposely excluded. The forcing is systematically spread through institutions, groups of people in power, and even policy. In this case, it is the dominate,hypermasculine type of masculinity that is the more powerful one, and the masculinities which are not, being sensitive, not violent, and being a gentle form of masculine, are exiled; forced to not be a part of the dominate.

This exclusion, by the very definition of toxic, is poisonous to men and women, and particularly young boys. Exclusion is one of the most power traits that keeps toxicity alive. Exclusion is learned from an early age, and if not corrected, it is taken into adulthood; the exclusion that makes fun of other boys for not being strong or playing American football; the exclusion that keeps those boys in a state of isolation (or other harmful associations with masculinity), which is very easily internalized and taken into adulthood.

If we are to displace, we must bring all forms of masculinity to the conversation. If we leave any form out, we further the toxicity. This may be a difficult notion to grasp. Harlene Anderson (1997), a postmodern thinker, offers a similar view on displacement; a philosophical view of language that offers us some help when thinking of how we displace and create a new concept.

According to Anderson, her language of solving problems is unique. She believes not in problems being solved, but rather in problems being *dissolved*. Even the language of "problems" is problematic for her since it implies a certain language that systems form around and adopt. Therefore, this creates a problem-maintaining system of language; problems live in language.

The connection to displacement is the use of language in the way Anderson conceptualizes it. Language, according to Anderson, supersedes problems. When language is used correctly, and when it is approached correctly, problems naturally dissolve.

This is a specific philosophical stance one takes, which tends to be post-modernist: language has the power to construct reality, and therefore how one experiences their lived reality. When we ask how someone has experienced something, we are interested in the language they choose to describe it in. The exploration and the attention to language that Andreson poses is the same process by which we displace. Displacement ought to be where all the possibilities of language around what it is we're deconstructing meet; and by way of our attention to such language, naturally will be displaced (or dissolved). The new concept is the outcome of the process by which, like Anderson's dissolving, will naturally be displaced with and through the exploration of language used to describe "problems."

There is a sense of positioning and openness to the possibilities of dissolving which we can translate into displacing. As Derrida describes it, it is an emergence and eruption of a new concept. But this does not happen without the philosophical stance, and the attention to language required for problem dissolution.

Before we visit the new concept emerging from this phase of deconstruction, let's first visit the data being collected for this project. The intent was to gather data and ideas from others who share about toxic masculinity. With their help, we can enhance the deconstruction strategy.

**Memo # 3 On Both and None**

It has to be both/and, as cliché as that is. One of the more confusing products of deconstruction is to produce a *thing* that is both a part of the original logical binary and that is also not a part of it.

Something bigger, something not able to put into words, something that is not a part of the systems that created the opposition in the first place, and that *something*, according to Derrida, is language.

First, both:

When we're talking about masculinity, toxic masculinity, we need to first sit with the two oppositions: toxic masculinity and what we're calling healthy masculinity. I think it's easy enough to conceptualize the two, and to even recognize their difference, both logically and in lived experiences.

The result or outcome of deconstruction needs to live and happen there: in the logical and experiential place of recognize the two opposites. At the same time, it has to be neither. That's where it gets tricky.

A masculinity that encompasses both logical oppositions, which we can probably easily see and think of, and at the same time a masculinity that doesn't encompass these.

We need to pay attention to what this exactly entails, which might be more difficult than we image. To see *both*, and to be in both, we need to be accepting of both, inviting of both. That is not to say to espouse toxic masculinity, or to even support or be it, but there does need to be some sort of inclusion of that part of the binary – I'd even dare to say spectrum. If the outcome of deconstruction consists of both, then there needs to be some sort of space for both of the opposites…

What does that space look like, though?

One of my favorite answers to the research question what the opposite of toxic masculinity is: it's a masculinity that doesn't exclude. Yes, we have our limits – we don't condone violence or abuse, there are limits to what we can accept, but you don't have to be toxic masculine to be abusive. So, there's that kink in that thought.

But a masculinity that is inclusive is a close argument to the deconstruction outcome; one part.

It must be and…and something more. We can't just espouse the spectrum of masculinity, the opposites and what is in between. Yes, that's inclusive, and that's well enough, but there is something more to that, it must be something else, we must go somewhere else to deconstruct.

This is where it gets really tricky. How do we practice inclusion of the possibilities of masculinities, toxic and not, and then on top of that make space for something that is more than that, in addition to that, beyond that?

A masculinity that is both the logical opposites of toxic and healthy, and then at the same time something more. How do we even do that? How is that possible? Inviting the opposites is difficult enough, but then to think outside that box of masculine possibilities…it's like the 4th dimension of masculinity. What does that even mean?

It operates in excess of the traditional form of conception. What? How do we operate in excess of the traditional conception of gender?

Is that merely gender fluid? I don't think so. Gender fluid would only fall into the first outcome of deconstruction, the *both*. We can happily accept multiple forms of gender and therefore be fluid in those choices. That, however unfortunate, does not operate in excess of our traditional conceptual knowledge of gender, it sufficiently operates between the logical opposites of the gender choice spectrum.

Then how?

An undecidable alternative that names a new possibility. Forever undecidable. Systemically undecidable.

Deconstructing toxic masculinity, then, is not "how to change masculinity," nor it is a set of standards that tell men and women how to be masculine – that's missing the point. Deconstructing toxic masculinity is something that changes inside you and me. It's something that will forever be something we want to be, exude, and live. We know it's not attainable, not because we don't believe in societies' ability to change, but because of our limits to conceptualizing what's beyond our experience of masculine and gender.

This isn't a bad thing. But it is something we will never achieve. It's the striving for that is worthy of pursuit. It's the working toward that is freeing, what deconstruction leads us to the want. It's the thing inside of us that naturally wants to change because of the process of going through deconstructing.

To deconstruct, then, is something that changes us. If it doesn't, we've missed the point.

## Notes

1  The deconstruction process is not one that comes to completion. To say "once we deconstruct" is only a phrase for our purposes of deconstructing multiple things: masculinity, gender, then toxic. The phrase is only to communicate the sequence of events before we get to the deconstruction of toxic masculine. Even then, we do not ever "finalize" the process of deconstructing toxic masculine. Instead, it is an evolving process that will always be in flux and in need of revisiting. Therefore, the current usage of the finiteness of words "first," and "once we," only describe the journey toward deconstructing toxic masculine.

2  Even though our attempt is to deconstruct toxic masculinity, the bigger picture of gender must be addressed. This is not meant to be a comprehensive review of gender – that is a different book entirely. This is to start the process of deconstruction so that we can enter masculinity, and then into toxic. This short aspect of gender is largely inconclusive and non-exhaustive. For a more in depth understanding of gender, see the Further Readings list at the conclusion of this chapter.

3  Genderless, in this case, is not simply choosing to not identify as one gender, and not asexual, but not having the option of a gender. Even though this word is made up for our purposes, it is communicating the idea of gender as non-existent.

4  For more on the masculine experience in not being socially acceptable to show emotion, and the way organizations, including other men, are trying to combat it, see the Netflix documentary *The Mask You Live In (2015)*.

# References

American Psychological Association. (2018). *Guidelines for psychological practice with boys and men*. Retrieved from https://www.apa.org/about/policy/boys-men-practice-guidelines.pdf

Anderson, H. (1997). *Conversation, language, and possibilities: A postmodern approach to therapy.* Basic Books.

Aspinwall, L. G., & Staudinger, U. M. (Eds.). (2003). *A psychology of human strengths: Fundamental questions and future directions for a positive psychology.* American Psychological Association.

Beauvoir, S. (1951). *The second sex* (H. M. Parshley, Trans.). Alfred A. Knopf.

Berggren, K. (2014). Hip hop feminism in Sweden: Intersectionality, feminist critique and female masculinity. *European Journal of Women's Studies, 21*(3), 233–250. https://doi.org/10.1177/1350506813518761

Brown, B. (2012). *Daring greatly: How the courage to be vulnerable transforms the way we live, love, parent, and lead.* Gotham Books.

Butler, J. (1988). Performative acts and gender constitution: An essay in phenomenology and feminist theory. *Theatre Journal, 40*(4), 519–531. https://doi.org/10.2307/3207893

Butler, J. (1990). *Gender trouble: Feminism and the subversion of identity.* Routledge.

Corvez, M. (1971). The structuralism of Jacques Lacan. *Revista de Psicología General y Aplicada, 26*(113), 711–741. https://psycnet.apa.org/record/1972-29247-001

Davis, A. (1981). *Women, race, & class.* Random House.

Derrida, J. (1981). *Positions* (A. Bass, Trans.). University of Chicago Press.

Derrida, J. (1981b). *Dissemination* (B. Johnson, Trans.). University of Chicago Press. (Original work published 1972)

Derrida, J. (1997). *Of grammatology* (G. C. Spivak, Trans.). Johns Hopkins University Press. (Original work published 1967)

Englar-Carlson, M., & Kiselica, M. S. (2013). Affirming the strengths in men: A positive masculinity approach to assisting male clients. *Journal of Counseling & Development, 91*(4), 399–409. https://doi.org/10.1002/j.1556-6676.2013.00111.x

Gunkel, D. (2021). *Deconstruction.* MIT Press.

hooks, b. (1981). *Ain't I a woman: Black women and feminism.* South End Press.

hooks, b. (2004). *The will to change: Men, masculinity, and love.* Washington Square Press.

Kiselica, M. S., Benton-Wright, S., & Englar-Carlson, M. (2016). Accentuating positive masculinity: A new foundation for the psychology of boys, men, and masculinity. In Y. J. Wong & S. R. Wester (Eds.), *APA handbook of men and masculinities* (pp. 123–143). American Psychological Association.

Lerman, L. (2014). *Hiking the horizontal: Field notes from a choreographer.* Wesleyan University Press.

Levant, R. F., & Richmond, K. (2007). A review of research on masculinity ideologies using the male role norms inventory. *The Journal of Men's Studies, 15*(2), 130–146. https://doi.org/10.3149/jms.1502.130

McDermott, R. C., Borgogna, N. C., Hammer, J. H., Berry, A. T., & Levant, R. F. (2020). More similar than different? Testing the construct validity of men's and women's traditional masculinity ideology using the Male Role Norms Inventory-Very Brief. *Psychology of Men & Masculinities, 21*(4), 523–532. https://doi.org/10.1037/men0000251

Nagayama Hall, G. C. (2017). *Multicultural Psychology.* Routledge.

Newsom, J. S. (Director). (2015). *The masks you live in* [Film]. The Representation Project.

O'Neil, J. M., & Luján, M. L. (2009). Preventing boys' problems in schools through psych-oeducational programming: A call to action. *Psychology in the Schools, 46*(3), 257–266. https://doi.org/10.1002/pits.20371

Roberts-Douglass, K., & Curtis-Boles, H. (2013). Exploring positive masculinity develop-ment in African American men: A retrospective study. *Psychology of Men & Masculinity, 14*(1), 7–15. https://doi.org/10.1037/a0029662

Seidler, Victor J. (1991) *Recreating sexual politics: Men, feminism and politics.* Routledge.

Simons, M. A., Benjamin, J., & de Beauvoir, S. de (1979). Simone de Beauvoir: An inter-view. *Feminist Studies, 5*(2), 330–345. https://doi.org/10.2307/3177599

Thompson, E. H., Jr., & Pleck, J. H. (1995). Masculinity ideologies: A review of research instrumentation on men and masculinities. In R. F. Levant & W. S. Pollack (Eds.), *A new psychology of men* (pp. 129–163). Basic Books/Hachette Book Group. (Reprinted in modified form from "Sex Roles," 27, Dec 1992, pp. 573–607).

Waling, A. (2019). Problematising 'toxic' and 'healthy' masculinity for addressing gender inequalities. *Australian Feminist Studies, 34*(101), 362–375. https://doi.org/10.1080/08164649.2019.1679021

# 4  How Masculinity Becomes Toxic

The approach to this work is a combination of philosophical thought and inquiry, along with qualitative research methods. The traditional thought from Derrida's deconstruction is the central focus of the study. In addition to this philosophical approach, I am combining it to qualitative inquiry.

As a qualitative researcher, I place value in people, their experiences, and their spoken words to describe their experiences. I believe researching people requires a personal component to gathering data. Therefore, that data gathered in this work comes from surveys and interviews. Surveys were given through various means: social media groups, email, and word of mouth. Interview participants were recruited through the survey, which gave an option to volunteer.

The following were both survey and interview questions:

1  What is your definition of masculinity?
2  What, if any, are some positive aspects of masculinity?
3  How, if at all, can masculinity be problematic or toxic?
4  What is the opposite of toxic or problematic masculinity?
5  How, if ever, have you dealt with problematic masculinity?[1]

My position as a researcher is postmodern. As such, I ask questions with the stance, and view of "truth," as there is no objective truth that is definable or measurable. "Truth," such as it is, is experienced by everyone in different ways. Therefore, I am not concerned about objective reality (in our case, toxic masculinity), the larger concern lies in how individuals experience such truths, events, ideals, hardships, etc. By asking questions about toxic masculinity, I am inquiring into people's thoughts, beleifs, and how they have experienced such things.

Data, then, largely relies on participants and their own language to describe their experiences. The postmodern stance in data interpretation attempts to "let the data speak for itself." The researcher is merely an instrument in which they are conveying data to an audience. Interpretation is minimal, rather, the researcher organizes and makes sense of the data with the help of participants to accurately depict individual, unique experiences. Therefore, the data you see in this chapter is direct words from participants.

DOI: 10.4324/9781003464228-4

The postmodern researcher also does not believe in one standardized, scientific method. Most postmodern researchers do not believe in a methodological approach to research (Daly, 2007). Data does not have to necessarily come from participants, interviews, or surveys. It can come from any form of information, expression, or work that involves said topic. In this study, as we have seen in previous chapters, I am also relying on secular forms of news and articles that speak to toxic masculinity.

In the spirit of postmodernism, and not believing in a standardized approach to research, I am also combining the philosophical tradition of deconstruction. This means even though I am deconstructing toxic masculinity, the ways and strategy laid out by Derrida in which I am deconstructing involve qualitative methods and inquiry.

## Qualitative Deconstruction

Like the postmodern researcher who does not believe in a standardized way to research, deconstruction itself is not a method (Gunkel, 2021). Deconstruction does not exist in a structured, step-by-step process like the scientific method, nor does it offer a way to follow inquiry. Instead, deconstruction is highly contextual and involved. There is no exact process in which to follow, rather, it unfolds as we inquire and gain understanding about what it is we are deconstructing.

Deconstruction follows its own way, it shapes as we gather data, analyze, and explore our topic at hand. We, as deconstructionists, follow where the process leads us. It demands a sense of flexibility, open-mindedness, and tabula rasa to be led by and through deconstruction. There is no predetermined route, then. Only where the process itself takes us.

When we allow the investigation to lead us, the possibilities of an "end" are endless. This is like the postmodern researcher: we allow data to unfold in front of us, and as we collect data, we are informed and ask more questions. As we ask more questions and collect more data, more questions arise. We are always being led by data, shifting, pivoting, and readjusting our stance based of what we uncover.

Even though there is no set method to deconstruction, there are important components to it. Derrida (1981) calls deconstruction a "general strategy" by which we respond and engage with the binary opposite of the metaphysical. According to Derrida, binary opposites do not allow us the full range of possibilities when engaging with our reality: alive/dead, black/white, in our case, man/woman. The binary opposites in which our world is created limit our understanding and possibilities of reality. Therefore, like postmodern research, deconstruction aims to go beyond these binaries and intentionally reverse the order that creates a power imbalance.

This is referred to as "overturning," where the inherit power by which binary opposites are placed is reversed, and therefore not given their positions of power; both the dominate and lesser. Deconstruction, like the postmodern researcher, is not interested in the "what" of binary opposites and power. Rather, we are more interested in the "how" of these experiences. The "how" of deconstruction, then, lies in how people experience this overturning.

In the last component of its strategy, displacement, we explore the possibilities of what exists without the constraints of binary opposites. For a postmodern researcher, this is the "how" of the experience that lies in deconstruction. This is the point in which we are to be led by where the process takes us, and where our participants lead us.

I am combining qualitative inquiry into deconstruction by asking participants questions about toxic masculinity at each point of the deconstruction strategy. The data itself, then, is the deconstruction process where I am letting participants do the deconstructing for us. Like the postmodern researcher, and the deconstructionist, it is important to allow the data and the deconstruction process to lead us. All the data collected was an evolving series of refining questions, follow-up questions, and letting things unfold while investigating.

## Definition of Masculinity

A part of the design of this project was to gather data from individuals, both men and women. In deconstructing toxic masculinity, the process, or the steps of deconstruction are easily laid out, where each step can become an opportunity for questions and answers. For example, deconstruction begins with defining the terms being deconstructed. In our case, we start with toxic masculinity. But as already seen, deconstructing toxic masculinity also means deconstructing and defining masculine. Therefore, the definitions of both were opportunities to gather data.

The following is collected from surveying both men and women, of varying ages and background and education levels. The responses given here are my version of the most given answers to questions. When asking "what is your definition of masculine," the answers were straightforward. Answers commonly revolved around Physical Characteristics, Biology (biological make up), or certain Behaviors labeled as masculine. Participants also referred to the Social Construction of masculine. For example, physical attributes and characteristics:

### Physical Characteristics

*Physical and emotional strength and the ability to provide for others.*

*Physical, emotional, psychological, or social traits that are associated with people who consider themselves male. Someone who is strong, courageous, compassionate, and tough, yet well-mannered and in control of his thoughts, speech, and actions.*

*Integrity. Assertiveness. When saying something, giving your word to someone, making a commitment, following through with it.*

*Strength, courage, independence, leadership, and assertiveness.*

*The temperament, roles, sentiments, and emotional and social needs typically pertaining to men. Fundamentally it would be the use of strength, backbone, and discipline. It would be the longing for adventure. Ideally, a man should find sentiment, either on a hero's journey or the journey of romance and marriage, such that he has something he values to put his strength in service to. To become a protector, a provider, and a leader.*

*Masculinity is the qualities defining a male. A male differs from a female in that he is "typically" stronger, faster, and thinks differently. Thinking involves being more protective, being a provider, and making sure everything is taken care of.*

Of the physical attributes shared, physical strength and appearance of being masculine were the most common responses to what masculinity is.[2]

### Behaviors

Participants also shared how they believed certain behaviors are what defines masculine. For example:

*Masculinity is a term used to describe behavior that is typical of men.*

*Masculinity is umbrella covering the behaviors that we associate with a person playing the character of a man.*

*Physically strong, engages in hobbies and sports traditionally associated with men (e.g., hunting, fishing, combat sports).*

*The behavior or aesthetic that a man is expected to display in public.*

*Play acting regurgitated media, not crying, animal hierarchy hyping.*

Even though the above responses share behaviors which are arguably upholding harmful forms of masculine, like not crying, the idea stands for assigning certain behaviors to what masculinity is. In this case, the participant supports the idea of not showing emotion as something masculine.

### Biology

The following responses support the biological definition of what is masculine:

*Appearing biologically male. Being willing to get dirty, get hurt, and be uncomfortable in order to get things done that have to be done. Shouldering the blame for when things go wrong whether you are responsible or not. Not looking for recognition when things go right because of something you did.*

*Masculinity is a term to describe traits or attributes generally associated with biologically, traditionally, and socially viewed "male" sex and or gender. While what is male is associated with a specific genetic trait, such as male-associated body parts like the penis, testicles, and maturity traits such as lowered voice, generally a larger stature, pubic hairs such as a beard, mustache, or groin regional hair. Masculinity may also be formed in the actions, expressions, or ideas done by males that are male biologically from birth. Those traits of masculinity however are not entirely restricted to biologically male from birth individuals but may also be found in women who may share more masculine traits through their actions, thoughts, or expressions that fall closer to what on average socially, a biologically male individual's feelings, actions, or thoughts reflect.*

*The gift of having male genital organ and being able to behave appropriate toward women and controlling, but also being able to express emotions. As well as keeping yourself physically different than women.*

*It's when you are a man and portray traits that men have like having a penis or growing beards and the more beard you grow and the more penis you have the more masculine you are.*

Of note, the above participants may or may not have supported the idea of toxic masculinity. For example, the last comment, insinuating size of penis equates to more masculine. Even though this might be true for "locker room" jokes, the definitions above do not speak to anything toxic, yet.

### Socially Constructed Masculine

Participants also shared how they believe the idea of masculinity to be a social construct, something driven by culture and society along with its expectations. For example:

*Masculinity is a gatekeeping term designed to create cohesion among the in-group and ostracize those in the out-group by choosing any of a number of details and claiming the out-group individual doesn't meet that particular metric.*

*Masculinity is a set of ideals constructed through the coevolution and conflation of socioculturally "normal" male characters, and biological male characteristics.*

*The performative gender and social role normally associated with the male sex. Typified by behaviors that demonstrate value to one's social relations within the cultural matrix one exists in.*

*It is the sum of culturally specific assumptions and expectations that are supposed to inhere and manifest in male-bodied/presenting individuals. In patriarchal cultures, the assumptions include dominance as positive (and subordination as negative).*

*Masculinity is a gendered expression that corresponds to cultural expectations of men, and then shifts based on context. It influences and is influenced by everything from the media, fashion, religion, food, and sports. Communication, intimacy, etc. Masculinity is associated with men, but not limited to men, and many individuals self-describe as masculine if they relate to things or presentations, they are stereotypically masculine in their culture.*

*Similar to what is usually defined in the West, except not showing emotions and being the main financial provider for the family (which in my culture it's about maturity not gender) and being physically active and strong (I found that lots of people who are the opposite of this have a strong "gentle" type of masculinity, maybe it's culturally related).*

*We divided human behavior arbitrarily in two categories. Masculinity is one of them. It's the one associated with the male sex in the binary division of sex, that "becomes" gender, the feminine and the masculine gender. What falls into masculinity and what doesn't is depending on time and space. It's a social construct, so it's not real, but it is an interpersonal fiction and a performance, so it is also real.*

### The Good

As mentioned before, not all aspects of masculinity are bad or harmful. There is nothing wrong with being physically strong or looking like Duane Johnson. The danger comes when masculine characteristics are used to hurt other people. To emphasize the point of not all masculine is bad, I wanted to know what others had to say about it. In surveying individuals on their experiences with toxic masculinity, one of the questions asked was "what are some good aspects of masculinity." Something reiterated in different ways was the "use" of one's masculinity; physically helping someone or using strength for leadership and courage. Participants had a lot of good things to say about it:

*Being tougher emotionally and learning to not let things affect you as much and on the flip side not being afraid to show love and affection for those you do care about.*

*I think more than anything else, men desire to feel respected, relied upon, and dependable. Insofar as that pushes him to act within a code of honor, and to be someone other people can depend upon, that is good. To enforce boundaries, to not burden others with his troubles \*if\* he can handle it on his own, to maintain composure where the situation calls for it. To be direct and not passive aggressive, all cards on the table.*

*Masculinity created the modern world, the "shut up and go to work" that built the cities, fought in wars, and did the dirty jobs others didn't want to do.*

*Positive aspects of masculinity include being more muscular, being someone that your community can rely on, and recognizing real danger vs perceived danger.*

*The competitive nature of it can pull others in your sphere upwards in mobility in every aspect of life. The disagreeable nature of it ensures optimal outcomes for self and others who fall underneath it's protection. And when stoic, it is the foundational structure the family unit will always depend upon.*

*Like I said in the previous question masculinity is nebulous and hard to define, so it's difficult to say what the positive aspects of masculinity are as I think that will vary from person to person. For me speaking on a personal level, I think I use my masculinity to help others; being someone people can depend on for emotional support and comfort. I do my best to maintain a degree of level-headedness and I think (hope) that when people ask me for advice I can better see a situation from all sides, and not allow my emotions to sway me too much. I also hope that the perceived level-headedness that I have allows me to better see and attend to the needs of loved ones. I lift weights and have been told that is inspiring to others so I suppose doing a hard task and being an inspiration to others is a positive. Again, hard to define without getting personal.*

## Binary Opposition

As part of the deconstruction process, the next step after defining terms would be to define their binary opposites. The survey and interview questions dealt with only one binary opposite: that of toxic masculine. The opposite of masculine of course would be, for most, feminine, as we saw in the previous chapter. Therefore, the survey and interview questions only focused on toxic masculine's opposite. When asked, "What is the opposite of problematic or toxic masculine," survey participants varied slightly in answer. Responses were gathered into main categories which were broken down into more specific subcategories, Qualities and Traits, Maturity and Growth, and changing Gender Constructs.

## Qualities and Traits

According to participants, the opposite of toxic and problematic masculinity are different kinds qualities and traits of masculinity. The first of those traits includes Confidence in one's own sense of masculinity, which also translates to Acceptance of both genders, including all things male/female.

### Confidence

For example, here is what participants had to say when it came to having confidence in oneself and their own masculinity:

*A clear understanding of self and one's connection to family and community.*

*Natural masculinity, like doing things because you want to and not to impress, true confidence not arrogance, strength in understanding and procession of emotions rather than blind repression and projection/perpetuation, inclusivity rather than bullying.*

*Letting go of self-judgement as to whether you are masculine enough.*

*Fully developing yourself in service of improving the world.*

*Someone who is confident in themselves and their space while allowing others to have their own space and be comfortable.*

*The opposite of toxic masculinity is the lack thereof. The acknowledgment of privilege by the men who benefit from it, and either the use of that privilege to benefit others, or the dissolution of that privilege.*

*A comfortable masculinity – being confident for being a man, but not confident to a degree where it harms yourself or others.*

If the opposite of toxic masculinity, according to participants, is a sense of confidence, a clear understanding of oneself, and a fully developed person, then anecdotally, toxic masculinity would mean someone who is not confident in their own self, are not a fully developed person, and even insecure. This will be visited in a later chapter, but the very show and act of a domineering, overpowering masculine is arguably at its root a major fear and insecurity.

### Acceptance

Survey participants also shared how the opposite of toxic masculinity is a sense of equality across genders, a masculinity that both accepts and believes in men and women being equal. For example:

*The opposite of toxic masculinity is a true masculinity that respects and compliments the feminine.*

*To me the opposite of toxic masculinity is intersection feminism. Feminism in the sense of fighting to dismantle sexism. In other words, dismantling patriarchy would not only help women/nonbinary folks but men as well, by helping to free men of the societal expectations of masculinity and manhood, allowing people to explore masculinity in a more healthy context.*

*Egalitarian respect. Accepting that masculinity is a state of being and not "maintained" by performing narrow, societally defined ways of doing gender.*

*Being open to other people's expressions and ideas of masculinity. Helping to cultivate the idea that not one-size-fits all for masculine people. Using your masculinity (in whatever way you define it) to help others in some way, even small.*

*Being a mensch.*[3]

*Living with what you believe to be masculine and helps you, not forcing it onto others.*

*Not being toxic and being female because these adjectives are independent.*

## Maturity/Growth

However, at the same time, to have such qualities and traits, there needs to be a sense of individual maturity and growth. This sense of growth comes with the positive spin on masculinity (Positive Masculinity), a Wholeness and Balanced sense of masculinity, and Self-awareness.

### Positive Masculinity

The overwhelming answer, when asked the opposite of toxic masculine, was positive masculinity. This answer slightly varied in how they describe what it means, but the sentiment was the same throughout these responses:

*Positive masculinity, I guess. I don't like the word for either. It should be you're either being a good or terrible person.*

*(positive) masculinity*

*Positive masculinity has the advantages of masculinity but none of its disadvantages.*

*Having a positive sense of oneself as masculine that is authentic to you and not imposing on other people.*

*The opposite of toxic masculinity is positive masculinity or better yet, correct masculinity. Masculinity done right.*

### Balanced and Wholesome

There is a balanced view of masculinity that comes with individual maturity, a balance encompassing both masculine and feminine. Some participants referred to this balance of masculine and feminine as wholesome. For example:

*Toxic masculinity is opposed by wholesome masculinity.*

*Healthy masculinity? Where the individual does not feel attacked by everything that is different from the identity he has chosen.*

*The opposite of toxic masculinity is positive masculinity or better yet, correct masculinity. Masculinity done right.*

*Using the traditional masculine traits in a way that uplifts others, supports women and marginalized groups. Basically, any masculine trait that is used to help others can be positive masculinity.*

### Self-Awareness

In the same regard, the idea of maturity and growth also included a sense of self-awareness of one's masculinity, or personal growth within one's sense of masculinity.

*A clear understanding of self and one's connection to family and community.*

*A fully developed personality and psyche.*

*Fully developing yourself in service of improving the world.*

*Being yourself, learning to understand yourself and disregarding the expectations and conditioning society has imposed on you. In a societal sense, treating people equally regardless of gender is the opposite. Note that it's a negation rather than a true opposite. There can't be a true opposite of toxic masculinity, because that would simply be another flavor of the same thing. Positive and negative sexism are both still just sexism and equally damaging, for example.*

## Gender Constructs

Once we have achieved this quality of growth and self-awareness, we can begin to create a new gender construct, one which is inclusive of masculine and feminine. These gender constructs involve an Inclusiveness of Femininity coupled with masculinity, along with a positive (Different) aspect of masculinity. For example:

### Different Masculine Constructs

*Positive masculinity. A culture and setting in which men are not antagonized for having feminine traits or expressing emotions generally considered to be feminine.*

*The opposite of toxic masculinity is altruistic suicide, which is again, the only option moral men have when they realize the #hivemindidiom culture of worshiping the most privileged exploiters. These are people who self-sacrifice to reveal the truth of our system, people who warn others about how we are lied too constantly by historical revisionism in academia. For more information search "unwitting colonizers."*

*The opposite of toxic masculinity is the lack thereof. The acknowledgment of privilege by the men who benefit from it, and either the use of that privilege to benefit others, or the dissolution of that privilege.*

*This is where I think my earlier answer becomes very relevant – all we are doing is talking about stereotypes here. So even if I can go back and list the same non-toxic traits, that's not going to provide a "roadmap" for men to follow because these are literally just stereotypes and not a solid basis for men to make life decisions.*

### Inclusiveness of Femininity

*To me, the opposite of toxic masculinity is intersection feminism. Feminism in the sense of fighting to dismantle sexism. In other words, dismantling patriarchy would not only help women/nonbinary folks but men as well, by helping to free men of the societal expectations of masculinity and manhood, allowing people to explore masculinity in a more healthy context.*

*The opposite of toxic masculinity is a true masculinity that respects and compliments the feminine.*

*Not being toxic and being female because these adjectives are independent.*

*Acknowledging and disavowing male privilege, magnanimity.*

*Gender abolition, by way of embracing feminism.*

The idea of gender abolition is deconstructive by idea, going beyond masculine to supersede gender. And at the same time, embracing the feminine to do so. While abolition of gender on its own is good in theory and a step toward equality, it is only one piece of a deconstructive pie since it excludes anything about its opposite of feminine. Therefore, including feminine with the masculine, and then abolishing gender is a closer way to its deconstruction. What would be lacking, then, is the new concept that is conceived by such abolition. More on the new concept in Chapter 5 (Figure 4.1).

The binary opposite of toxic masculinity, then, according to participants, includes certain qualities and traits like confidence and acceptance of an individual's experience in masculinity. Those qualities and traits, though, lead to a certain amount of maturity and growth. This growth includes positive views of masculinity, a balanced and wholesome life of masculinity and femininity, and self-awareness in one's experiences of this balance. It's only through the confidence and acceptance of one's masculinity that this can be achieved. This also leads to a different view of gender constructs – masculinity and being inclusive of feminine qualities in oneself. This inclusiveness in gender constructs leads us back to the qualities and traits of acceptance and confidence: it's only when we are confident in ourselves that we

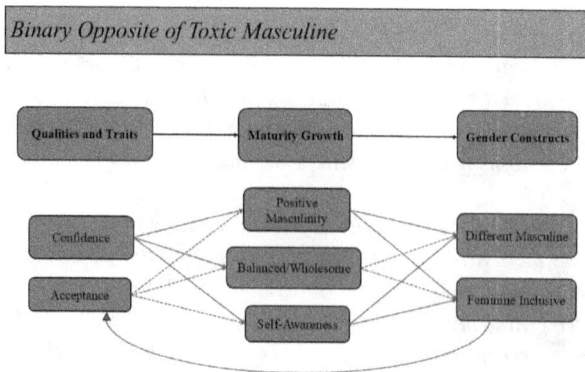

*Figure 4.1* Binary Opposite of Toxic Masculine

can accept other constructs of gender which may not be included in the dominate narratives we live in.

## How Can Masculinity Be Toxic

How masculinity becomes toxic was more involved to answer for participants. When surveying and asking the question: how can masculinity be problematic or toxic, responses focused on four categories with their own subcategories. Each category within this question can be seen as a part of a process in how masculinity can become toxic. It begins with Societal Expectations, which can encompass Patriarchy and the Performance of masculinity. This is followed by the Interpretation of those expectations, which include the Pressure to be masculine and the Emotional state that comes with it (or lack thereof). From those interpretations are its Applications, or the Misuse of masculinity, which include Bullying and Dominance. The Applications lead to forms of Aggression, which can be seen through Physical Violence and Competition. When referring to societal expectations of masculinity, and how it can be toxic, this is what participants had to say.

## Societal Expectations

The expectations to be masculine received from society can vary. It's these expectations which tend to turn masculinity toxic. Participants tend to answer about society's expectations in two main ways: society's influence of Patriarchy and how to Perform masculinity.

### Patriarchy

*It's toxic in that it's an aspect of patriarchy. Toxic masculinity is wielded toward women and men alike. Against women and nonbinary folks as a way of othering and putting them beneath men, and against men because they're forced to conform or be pushed to the out group.*

*By instilling harmful patriarchal ideals that inhibit the ability of men to express their emotions, leading to emotional repression and a disconnection from what it means to be truly human: to feel.*

*Masculinity can be problematic through the patriarchy in the intrinsic belief that men should be the head of the system whether in a business, group, or family. The competitive nature between boys and men can easily get out of hand and be dangerous for one, both, and/or multiple parties. The social self-regulation of men by men can pressure men to conform to expectations, even if unreasonable.*

*Since Genesis 3:16, masculinity has been problematic in that women sought to desire their husbands, but men (via Adam) want to be tyrannical toward them (and others).*

*It creates false conciseness in terms of men's collective interests. I think this leads a lot of men with more traditional values to blame women for societal problems affecting them.*

*Under patriarchy, masculinity demands the subject define their gender through creating a lesser class (feminine) and then defining themselves apart from that. This is done through means of permitted domination, meaning the masculine subject cuts off parts of themselves that are identified as feminine and hurts others through leveraging their power over them. Additionally, the masculinized subject may direct this domination at any people who threaten the Hegemony that maintains their power as men.*

*I think when people have a very rigid idea of masculinity, that it has to be a specific way and can't be anything else, toxic masculinity festers. To better answer your question, when people take on some "traditional" views of masculinity (who's tradition is rarely answered) and go to an extreme it becomes problematic. Many people think being confident is masculine, and it can be, but too much of that can lead to thinking you're always correct, other people are dumb or "haters," and not respecting other people's feelings. Being "strong" is great until you get to a point where everyone else is weak and not worth your empathy. Being "dominant" while sometimes masculine coded isn't necessarily masculine and can lead to some very dangerous situations both for the person acting overly dominant or people interacting with them.*

### Performance

*We lost the infrastructure of masculine pride and positive masculinity. Men don't know how to be "good men" because we have lost rites of initiation and therefore how becoming a man place one in a role that benefits their community. Instead, we're forced to slap together what it is to be a man from media without the benefit of elders' wisdom to guide us. Hegemony without wise guidance misleads our efforts from conquering the needs of our community to conquering each other.*

*Only when it is performative. Or, used unjustly to dominate weaker people to gain benefit in a harmful way. Actions should be taken in a way that is good for the individual in a way that is good for community and good for society at large.*

*It can provide a normalization for abuse or controlling behaviors. "Men are just like that" can be used to wave away harassment or rape, for instance. Additionally, the expectation of men's eternal stoicism means men frequently do not get emotional support. In extreme cases, abusive women can exploit that.*

The normalization that this above participant shared has been a common response. Both men and women believe how masculinity becomes toxic when dangerous characteristics become the norm for society at large. This is what makes masculinity toxic; normalizing dangerous behaviors spreads the belief of the "right" way to be masculine, even excusing dangerous behaviors. This leads to the belief in patriarchy being one of these mechanisms that normalizes dangerous masculine behaviors, where patriarchy pushes men to perform in a certain way. Consider the following:

*Masculinity can be problematic through the patriarchy in the intrinsic belief that men should be the head of the system whether in a business, group, or family. The competitive nature between boys and men can easily get out of hand and be dangerous for one, both, and/or multiple parties. The social self-regulation of men by men can pressure men to conform to expectations, even if unreasonable.*

*I don't think masculinity as I defined it is inherently problematic. But social pressure to conform to a \*specific\* masculine ideal can cause self-esteem issues, unhealthy coping techniques, and concurrence seeking can cause behaviors that are damaging to others and self.*

*I don't think that real masculinity is ever problematic, but I think that people attempting to mimic bad interpretations of masculinity can be. That's where we see the overly aggressive/entitled/fake tough personalities emerging from.*

The mimicking of this participant refers to supports the idea of learned behaviors. These learned behaviors are deeper, though. As mentioned in a later chapter, sometimes the characteristics of anger, macho, or stonewalling are ways to keep vulnerable things hidden, like the fear of being feminine or failing the masculine narrative. Hiding these with bad interpretations of masculine is very much a learned phenomenon. It's not so much that men mimic other harmful masculine behaviors; instead, they learn to hide their fears through these behaviors. What is really being mimicked is the emotional suppression of vulnerable fears, not the characteristics we see themselves.

### Interpretation

One of the ways, or a part of the process, in which masculinity becomes toxic is the interpretation of society's expectation on what it means to be masculine, and how to be masculine. According to participants, there is a certain quality of Pressure that men feel the need to conform to, and some of that pressure is interpreted in stereotypical ways, including certain Emotions pertaining to masculinity.

#### *Pressure*

There is a sense of pressure to "be" a certain type of masculine. This pressure tends to lead to forms of toxic and harmful masculinity. For example:

*Masculinity is absolutely problematic in that so many men feel the need to be "overly" masculine. Typically, when you come to a party there is one man being the "loudest person in the room." There are a few women who are drawn to that but everyone else chalks it up to be 'toxic masculinity', which is the correct assumption. It makes men in general look bad when it's only a few who act like that, but they're the ones who get all the attention.*

*If it's taken to the extreme, it can become toxic and hurt people who are not masculine or force men into stereotypes or pictures of what the "true man" should be. Examples are people like that bald dude who I forget the name of who got arrested in Romania and was a big thing on the internet.*

*It can lead to men changing their interests or beliefs out of a fear that they'll be shunned for acting unmanly, and sometimes those new "manly" beliefs that they adopt can themselves be damaging.*

*The stress of being looked at as someone who has to have all the answers when things go wrong, or being looked to be a primary provider, without recognition of the difficulty causes some men to develop substance abuse issues or treat others poorly as a way to lash out against those weaker than them when they feel powerless.*

What's interesting about this participant's answer is their use of being masculine to "show" a man how to be masculine. This is consistent with literature on positions of power and reducing inequality; it takes people in power to initiate change. In the case of changing the narrative of toxic masculine, it takes a "masculine man," someone inside the powerful narrative of masculine, to initiate the process of inclusion and tearing down the ideals that keep toxicity alive.

### Emotions

Another common interpretation of society's expectations of masculine is the emotional state, or the lack of emotions men are "supposed" to have. This is a common interpretation according to participants.

*I think both masculinity and femininity have toxic aspects to them that need to be unpacked, but men are undeniably in a power position to express that toxicity in more explicitly destructive ways. As an example, men's relationship to sexuality, in combination with their physical strength can easily turn expression of sexual frustration into threatening behavior that in turn (somewhat understandably) leads women to demonize male sexuality in a way that ends up biting men right back in the ass. Although I see it as something that women are equally complicit in, I also think men's insecurity around expressing their vulnerability is a huge problem that needs to be addressed. I don't think women have a good idea of what men's experiences or internal lives look like, but men certainly don't make it easy for women because most men just aren't very good introspection and voicing their feelings in productive ways.*

*It can be when traits considered masculine are present. For example, someone decides being emotionless is masculine. Another time it can be problematic is when someone decides that physical aggression is a way to solve problems or as a way to show how you feel.*

*When it melds with destructive fear. Teaching men to be dominant over their women partners (or that they should have women partners even if they like men more) because you're afraid of what non-heteronormative relationships may bring, to declare war on others for living in ways different from your own (even if they're demonstrably healthier in important contexts), when you ignore your own feelings of unhappiness and misery because it's "not manly" only to channel those feelings into self-destruction, that is when masculinity can be problematic (to put it lightly).*

*As masculinity seems to be pretty highly valued the problematic aspects seem to come from people trying to display or increase their masculinity.*

*Masculinity could be problematic if specific traits, usually behavioral or belief, override any reasonable actions, thoughts or choices to be made in usually extreme measures. Through extreme actions, beliefs, and or thoughts likely negatively impact the lives of others, or themselves due to exaggerated actions, beliefs, or traits of what is "masculine" and whether those actions, or thoughts, are done, or beliefs are, in the extreme or accentuated. Which usually leads to manipulative, egocentric, or even toxic behaviors inflicted to those who do not agree with their actions, or beliefs from the individual with what might be called problematic masculinity.*

*Masculinity as a construct is an issue because it tells men they all have to be the same way: unemotional, strong, brave, the breadwinner for a family, competitive, successful, etc. They have to meet expectations of appearance, muscular, large penis, chiseled cheekbones, etc. they have to fight or be angry instead of cry, they have to always protect and provide. If they don't act this way, they are considered effeminate and/or "gay" which still bothers heterosexual men.*

## Misuse/Application

After society's expectations are interpreted, those interpretations are then put into action. Or they are misused and applied to different lives and relationships. According to participants, this can be seen as Bullying and Dominance over others who aren't masculine, specifically women.

### Dominance

*If it's taken to the extreme, it can become toxic and hurt people who are not masculine or force men into stereotypes or pictures of what the "true man" should be. Examples are people like that bald dude who I forget the name of who got arrested in Romania and was a big thing on the internet.*

*When it is seen as superior to femininity and when it is seen as fixed box that men have to conform to rather than a toolbox of ways to relate to the world which anyone can pull from.*

*Masculinity is as varied as there are number of men on this planet. Therefore, masculinity should be defined by each one of them for each one of them. If one prefers to lift weights and provide for a family that is their individual definition of masculinity. If one prefers two crochet and be a stay-at-home partner, that is their individual definition of masculinity. Neither are less valid. By using the term to gatekeep for the in group, you inevitably end up with a large death of toxic peacocking behaviors in which men behave in accordance with what the end group deems is appropriate even when this may be counterproductive to their own progress and success. A perfect example would be the belief that emotions shouldn't be shown in public or to your partners.*

*When it is seen as superior to femininity and when it is seen as fixed box that men have to conform to rather than a toolbox of ways to relate to the world which anyone can pull from.*

*When it melds with destructive fear. Teaching men to be dominant over their women partners (or that they should have women partners even if they like men more) because you're afraid of what non-heteronormative relationships may bring, to declare war on others for living in ways different from your own (even if they're demonstrably healthier in important contexts), when you ignore your own feelings of unhappiness and misery because it's "not manly" only to channel those feelings into self-destruction, that is when masculinity can be problematic (to put it lightly).*

### Bullying

*Masculinity in itself cannot be problematic. Defining bad behavior as masculine behavior is the problem. For instance, if I bully or intimidate someone into getting my way, this is bad behavior on my part, not masculine behavior.*

*It becomes problematic without noble sentiment or interpersonal bonds or social ideals of honor to order it. Without something to put strength in service to and without a code of honor to maintain respect within, the desire for strength and respect degenerates into a very self-indulgent clout chasing, boorishness, and bragging and flexing. See the Andrew Tate phenomenon.*

*It can used against you in gender discrimination.*

*When it's acted out in a way of superiority.*

*When it's idolized or it's assumed to be normative.*

*When men use their masculinity to bully or deride others.*

*Traits can be misused. Being decisive can also mean someone may be stubborn or think themselves always right.*

## Aggression

The final piece of this process in which masculinity can become toxic is the outward misuse or application of interpretation, which tends to lead to acts of aggression. According to participants, aggression is shown through Physical Violence and Competition, which seems to be a central component in toxic masculinity.

### Competition

*Most masculine traits can cause problems when taken to the extreme: stoicism, leadership, risk-taking, competitiveness, willingness to fight.*

*It can encourage men to adopt needlessly competitive attitudes with other men. It can discourage men from expressing themselves emotionally and adopting traits that aren't considered traditionally masculine. And many men feel that they have to be providers for their family and feel weakened when they don't earn as much income as their wives/girlfriends.*

*When it becomes a contest.*

*It can manifest as hyper-competitiveness, emotional repression, social segregation based on gender identity and conformity, and punish those considered less masculine.*

### Physical Violence

*Asserting masculinity through displays of dominance and aggression is clearly problematic, and the same can be said for asserting masculinity through sexist behavior and remarks. Attempting to suppress your feelings in order to be a man is also problematic. I don't think that men initially choose to suppress their emotions – in my case, I started doing it because when I shared my emotions, they were dismissed, although I've since found ways of opening up again. So, one problematic aspect of masculinity is that some people (men and women) will dismiss your valid emotions because of your gender.*

*Maybe when groups associate aggression with masculinity too much it can become problematic.*

*Being taught that no one will care about you – or your suffering – if you are a failure lends itself to high-risk, aggressive strategies in all realms of life, often causing harm or conflict.*

*By being antagonistic – looking for fights, treating women like they're lower beings.*

*Can result in violence, hatred, and tribal behavior, when it's thought of as purely physical.*

*I don't think that real masculinity is ever problematic, but I think that people attempting to mimic bad interpretations of masculinity can be. That's where we see the overly aggressive/entitled/fake tough personalities emerging from.*

*Mostly aggression, self-destructive self-reliance, isolating yourself to the point it's detrimental. Men are falling behind in education. Suicide is increasing because we often feel stigma around seeking mental health treatment.*

*Masculinity, as a social construct in America and Western cultures (Eastern too), can have very problematic traits. These include using violence to solve problems, seeing anger as an acceptable emotion to use to manipulate or win arguments, believing that men must repress all other emotions except for anger, believing that anything outside the narrow definitions of "masculinity" is "gay" (and that being gay is inherently negative), and seeing anything deemed "feminine" as weaker or inferior.*

(see Figure 4.2).

There are certain societal expectations, then, which mainly come from the already established patriarchy; expectations to perform in a specific way of being a man. Those expectations can be misinterpreted through that pressure to perform and to be a certain type of emotionless person. Those interpretations then become a

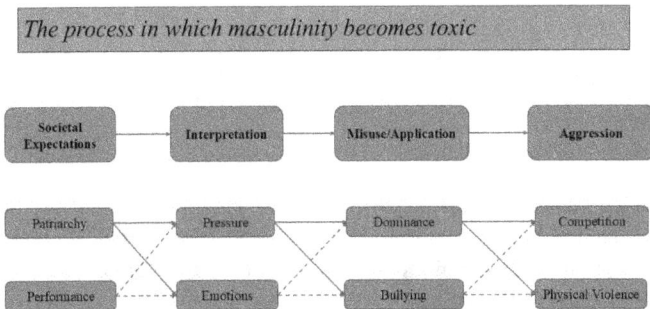

*Figure 4.2* The Process in which Masculinity Becomes Toxic

misuse of masculinity, which usually includes dominance and bullying, but are also done through the previous interpretations of society's expectations. Misuse can also lead to aggression, competition, and physical violence, which are commonly stereotyped as toxic masculinity.

One of the key components to our definition of toxic masculinity lies at the center of this book's argument; as participants have shared, it's the sort of masculinity being forced onto someone where they don't have a choice in it. Specifically, though, it's the sort of masculine considered to be harmful: aggression, violence, abuse, domineering. The traits we've come to call toxic are dangerous. And as a description, this is an acceptable way of approaching it.

However, I want to move past the description of toxic masculine into the process of toxicity, how something becomes toxic. Which means these harmful traits we've come to know to be toxic are forced on society, by expectation, or through other avenues of rhetoric. It's the sense of these traits being the "right" way to be masculine, and the rejection of other forms of masculine which then become toxic. The process by which these harmful traits are upheld, taught, believed, and reproduced is what makes toxicity.

My definition, then, is as follows:

*Toxic masculinity: The harmful traits of masculinity, such as violence, bullying, domineering, or intimidation through physical force or appearance to cause forms of oppression, which are disseminated through beliefs, institutions that uphold these beliefs, or other societal means, and are spread to the point where they infiltrate parts of society and relationships.*

Having defined it, and having laid the groundwork for Derrida's double science, we now proceed to the second portion of the strategy, displacement, to make a new concept of toxic masculinity deconstructed.

## Limits

To my knowledge, there is no such approach like "qualitative deconstruction," where the strategies of deconstruction are translated into qualitative inquiry. This attempt for something new is the first step to this approach. Having laid out the deconstruction strategy – defining binary oppositions, overturning, and displacement (new concept) – the current work only met the first two-thirds of the strategy. Displacement was not a part of the current work. Participants only aided in the defining and overturning portion of the strategy. Therefore, there are more studies to be had from the remaining portion of the deconstruction process.

### *Memo # 4 On Being Numb*

I'm currently listening to Brene Brown's podcast, and her guest is Vice President of the United States, Kamalah Harris. It's a very interesting episode if you haven't listened to it yet. In one portion of the episode, Brene talks about how society lives in a state of numbness, going back to the COVID years. She thinks there is too much going on emotionally that we start to be numb to basic emotional things. I don't disagree.

What's especially interesting is how we are constantly, slightly emotionally numb, because we haven't processed a lot of what's happened in the last 8 years, we "need" something very emotionally outstanding to get our attention. Which is why Donald Trump is seemingly successful as a presidential candidate. He's loud, emotionally, with his racist remarks and bigotry. And it works.

Two things about this:

First, so many people seem to be living under this emotional state of numbness. I can see how the 2016 election and COVID-19 were a lot to deal with. On top of that, the #metoo movement, and right before that the #blacklivesmatter movement. It has been a lot of emotional stuff in the past decade. COVID put a damper on things because we didn't have to see each other. It was an abrupt halt to the emotional chaos around us. Sure, COVID came with its own intensities, it was a political fandango. But it forced us to expend our emotions elsewhere - we going to die if we catch COVID.

If Brene's theory is true, and I think it is, then a lot of Americans are living under this slightly numb state. This offers a lot of explanation as to why so many people follow Donald Trump, or other emotionally loud people: Jordan Peterson, Andrew Tate, and Joe Rogan. It catches our attention because we need this sort of loudness given our emotional state.

Second, this also makes sense as to why things like toxic masculinity are still a thing. In a society where most people, if not the majority, are emotionally numb because of all the termoil we've endured, and if loudness is what captures our attention, then it's no wonder why toxic masculinity like aggression, violence, domineering, sexism, and misogyny are so rampant. Toxic masculinity is emotionally loud in the wrong way. Our slightly emotionally numb state is a perfect recipe for toxic masculinity to be given the spotlight. Toxic masculinity is just loud enough that it breaks the numbness.

The problem with this is our aversion to numbness. We don't want to feel numb.

This is an unconscious cycle. I think a lot of people are not emotionally aware enough to know how much a toll the past decade has had on our emotional states. Therefore, the awareness of the emotionally loud tactics, like a Trump rally, is also lacking. The fact that so many people follow this sort of emotional loudness speaks to how unaware we are as a nation.

In the context of toxic masculinity, the same amount and quality of unawareness is present. If we don't know we're being "sucked into" an emotional frenzy because we "need" it for a spark, or to get us out of our numbness, then we will never win the battle over it.

Over and over again I've seen people say the opposite of toxic masculinity is healthy masculinity, or a masculinity that is emotionally in tune with femininity. Not only does it require emotions to combat toxic masculinity, but it also takes the inner workings of self-reflection and awareness to combat it. It takes the realization of being emotionally numb and recognizing the emotional trap we fall into when we see things like toxic masculinity.

I'm worried there are not enough individuals willing to do that.

## Notes

1 This question was not included in the final analysis we see in this chapter. However, the data to this question was initially analyzed. To see this analysis, see Appendix 8.
2 For more definitions of masculinity from participants, see Appendix 3: What is Masculinity.
3 The Merriam-Webster Dictionary defines a mensch as a person of integrity and honor. Coming from a Yiddish background, it can also mean someone of upright character, responsible, complimenting individuals with the upmost qualities of a person.

## References

Daly, K. J. (2007). *Qualitative methods for family studies and human development.* Sage.
Derrida, J. (1981). *Positions* (A. Bass, Trans.). Chicago: University of Chicago Press.
Gunkel, D. (2021). *Deconstruction.* MIT Press.

# 5    New Concept

## Postmodernism and Postmodern Masculinities

Postmodernism does not believe in objective truth. Instead, truth is in the experience of those experiencing any phenomena. The goal of de-constructing or exploring ways in which we arrive at different "truths" focuses on where and how participants came to experience their experiences. Therefore, the postmodernist is more interested in "how" people experience certain phenomena, rather than "what" they are experiencing; "How was it for you to go through a divorce?" As opposed to what the rates of divorce are at any given time. Or, in our conversation, "how" do you experience masculinity and its toxicities? There is an underlying skepticism about what we know to be true, or that we can know anything at all with certainty (Rosenau, 1992). The postmodernist is willing to accept conclusions and positions as inconclusive and a process that continues to seek to understand; subjects trying to understand subjects (Wilber, 1998).

Postmodernism challenges the obtaining of objective knowledge. This challenge arose from questioning the scientific method, believing there is more than one way to know what we know. This becomes especially true when we speak of social norms of masculinity. As we've discussed, societies tend to agree on a hegemonic form of masculinity – a prototype, if you will. There is an accepted truth of such masculinity, and because the masses agree to it, it becomes an internalized truth. Postmodernism challenges this social norm of masculinity, how it is we come to establish such norms, and there too any rigid definition of masculinity.

*These prototypes of masculinity are not inherent, they are constructed by structural powers created by societal norms, and then adopted by men and women as the rules of what masculine ought to be.* Once we begin to believe this, the possibility for other masculinities presents itself as an opposing force, one which will continuously be against its oppressor.

Postmodernism also holds a skepticism toward grand narratives or metanarratives. Jean-Francois Lyotard (1984) poses the idea of no such thing as one unifying truth. This is especially true for interpretations of history, culture, and knowledge. The rejection of metanarratives also points to major institutions, like religion or policies, that tend to uphold their ideals as overarching truth. Lyotard describes this as "incredulity toward metanarratives." The danger in grand narratives, especially

DOI: 10.4324/9781003464228-5

in the case of gender, is one unifying way to "be." Whether one chooses to identify as male or female, or neither as non-binary, grand narratives limit the possibilities of existing.

When it comes to masculinity specifically, a central agreement of this book is how institutions and social structures have kept certain narratives of masculinity alive, harmful aspects of masculinity at that. What it means to be a man, according to grand narratives, means being dominate, aggressive, and even violent, which then by default excludes other options for living outside of those narratives. This turns into an exclusionary way of life; if you're not *this* type of masculine, you're not a man.

Closely related to the skepticism of metanarratives is the rejection of binary opposites. Postmodernism, like Derrida, also believes in the breaking down of binary opposites. When it comes to gender, the postmodernist believes in the limiting aspects of two binary genders, male and female. Rejecting this also means accepting the multiplicity of genders, along with all other "truths." We can only be as "real" as our experiences. And if we experience things outside metanarratives and binary opposites, then those experiences are important to the larger conversation of truth.

Michel Foucault is a dominant postmodern thinker who challenged the notion of universal truth, and at the same time examined the socially constructed aspect of truth. He argued that truth and knowledge are shaped by people in power, by the rules and politics that make up our society (Foucault, 1979). "Truth," then, is of course, relative. This translates well to our conversation of gender; everyone can have different experiences of being a man or a woman, and their experiences make their reality, not having one said reality needed to be lived by. But when the expectations are placed on anyone to *be* a certain way, and when those expectations breed a certain prototype of masculine, and therefore man, it becomes toxic.

*We remove toxicity through postmodernism by removing the lack of choice to be any one gender. When we accept everyone's experiences as different from our own and everyone else's, the spread of harmful traits is also removed.*

When it comes to the way metanarratives are shared, communicated, and believed, language becomes a central component in the mind of postmodern thinkers. How metanarratives are shared and the expectations placed on individuals are all transmitted through language.

The postmodernist also believes in the power of language and how it can shape our experiences. For example, the phrase "be a man" has historically been associated with a boy's ability to silence emotions, repress any form of femininity, and believe how "boys don't cry." Of more damaging effect, the phrase "don't be a pussy" has double the implication: it further emphasizes the fear of femininity and simultaneously degrades women. These phrases and rhetoric have the power to shape the experiences of men and women. Postmodernism challenges these languages and tries to be inclusive of other ways of languaging masculinity, other rhetoric that can also describe masculine experiences. In the case of deconstructing toxic masculinity, this presents the possibility of multiple masculinities to the process.

How one experiences masculinity, specifically outside the dominate narrative of masculinity, is where postmodernism focuses. Toxic masculinity tends to be a part of essentialism; it's a rigid form of masculinity, one that tends to exclude other forms and experiences of masculinity. "If you're not this kind of man, then what kind of man are you?" Being physically strong, or aggressive, tends to be the common trait that lives within toxic masculinity. Postmodernism, though, challenges the essentialism behind the expectations of masculinity, realizing the traits of toxic masculinity themselves are socially constructed, therefore challenging the norms themselves which constructed the traits.

*What if there are other forms of masculinity? What if there was a place in which all forms of masculinity can be invited to be a part of the bigger narrative of masculine? Postmodernism helps us get there by its views toward all rhetoric of all masculines.*

Postmodernism also gives us a philosophical stance when it comes to creating a non-dialectical third term, a new term that does not exist, yet already exists at the same time. The philosophical stance is considered *co-construction.* This term is common in the world of postmodern therapy and counseling, as well as social science qualitative research. The stance positions the researcher/therapist in a co-constructing relationship, language construction; language is generated through the interactions of the research and therapeutic process. Therefore, the interactions that share languages of the participant and researcher and therapist and client become generative (Perez, 2021).

Co-construction happens when people like you and me, people who want to change the narrative of harmful masculinities, are intentional about creating space to welcome other forms of masculinity. By acknowledging and using language outside the dominate narrative of masculine, we form language into the possibility of experience; an experience for others to live in other than the normalized expectations of being a man.

Social psychologist Kenneth Gergen (1985) challenged the notion of our amount of autonomy by arguing how our beliefs are fluid and constantly changing by the influence of our surroundings and contexts. Social constructionists believe we are constantly sharing meaning-making interactions. Our meanings and realities, even the meaning we give masculinity, are made through social availability and shared understandings (Daly, 2007). This is an encouraging thought, though.

This becomes more than a simple philosophy, or a way of conceptualizing masculinities. It becomes a way of believing; a way of interacting with the world around us. The postmodernist believes in the generative process found in interaction. They also believe in the power of language and how it's used to communicate truths and experiences. The postmodernist *believes* that language is what organizes and constructs experiences, and trusts in how an individual experience their truths, and so too trusts in the ability to experience individual truths outside the normalized narrative of masculinity.

Postmodern masculinities, then, are a conceptual step in the right direction when deconstructing toxic masculinity and displacing its binary opposite. Because the postmodernist challenges the norms around masculinities, it's an easy segway into the possibilities that arise when deconstructing toxic vs. healthy masculinity. The challenge lies in formulating a new term, an outcome of the deconstruction process.

## New Concept

Now that we've named our binary opposites, reversed their hierarchical order, and marked the intervals within that inversion, the remaining part of the deconstructing strategy is to explore the unexplored within and outside of this process, a new concept.

Gunkel (2021) helps articulate the abstractness of this third term, this new concept. This third term needs to encapsulate all the things within the possibilities of the toxic/healthy masculinity binary. At the same time, it cannot. The term we're looking for must exist within our realm of the theory of masculinity, at the same time it needs to exceed it. We need something that is everything about toxic/healthy masculinity, and nothing at the same time. The product that we find ourselves seeking needs to be where the deconstruction strategy leads up, both conceptually and in practice – everything and nothing at the same time.

However, as soon as we create a word to accomplish this, we put it in the box of theory, along with its potential binary. For example, a centaur. It's half man, half horse. It's both. But since we gave it a name, we now have the potential to describe what it's not, along with its potential opposite. What's the opposite of a centaur? A unicorn?

Therefore, we need to settle on one notion: whatever word we choose for this new concept, we must agree that it lives beyond our knowledge of our masculinity theory box, and that it tries to be all and none of the masculinities at the same time.

As recalled from before, when we deconstruct toxic masculinity, we also need to deconstruct masculinity – the gendered part of this puzzle. Therefore, this new concept needs to do two things for us: encompass the deconstruction of masculinity, and the deconstruction of toxic masculinity. As if one wasn't difficult enough.

What happens, then, when we explore all the possibilities that lie within the dimensions of masculinity, specifically within the sphere of toxic masculinity? Consider Figure 5.1. What do we get when we explore all the options of all possibilities of masculinity, and then reconfigure our options as far as new terms go?

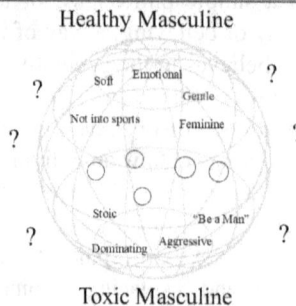

*Figure 5.1* The Process of Overturning and the Exploration within Displacement

There is an inherent deficit when approaching deconstruction in such a way. As we will see in the next chapter, there are shortcomings, or limitations to how we "end" the deconstruction process. Deconstruction never ends, just as Hegel dialectics (1977) are a constant cyclical attempt to resolve the tension between opposites. Deconstruction does not "end" because the possibilities of creating new concepts, the result of the *double science* (1981), are endless. As we will see, each concept cannot fully capture the essence of a new concept because we are limited by language, the very thing we use to create concepts. In actuality, concepts are concepts, once put into words, they become something different.

We must also make the distinction, though, between Derrida's and Hegel's[1] views on a non-dialectical third term. One outcome or process of Derrida's deconstruction is a "new term," one that both "inhabits and operates in excess" (Gunkel, 2021, p. 63) of what we are trying to conceptualize. Hegel's approach to dialectics is somewhat different from Derrida's. For example, one Hegel is famous for, is the dialectics of *being* (1989). According to Hegel's dialectics, anything's beginning is determined by the *other* of itself. Therefore, *being's* other can be considered *nothing*. This is his first negation, defining an *other*. The second negation comes by way of "sublation," or in its original language *Aufhenbung*. Sublate has two meanings, to preserve, and to put an end to. So, the sublation of *being* and *nothing,* according to Hegel, is *becoming.* Becoming solves the opposition of *being* and *nothing,* and at the same time preserves them both, or describes how they are both "used" to solve their opposition. "Becoming is the unseparateness of being and nothing, not the unity which abstracts from being and nothing; but as the unity of *being* and *nothing* it is this *determinate* unity which there *is* both being and nothing" (Hegel, 1989, p. 105).

The problem with this, however, is one that deconstruction aims to resolve. For Hegel, the process of his dialectics is ongoing, cyclical. His "third term" is the beginning of a new cycle. This means that the resolving of *being* and *nothing,* which is *becoming,* now starts the process over. What is the "other of itself" of *becoming?* And that resolution will take us to another third term that will repeat the cycle.

Derrida's deconstruction takes this approach through a different process, one that separates it from Hegel's. His double science is different from Hegel's process, the double science that overturns binary opposites. This step specifically calls out the "violent hierarchy" of binary opposites. Therefore, this part of the deconstruction process does more than reverse words or find opposites, *double science is an existential call to understand the power our own language has on our internal narratives, and therefore explore new spaces that don't exist between the possibilities of binary pairs.*

Whereas Hegel's process results in the sublation of two terms, his process does not involve overturning, nor does it recognize the inherent hierarchy that comes with positioning opposites. This does distinguish it from deconstruction. Derrida's goal in a non-dialectical third term is for it to be organically produced through the process of the double science: defining opposites, and their overturning. It is the disruption that occurs in this overrunning that is central to the new third term, the new concept. There is a space produced when overturning that ought to naturally lend itself to the new third term. When done well, a new concept will erupt and emerge within this space.

With the agreement of this new concept being a term existing beyond the box of our gender and masculine theories, and beyond what we experience today, let's explore the following. To my knowledge, these concepts are not "real" words but are words derived from the language and definitions and other words we use today and therefore used to try to grasp something beyond our language today as well. We will discuss the terms along with their potential shortcomings to arrive at a deconstructed toxic masculinity.

## Concepts

The process of creating this new concept is limited because of our system of language. However, Gunkel (2021) presents the useful idea of remix, which is what we will be attempting. Remixing is close to deconstructing, and the outcomes are similar. For example, take the remix of one of your favorite songs. The remix consists of two songs, independent of each other, but when put together, they become something differently entirely, also independent from the original two songs. Therefore, the remixed song is something that both encompasses the original songs (or in Derrida's deconstruction, the binary opposites), and simultaneously transcends both songs, making something new. The small piece lacking here is the step of overturning, and the acknowledgment of a hierarchy existing because of the order of opposition. This step is necessary as we pointed out in the earlier chapter, because without the recognition and overturning of the hierarchy, we have the same problem in the reversed order.

When displacing, though, and creating a new concept, remixing is a helpful exercise in imagining what already exists when we deconstruct, and the mental space needed for two opposites to live together, and therefore to create something new. With the idea of remixing in mind, the following are multiple attempts at a new concept, one where we have completed the phases of overturning to deconstruct toxic masculinity.

## Masculine New Term

First, masculinity. Given the feasible options of masculinity that lie within masculine and feminine, once we overturn their oppositions, and once we displace their possibilities, a few options present themselves.

*Omnimasculinity.* Omni comes from the Latin word for "all," or "every" or "all at once." The inclusion of masculinity is to communicate the traits associated with masculinity. In my definition, this is to include the less common forms of masculinity, such as gentleness and nurturing. Therefore, "all" forms of masculinity. The hope is to reject the rigid rules and ideas of gender, and to be more inclusive and equal of all aspects and experiences of gender. This term is also an attempt to provide flexibility and fluidity between all aspects and traits of masculinity.

The shortcoming of this term is the gendered assumptions associated with masculine and feminine. It is usually the common assumption that women are the nurturing gender. Therefore, even though *Omnimasculinity* tries to displace and to arrive a new term, it has its challenges.

Next, *Variousculinity.* This is a combination of the word "varied" or "various," and the term masculinity. The hope is to communicate a diversity of masculinity, acknowledging that there are diverse ways to express and experience masculinity. The hope is to also communicate the various identities that might live within the realm of masculinity, and beyond, but still including, stereotypical forms of masculinity.

The challenge with this is the exclusion of femininity. This does come closer, though. There is the possibility for femininity to live within the realm of masculinity; one can be feminine and masculine at the same time. That possibility is not clearly communicated through *Variousculinity*, though.

A term that may include the possibility of femininity existing within the realm of masculinity may be *Plurimasculinity*. This comes from the Latin word "plurimus," which means multiple, or many. This can include a broad range of masculinity, even multiple spectrums of masculinity, which can include the possibility of a "feminine masculine." This term ought to communicate the coexistence of all masculinities in their diversity and multiplicity.

Again, the lack of the word feminine is problematic. As well as the word masculine. To include the word masculine in any phrase, by default, tends to exclude anything feminine.

Therefore, to try to remedy that, let's consider *Magnamasc.* Magna comes from the Latin word meaning great, or vast. *Masc* is an entirely made-up word: short for masculine, simultaneously attempting to only communicate masculine qualities. Therefore, the goal is to welcome the vast concept of masculinity – forms and experiences. *Masc* is a way to strip away the gendered form of masculinity to include anything possibly feminine in it as well – any gender can be masculine, therefore, *masc.*

*Esymasc.* The prefix "esy" is not a real word, but it is meant to sound like *easy*, insinuating a fluid or evolving form of masculinity. As above, *masc* shows the traits of masculine, attempting to remove the gendered male assumption of masculine, of which *Esymasc* is a great attempt at doing so.

We still need to communicate something all-encompassing and not at the same time, "either/or and neither/nor." For this, let us try *Novamasc.* Nova comes from the Latin word "new" or "novel." This word is intentionally trying to break down the binary of masculine/feminine, creating something "new" instead, while combining it with *masc*; a novel form of *masculinity*. *Novamasc* does come close to attempting a new third term, however, it only communicates the newness of a word, it does not communicate the nothingness of the deconstruction, the term that is both all of masculinity, but at the same time none of it.

Next, *Nullimasc.* Nulli comes from the Latin word "nullus," meaning none, or nothing, the absence of anything fixed. This is closer. *Nullimasc* can exemplify an all-encompassing form of masculinity while embodying none of the forms. This can potentially be an undefinable form of masculinity that lives outside the boundaries of our definitions, and at the same time standing for the traits of masculinity, *masc.*

We could go on. The possibilities for words that communicate all genders and none at the same time are limitless. The attempt to evolve a word will continuously, in my opinion, be met with some form of challenge because of the limited vocabulary we have as a western society to communicate genders, specifically masculine and feminine traits of gender.

### Toxic Masculine New Concept

When it comes to the concept of Toxic Masculinity, the same challenges present themselves as deconstructing only gender. The limit on gender will inevitably be present. To attempt a new concept, let us consider the following creations. The ideal use of the following terms is to transcend the entire notion of gender, and therefore the idea of toxicity. If one of our primary definition of toxic masculine is a rigid idea of masculine, one without choice, where that choice is to only be stereotypical and harmful forms of masculine, then these terms strive to move beyond that. One preface: there is no one "right" phrase in the following list. These are all attempts to reach a non-dialectical third term.

First, *HumaUnity*. This word has several goals. The first goal is to break away from gender all together, transcend the binary opposite of male/female, and masculine/feminine: humanity. In several points of data collection, participants asked and responded with the need to even define masculinity – to do so might even arguably be toxic. Therefore, we need to think beyond masculine, feminine, male, and female, to think in terms of "humanity." This is a good example of going beyond the theory box of masculine, along with its binary opposite, feminine. However, *humanity* is a word that already exists. Hence the addition of *Unity*. *HumaUnity* moves beyond male/female, and unites the two, creating one possibility of only being human. Then why not simply call it being human?

One challenge with this term is the exclusion of the absolving of "toxic." Since the description of toxic has been important to our conversation, to leave that out of the new term does not try to move beyond the "toxic" part of masculinity.

Next, we have *Harmoneity*. This is a combination of "harmony" and "identity." This term suits us well for several reasons. First the philosophical stance of being in harmony with one's own self in their choice of masculine. Again, this intentionally leaves out the rigidness of "needing" to choose any form of masculine. Harmony also implies the lack of needing to be identified by any one gender, trying to transcend the binary state of toxic masculine where the choice is made for you. The identity part of the word implies how one chooses to identify. This extends the masculine construct into anything else one chooses to identify as. Therefore, deconstructing both toxic masculine and masculine at the same time; one can choose to be any form of masculine and have a harmonious experience in that, and one can choose to identify beyond the masculine ideal, even beyond its opposite feminine.

I find few challenges with this term as well. One small lack is the term harmony. Even though it is well suited for our new concept, the term can imply the choice of only one possibility of masculine identity, such as it is despite the harmony one experiences with it. This can move away from our efforts to simultaneously encompass *all* and *none*. If we are transcending toxic, then we ought to be all things as opposed to only one thing. When we choose one thing, we run the risk of meeting its opposite with rigidity.

Therefore, let us consider *Essentium*. This combines "essence" and "continuum." Ideally, one is able to express their own selves along a continuum of gender, from masculine to feminine. This is trying to encompass the entire spectrum, or continuum of gender, from masculine to feminine, covering the binary opposition. Therefore, one can be flexible and fluid with their gender experiences. Essence attempts to move beyond that continuum, grasping at the essence of more than what it means to be masculine or feminine, but the essence of the entire continuum itself, the essence of *all* the gender choices. This too removes the rigidity of having to "choose" one masculine, which alleviates our challenge with toxic.

This possibility is also well suited for our conversation; I have small challenges with it as well. Even though "essence" captures a state of being that communicates our goal in moving beyond binary opposites, "continuum" is too two-dimensional. It does not attempt to displace, or "flip the script" of the power in which the masculine/feminine binary is ordered. Even though a continuum gives the freedom to be fluid and experience more than one area of masculine or gender, which also relieves the toxicity of masculine, there is the possibility of power also being de-constructed[2] with the fluidity, which is not our aim.

Next, we have *Unifidenity*. This is a remix of "unified" and "identity." The mixing of these two tries to grasp the state of diverse traits, from masculine to feminine, covering the span of the binary, and cohesively weaving them into one, creating something new. As one single trait, one can transcend gender expectations into their sense of identity. With *unifidentity,* we have a mix of all the traits from masculine to feminine, working together, for a unified state of being all the traits, which in combination makes one trait.

The combination of unified and identity also removes the toxicity of "needing" to be a set of traits of masculine. However, like the previous term, this term is two-dimensional. Even though we are encompassing all the traits into a unified one, the traits come arguably from a binary, not the overturned nature of the "flipped script."[3] This is a constant lacking when trying to create our own term to reach the ending states of deconstruction.

When attempting to include all forms of masculinity in a new concept, all forms which also span the possibilities of masculine and its binary opposite, the plural form of masculine is a good start. The plural form of masculine can be *masculines*. Sofia Aboim (2010) also emphasizes the idea of a plurality of masculinities. Even though she presents a wide array of masculine possibilities and contextualizing them within family and a relationship to the feminine, the resolution for Aboim is not a new concept as it would be for deconstruction.[4] To reach a new deconstructed concept, we would need a plural form of the plural form of masculine; a plural of plurals. *Masculi* can be more than only presenting multiple masculinities, and more than the simple plural of masculine. This communicates the idea of multiple possibilities for masculine, but also the options for both/and other pluralities to exist at the same time. Pluralities of masculine also gives us the possibility for masculinity to exist with femininities. However, another challenge with *masculi* still lies within the limiting aspects of gender, the exclusion of the word feminine. To truly deconstruct toxic masculinity, we need to also transcend gender.

One possibility to try to transcend gender would be to use conjugations like the Spanish language. It has been recent, when speaking of Latino individuals, that Latinos was used to signify men and women. The term evolved to Lantinx to signify multiple races and nationalities among the American and South American cultures. However, this also evolved into a gender-neutral term Latines, communicating a non-binary feminist community of Spanish-speaking countries. The use of "es" in Latines comes close to our purposes.

The word masculines does exist in the English language. However, when pronounced similar to Latines, we come with *Masculin`es*, a combination of *masculine* and Latin*es*. Like the Latines, the intention of masculin`es is to present the choice of a non-binary term, even a feminist term. Adding this feminist component also give the intention of creating an equality between genders, making no one gender more "powerful" than the other. This also removes our problem with toxicity; *when we create equality among gender, and when we address individuals as a non-binary person, we remove the toxicity of "needing" to choose between any with gender. It is inclusive of all genders, and removed any hierarchy we might have, resolving our overturning phase of deconstruction.*

Once again, the challenge we face here is still the involvement of gender, specifically mentioning the partial phrase of masculine. The new concept, even though successful in other efforts to neutralize gender, is not the goal of deconstruction. To neutralize would be to de-construct, to take something apart, to strip it away of its parts, and "neutralize" it. Even though these efforts are worth of pursuit, especially for a feminist approach to masculinity, they fall short of deconstruction.

One possibility could be *Metamasc*. The idea of "meta," according to its Greek etymology, signifies "after" or "beyond." This presents an option for us that would offer something "after" masculine, or "beyond" masculine. This is very close to what Derrida's purpose of a new concept would be, something that is "more than" its original use and its binary opposite. According to the Merriam-Webster Dictionary, meta can also mean transcending, or something altering. This also presents a close deconstruction possibility; a masculine transformed, changed, or beyond our idea of masculine. As above, the abbreviation of *masc* is to not include the entire word masculine, to remove the direct tie back to masculine, moving beyond masculine but still including some of original meaning. Therefore, we're attempting to be either/or by using *masc*, and neither/nor by using *meta*, communicating something beyond or transformed.

Even though close to the arrival of a concept, *Metamasc* does fall a little bit short of our resolution of the double science. As Gunkel (2021) describes it, "Deconstruction cannot come to speech, be spoken about, or appear in writing, without redeploying and remixing the available set of words and concepts" (p. 83). The very fact of creating novel words, words that don't exist, or a combination of already used words to create something original, will always fall short, hence our agreement at the beginning of this chapter. *Metamasc* falls short because of the very fact of providing the term language and writing. As is the case for all our terms; putting it into writing provides us with the space to argue its binary opposite. For example, the binary opposite of *metamasc* could arguably be *inframasc*, a masculinity subset of masculinity, the opposite of the transcending nature of meta. This could be the case for any new concept we create.

Another term to consider, one having a positive outlook on masculinity along, is *Tonic Masculinity* (Groth, 2021). The term has two connotations. One being that of a musical harmony, where the tonic chord is the root to a melody of a song, usually a triad of notes from which a song's melody is central to. The key idea behind this connotation is the harmony and foundational elements of music found in the tonic chord. What if there is a sense of masculinity that is harmonious with other masculinities and genders?

The other connotation of this term is the idea of a substance or an influence, a "healing" tonic. This sense of tonic is what Groth refers to as a homo ludens (playful man). There is a certain type of man that does not fit the traditional mold of a man; a "warrior" or a "head of the family" as seen in many Christian narratives, for example. Instead, this is a type of man that holds deep and long friendships with other males, it is also seen in homosexual men who do not identify as a feminine homosexual but are "proud" to be masculine homosexuals.

Tonic masculinity is a good description of a masculine that goes beyond the ideals of traditional masculinity. What does it take to achieve this sort of harmony, though? What do we need for men and women to be at peace with this type of masculine?

Like the concepts before this, there is a limit to tonic masculine. Although a worthy effort, this falls short of exceeding what deconstruction attempts: the idea of a new concept that goes beyond our theory box of gender. Tonic masculine, then, still encapsulates masculine, which automatically puts it in a vulnerable place of introducing its binary opposite.

**Masculine with Choice**

If one of the key tenets to our definition of toxic masculinity is masculinity without choice, and with that, the spread or infestation of the lack of choice to be masculine, we also need to find a new concept for those aspects of our definition. This would be the outcome, or the product of the overturning of the binary opposites, of masculinity with choice and without choice. One side of this binary opposition communicates the expectations society places on masculinity, where it is acceptable to be domineering or bullying. And in that, there is no choice or room for any other form of masculine. On the other side of this opposition we do have choice in the form of masculine we feel most comfortable living, one where there is no judgment or societal expectation. Overturning can produce these following new concepts. Like the concepts above, each has their own limitations:

For example, *Fleximasc*. This is a combination of "flexible" and "masculinity." Flexible tries to communicate the amount of freedom one has in choosing their experiences with masculinity, and at the same time trying to break down the rigidity of masculine expectations. And of course, when combined with masculinity, there is a broader range of masculine expressions by not calling it "masculinity."

The challenge with this concept is the idea of choice. Even though flexible communicates an acceptance of choices, to properly deconstruct this definition of toxic masculinity, we would need to move beyond the binary of choice/no choice. Flexible does not allow us to do so.

Another concept, then, could potentially by *Mallemasculinity*. This is remixed from the combination of malleable and masculinity. Malleable tries to depict something altered, or shaped from its original form, even easily changed or moldable. I use the term masculinity intentionally with this concept because of the malleable aspect of it, communicating this can potentially exceed gender limits, where even women can be a type of masculine, and even feminine can be masculine.

This term comes closer to the deconstruction result, where masculinity can be altered and changed, and so too can the aspects and genders be molded and changed where we include men and women. With this concept, we are aiming to go beyond the gender theory box and at the same time *try* to move beyond the limits of choice/no choice. However, even if something is molded or altered, it does imply some sort of choice. Who is doing the molding? Or, if something is altered without consent, it communicated something without choice.

Next, let's try *Automasculinity*. This remixes words autonomous and masculine. Specifically with autonomous, there is an internal process to be explored. Instead of having a choice or not, living inside or outside the dominant narrative of masculine, there is an ongoing negotiation about what is offered as a masculine choice by society's standards, and what we want for ourselves. There is an active tension and negotiation between being one's own self in the face of external pressures. Therefore, the masculine one lives in is the result of the discernment that comes from being an autonomous self.

Even though a good concept, there is still a small hint of "choosing." Despite the fact it being a well-thought-out decision, it is still a decision, nonetheless. And with the process of deconstructing choice/no choice, we fall a little bit short of the concept exceeding that.

What is needed is a concept which takes us beyond gender, and beyond the idea of choice. Be it a social construction of gender, or an intentional "against the norm" of gender, the aspect of choice is one we're trying to transcend.

Consider *Exogenity,* from the Greek word "exo" (ἔξω), and a combination of "*gender identity*." Exo symbolizes something that transcends, something that goes beyond or outside conventional thought. For example, an *exo*skeleton. With this combination, we're trying to move beyond choice, removing it altogether. If we're moving outside or beyond gender identity, we're also trying to alleviate any potential negotiation one faces with internal experience and external pressures received from masculine standards. Therefore, moving outside or beyond choice, one's gender identity is constantly emerging, and there too their expressions of masculinity, where masculinity is constantly evolving and in a process of discovery.

At the same time, *Exogenity* also moves beyond an individual into the idea of being relational. If society, ideals, and beliefs are constantly shaping gender identity and masculinity, then we need to consider both sides of this phenomenon – the shaper and the shaped. There is a relational aspect to how our gender identity and masculinity are constantly influenced on both sides. With *exogenity*, masculinity shifts, changes, and forms the interaction between internal self-reflection and external motivators.

With *Exogenity*, we're also trying to transcend masculine to gender. We're pushing past the labels of *who* can be masculine, and what gender it belongs to. Masculinity, like gender, is an open door to a multitude of possibilities not defined by society's norms or language (even though we're putting language to it.).

*Exogenity* is very close to a concept we're trying to reach, one encompassing the action of moving beyond choice when it comes to masculinity (which removes the toxic part of the definition), and at the same time moving beyond gender itself, meaning our gender identity and how we chose to "do" masculinity is no longer a position of "this or that."

### Toxicity of Masculinity

As per our definitions of toxic masculinity, we also need to be mindful of its spread, how toxic is something infectious and how it infiltrates. The infection of harmful masculinity, and how those qualities become widespread is one of our key definitions of toxic masculinity. Therefore, we also need to attempt to resolve its new concept; one resulting from the double science of the infectiousness of harmful aspects of masculinity and its opposite, the opposite of spread – to be still, to be one, whole, healthy. This action part of this term is central to the new concept, which communicates a process of becoming infectious, and therefore becoming the opposite of it.

The term *Unmasculate* communicates several processes that try to reverse the spread of harmful masculinity. *Unmasculate* attempts to increase the awareness of how masculinity can be harmful, manifesting at the individual and societal level, this includes misogyny, emotional suppression, hypermasculinity, and other harmful aspects of masculinity. This also communicates an intentional doing away or separation from such traits, hence the "un" in masculate, where masculate is a verb. The process, then, becomes an active disengaging from harmful patterns, and an intentional exposure to other possibilities of masculinity. The action also ideally consists of rebuilding the newfound aspects of masculinity in relationships with other men and women.

One area of critique with *Unmasculate* is the lack of gender-neutral language. Since we're deconstructing toxic masculinity, and therefore masculinity and gender, the new concept we're seeking ought to encompass the effort behind each of those. Even though nice in theory, *Unmasculate* leans specifically to the masculine, male-gendered side.

Consider, then, *Eqlibrium*. This is a remix of "equality" and "equilibrium." Given the last concept, equality is intentional, attempting to recognize the inequality between genders. This also attempts to rebalance, or create an equilibrium of masculine and feminine traits, also equalizing them. Therefore, there are no gender constrains to traits like vulnerability, empathy, strength in caring, physical strength, or any other stereotypically gendered trait. *Eqlibrium* also recognizes the intersectionality across masculinities – race, class, politics, culture, media. This recognition also gives attention to the spread of harmful aspects of masculinity, while trying to interject in the intersections where we find its toxicity. Therefore, there is celebration in intersections, community, and therefore, accountability. Finding the right access points to healthy forms of masculinity, growing those communities, and rethinking the intersections where masculinity becomes toxic is the exact opposite of its spread.

Similarly, let's also consider *Recalibra*. This communicates the transformative process of "recalibrating" gender norms associated with masculinity to include things like emotional authenticity while letting go of other traits like aggression and hypermasculinity. This also communicates a merging, or recalibrating, of traditionally "feminine" qualities, like nurturing and gentleness. The bigger picture with *recalibra* is to envision a larger societal recalibration, one where there is collective healing to hurtful masculinity, and an adjustment toward an inclusiveness of all aspects of all genders.

Like the above two concepts, we can also remix *Gentlecode*. This tries to communicate the literal rewriting of the "code" of masculinity and femininity, deprogramming their inherited beliefs and expectations. The rewriting would include normalizing characteristics that aren't traditionally acceptable for men: nurturing, vulnerability, and gentleness. Rather than promoting the "hard" traits of masculine, *gentlecode* rewrites the narrative of masculinity to include the "non-hard" points as well.

Even though these concepts remix well, and communicate a seeming deconstructed version of toxic masculinity, they all fall somewhat short because of the nature of language in deconstructing, and the multiple aspects of toxic masculinity. Therefore, we will visit one last term, one which comes the closest to deconstructing toxic masculinity.

## Cyborg Masculinity

By simply creating concepts and putting them into writing, we inevitably fall short of the "resolution" to the deconstruction process. Even though we're moving beyond gender and masculinity, we are still including the aspects that encompass the two at some point of the process. This will be a constant struggle: creating words themselves that describe the very thing we're trying to deconstruct. The limitations of our language will always be a roadblock when it comes to deconstructing.

The following concept is no exception. The last concept we will explore creates the same challenges but also gives us some resolve in what we can describe in deconstruction. We will still be creating a word or remixing two concepts. However, we do so with the agreement from earlier: we're agreeing to breaking the rules of deconstruction to reach a term to help us conceptualize toxic masculinity deconstructed.

Derrida (1981b) refers to this as "bifurcated writing," where the existing terms we use to deconstruct are used against themselves; we must use the words against themselves to deconstruct. As Gunkel (2021) reminds us, "deconstruction cannot come to speech, be spoken about, or appear in writing, without redeploying and remixing the available set of words and concepts" (p. 83).

With that in mind, let us examine one more concept, one that will try to encompass the bifurcated writing Derrida explains, and one that will also help us "resolve" the deconstruction process, only for the sake of calling it resolved.

Before we review the final concept of our conversation, however, let us remind ourselves of the strategy of deconstruction in which we find ourselves in: displacement, or finding a new term. The consistent challenge in finding new terms is twofold: one is the recurring cycle from Hegel's dialectics, where it's easy to find a new term, and then fall into the trap of finding its opposite, which starts the process over again. We seem to have alleviated that – for now – by creating the above concepts to try to reach deconstruction. The other part of that challenge is the lack of a word that encompasses all deconstruction aims to achieve.

As Derrida (1981) describes,

> The irruptive emergence of a new 'concept,' a concept that can no longer be, and never could be, included in the previous regime...it can no longer be included withing the philosophical (binary) opposition but which, however, inhabits philosophical opposition, resisting and disorganizing it without ever constitution a third term, without ever leaving room for a solution in the form of 'speculative dialectics.'
>
> (p. 42)

As mentioned before, and as Gunkel (2021) puts it, this new concept is simultaneously neither/nor, and either/or. While the concepts above can reach a place of either/or, the challenge that keeps presenting itself is the simultaneous neither/nor. This is quite impossible to achieve with words. Even though impossible, we find ourselves using the only tools that we have to communicate this new concept and the outcome of deconstruction: words. Therefore, as agreed on before, the words we choose are an understanding that we cannot achieve deconstruction without words, even though words are not the end goal. Bifurcated writing helps us intentionally leave our understanding of a word to arrive at a new concept, even though the new concept is insufficient and incomplete, but still necessary to articulate for the sake of deconstructing.

How do we articulate something that is, and is not? How do we articulate something that is neither/nor, and either/or?

### Both and None

It is difficult to conceptualize something which both occupies the words we use in everyday language, and at the same time (in the same words, even), imagine words that do not exist. As soon as we create a word, we are left with the challenge of finding its binary opposite, or at the very least we leave a word vulnerable to its contrary. For example, the gender spectrum. Yes, there is such a thing a fluidity on the gender spectrum, one can fluctuate between any given point on the spectrum, one day leaning toward masculine, and another day leaning toward feminine. These two days of leaning on the spectrum are arguable independent from each other. What about two different points at the same time? What about one point leaning toward masculine, and the other point simultaneously leaving toward feminine? This is beyond Queer theory, or the ambiguity of gender. Deconstruction calls us to imagine multiple points on the gender spectrum at one time, at any given moment, and because multiple points are occupied, none are. This is not a negation or an oversight of the points on the spectrum, it is something beyond our comprehension of gender, something that has not been conceptualized.

One term to consider, one which has the potential to be neither/nor and simultaneously either/or, is the cyborg. According to the Oxford English Dictionary, a cyborg is a "fictional or hypothetical person whose physical abilities are extended beyond normal human limitations by mechanical elements built into the body." According to Encyclopedia Britannica, a cyborg is a "term blending (or remixing) the words cybernetic and organism, originally proposed in 1960 to describe a human being whose physiological functions are aided or enhanced by artificial means such as biochemical or electronic modifications to the body."

A cyborg, then, is both human and machine. It is not fully machine, nor is it fully human. It's also beyond both humans and machines individually and put together. When applying this to the gender conversation, this becomes a close option to a new concept. Even though cyborg is not a new concept, combining it with masculinity might be something new. Something that is both masculine, and feminine, and not. It's potentially something that ought to transcend masculinity and gender altogether.

Our final term to consider, then, is *Cyborgmasc.*[5] This term combines the word cyborg and the short of masculinity, *masc,* to attempt to take away from the gendered word "masculine," but still keep traits of the masculine gender. Taken from Donna Haraway's (1985) work *The Cyborg Manifesto,* she describes the cyborg as a hybrid of machine and organism, but adds the social reality of the "creature." As it pertains to a woman's experience, "the cyborg is a matter of fiction and lived experiences that changes what counts as women's experiences in the late 20th century" (p. 66). She goes on to say how the cyborg is our ontology, it is a "condensed image of both imagination and material reality, the town joined canters structuring any possibility of historical transformation" (p. 66).

The cyborg is something that enhances the state of being human when remixing it with human and mechanical aspects. So much so, the new creation is something beyond human, transcending what it is to be human, and is something entirely different from "only" being human. By way of creating a word, the cyborg is one of the closest things we can come to at the end of the deconstruction process.

When thinking of the cyborg in terms of masculinity, just like a cyborg is something more than human, the cyborg masculinity is also something beyond masculinity. Just like the cyborg enhances being human to the point of being something other than human, but human at the same time, this is also true for gender and masculinity. *Cyborgmasc* is something beyond gender, and enhances gender to the point of being something more than gender, but gendered at the same time, therefore moving beyond masculinity.

Haraway goes on to say about the cyborg:

> The cyborg is a creature in a postgender world; it has not truck with bisexuality, pre-oedipal symbiosis, unalienated labor, or other seductions to organic wholeness through a final appropriation of all the powers of the parts into a higher unity. In a sense, the cyborg has no origin story in the Western sense – a "final" irony since the cyborg is also the awful apocalyptic *telos* of the "West's" escalating dominations of abstract individuation, and ultimate self-united at last from all dependency....
>
> (p. 67)

Haraway's description of the cyborg is both complete and non when it comes to the gender argument she presents, which ties perfectly into our efforts to deconstruct toxic masculinity. Since her image of a cyborg consists of no origin, not concerned with bisexuality, and supersedes the domination over the abstract, the cyborg is one of the best attempts to deconstruct.[6] Haraway's description of the cyborg being specifically postgender is one of the better definitions of the cyborg. I relate this to postmodernism; a challenge to the overarching way of knowledge, questioning the supremacy of the scientific methods of "knowing what we know." The postgender cyborg questions and challenges any notion of gender altogether, how we come to know gender, and the rigidity of the construction of gender altogether.

By taking the philosophical stance of "post" (be it modernism or gender), we are also removing the idea of toxic. When it comes to toxic masculinity, "toxic" can only live when the standards of masculinity are enforced on societies, when we are forced to conform to the social constructions of what it means to be a man; playing American football, rugby, shooting guns...pick your standard. *When we look beyond gender, beyond masculine and feminine, and all the rigid expectations that come with both, we organically remove toxicity from the conversation.*

Hence the term, *cyborgmasc*. The cyborgmasc is the philosophical use of Haraway's cyborg when speaking of the feminine. It combines the shortened *masc* from our word exercises above, removing the "traits" of masculine while still referring to it. The cyborgmasc, therefore, does not associate itself with any narrative of masculinity, it is a neither/nor, and either/or. It is one of the closest words that describes the final processes in deconstruction: something that is, and that is not. It is removing all the expectations of masculine while holding onto what they describe. And by doing so, we remove toxic, the rigid expectations of "needing" to be one.

*It is by and through deconstructing we take away any option of toxicity to masculinity, and there too from gender altogether.*

## Post-gender and Queer Theory

To mention post-gender is to also mention Queer Theory. The post-gender movement was a following of Queer Theory, also within the realm of post-structuralism, which believes in the challenging of heterosexuality as the societal norm (Warner, 1993). This belief tried to lean away from essentialists views of heternormativity, sexuality, and gender all together. More than that, Queer Theory is also largely political.

The belief that those living outside the norms of heterosexual relationships are often labeled as "queer" is what is challenged in Queer Theory and post-gender thought. However, queer theory focuses on specific rhetoric which defines the difficulty in categorizing gender and sexuality. Socially and culturally, structures have been made to "police" the discourse and rhetoric describing sexuality (Foucault, 1978). As a result, heterosexuality is normalized, and homosexuality, or anything "queer," is stigmatized. Terms like "gay," "straight," and "lesbian" have been used to drive political agendas and to stigmatize individuals living in those terms.

Regarding toxic masculinity, Queer Theory intentionally challenges the traditional forms of gender, specifically masculinity. The binary system in which gender is conceptualized – male/female, masculine/feminine – is seen as limiting and marginalizing. Since toxic masculinity arguably enforces these rigid expectations of gender, Queer Theory aims to dismantle the binary of gender, and therefore the toxicity that comes with those expectations.

With the addition of the cyborgmasc, the conversation of transcending gender becomes more central to the deconstruction process. Given the characteristics of the cyborg, and there too cyborgmasc, gender becomes something challenged and questioned. The term post-gender, though, is not widely used, and therefore needs further attention for our conversation.

Post-gender can be considered in interpretation of the feminist critique of gender, specifically the patriarchy which has traditionally oppressed genders that do not fit the dominate narrative of masculine and feminine. Post-gender is also an interpretation of the genderqueer critique of the constrains of binary gender, which limits our capacity to relate to others. The goal of post-gender is to transcend the social construction and social norms of gender, freeing societies from the rigidity of gender, which is largely held by the gender binary. Therefore, when thinking of toxic masculinity, post-gender aims to think beyond the limiting options for what it means to be a man – all the traditional, stereotypical traits associated with manhood and masculinity, especially those deemed harmful.

Post-gender goes beyond a gender continuum and beyond gender equality. The philosophy behind post-gender is also more than gender tolerance, be it transgender or pansexual, but to challenge the entire notion of gender itself. Judith Butler (1990) was one of the first gender philosophers to challenge all gender binaries in her work *Gender Trouble: Feminism and the Subversion of Identity.* A deconstructive approach, Butler argues to move beyond the binary of biological sex, performative gender, and heterosexual narratives. This calls for the intentional subversion, or deconstruction, of a gender binary. Another key gender philosopher that promoted post-gender thought is Kate Bornstein (1994). Her work, *Gender Outlaw*, promoted and supported transsexuality, and argued for more policy to be made in favor of gays, lesbians, and transexuals, and to politically think beyond the confines of gender.

Some social scientists agree that post-gender refers to multiple areas of being, an ontological assumption. This can mean a technological state eroding the biological makeup of sex; artificial wombs and gender re-assignment surgeries (Hughes & Dvorsky, 2008). There are also psychological implications post-genderists assert: post-gender moves beyond gender essentialism and social construction, asserting that freedom from gender will require social reform and biotechnology.

The cyborgmasc is post-gender. With some post-gender theories inviting technology to transcend our gender abilities and experiences, the cyborg metaphor can be more than a metaphor, but a living reality.

The cyborg is more, though. While the idea of a cyborg can lead us to a post-gender philosophy, and way of existing, post-gender only takes us so far, specifically in the deconstruction process. Cyborg, and cyborgmasc is more than an ideal, utopian philosophy of gender, one where gender is so fluid there is no sense of boundaries or limits for what one can be.

To truly deconstruct toxic masculinity, the cyborg brings us to a different area of thought. As we've said before, to deconstruct toxic masculinity, we also must deconstruct masculinity. It does not stop there; we also need to deconstruct gender. And cyborg helps us do this, reaching the philosophical lens of postgender. However, it does not end there. To deconstruct gender, we would also need to deconstruct what it means to be human. Just like the character of Robocop, who is both human and machine, we also need to deconstruct humanism. This is not the book for this, but the point stands: deconstruction does not end.

There is something to say about posthumanism, though. Haraway argues how the boundaries between humans, animals, and machines have all been already blurred (Haraway, 1985). With the rise of technology, transhumanism, and Artificial Intelligence, the very concept of existence is constantly being questioned.

The ontological assumption of the cyborg and what it means to be a human, or what it means to exist, or the nature of existing itself, ought to ask what it means to live in a state of posthuman, of the cyborg. What is the nature of *being* if we were to live in a cyborg state, a state where gender doesn't exist? Even though we cannot "live" as both machine and man (even though we come close to it with our advanced state of technology), this is a philosophical exercise more than a physical existence. The nature of a cyborg is not Robocop, a mix between a man and a machine, but a thought comprising a duality and more, a place of multiplicity of existences when it comes to being human, masculine, feminine, or gender.

### Memo # 5 On the Cyborg

The cyborg is an interesting idea when thinking of toxic masculinity. I remember the movie Robocop. It was about a man who was killed in the line of duty, but not completely dead. There was some new science that made someone like him, someone who needed help staying alive, into something different. Not a man, and not a machine. He was both, but he was neither. He was a cyborg.

The cyborg ought to be something beyond what we consider to be human; a mix of human and technology, and at the same time both of those things while neither of those.

It's the perfect "word" we can use to describe the deconstruction process, or the outcomes of it. All the while realizing we can't use it either. Because as soon as we use a word, we fall back into the classic Derrida trap. But we can pretend to use this word to describe a place we want to be.

Deconstruction needs to lead to a place we strive for, a place we cannot comprehend or reach. It will always be something unattainable. As soon as it's reached, we place it into our systems of knowledge.

## Notes

1 This is not meant to be an exhaustive review of Hegel. For more of his readings and approach to dialectics, see the further reading section at the end of this chapter. Hegel's mention here is to point out the difference between him and Derrida, and to highlight the difference in the result of the two non-dialectical third terms: sublated and deconstructed.

2 I use the term de-construct intentionally to emphasize the "dismantling" of power that may come along with this term. The breaking down of power may be the experience when thinking of the essence of a continuum. This is not the term deconstruction as we have been philosophically attempted this far.

3 The overarching difficulty in creating new terms is the lack of ability to encompass the "flipped script" in the deconstruction process. Having these terms serves us well to create something that is not yet created. However, the earlier chapters do serve as the process of deconstructing. The current chapter only serves to attempt the latter/end stages of deconstruction.

4 Aboim (2010), is a great resource for our conversation, being one of the closest works to deconstruction of gender and masculinity. Her aim is not to deconstruct, but she places the phenomenon of masculinity within several binary opposites, that being specifically the feminine within a familial context. She also presents several ways in which society today can change the rhetoric and discourse for men and their experiences and identities. See *Plural Masculinities: The Remaking of the Self in Private Life* for more detail on how the narrative of men and masculinity is changing into multiplicity of options.

5 I cannot take full credit for *cyborgmasc*. In a conversation with Daivd Gunkel, where we spoke about the deconstruction process, he reiterated his studies on Haraway's Cyborg Manifesto. It was in that conversation, where we were "spit balling," he made up the word phrase *cyborg masculinity*. That phrase was very close to what I had originally wanted for deconstructing toxic masculinity. In thinking through the process further, and and after "creating" the *masc* form of masculinity, I tailored *cyborg masculinity* to *cyborgmasc*.

6 To reiterate: this chapter began with the agreement of attempting to find a word that best suits our non-dialectical third term and new concept, even though using words puts us in the original place of the system in which we are trying to deconstruct, putting us back in a place of binary opposites. Using any word is only under the agreement that we are looking beyond that place of inevitability in the deconstruction process.

## References

Aboim, S. (2010). *Plural masculinities: The remaking of the self in private life*. Routledge.
Bornstein, K. (1994). *Gender outlaw: On men, women and the rest of us*. Routledge.

New Concept 115

Butler, J. (1990). *Gender trouble: Feminism and the subversion of identity*. Routledge.

Daly, K. J. (2007). *Qualitative methods for family studies and human development*. Sage.

Derrida, J. (1981). *Positions* (A. Bass, Trans.). University of Chicago Press.

Derrida, J. (1981b). *Dissemination* (B. Johnson, Trans.). University of Chicago Press. (Original work published 1972)

Foucault, M. (1978). *The history of sexuality: An introduction* (R. Hurley, Trans.). Pantheon Books.

Foucault, M. (1979). *Power, truth, strategy*. Prometheus books.

Gergen, K. J. (1985). The social constructionist movement in modern psychology. *American Psychologist, 40*(3), 266–275. https://doi.org/10.1037/0003-066X.40.3.266

Groth, M. (2021). Tonic masculinity in the post-gender era. *New Male Studies, 10*(2), 49–62. https://research-ebsco-com.lcu.idm.oclc.org/c/5pgmkm/search/details/aej2b4xlbr?db=asn&proxyApplied=true

Gunkel, D. (2021). *Deconstruction*. MIT Press.

Haraway, D. J. (1985). Manifesto for cyborgs: Science, technology, and socialist feminism in the 1980s. *Socialist Review, 80*, 65–108. chrome-extension://efaidnbmnnnibpcajpcglclefindmkaj/https://monoskop.org/images/4/4c/Haraway_Donna_1985_A_Manifesto_for_Cyborgs_Science_Technology_and_Socialist_Feminism_in_the_1980s.pdf.

Hegel, G. W. F. (1977). *Phenomenology of spirit* (A. V. Miller, Trans.). Oxford University Press.

Hegel, G. W. F. (1989). *Science of logic* (A. V. Miller, Trans.). Humanity Books.

Hughes, J. J. & Dvorsky, G. (2008). Postgenderism: Beyond the gender binary. *Institute for Ethics and Emerging Technologies*. https://ieet.org/index.php/IEET/more/postgenderism

Lyotard, J.-F. (1984). *The postmodern condition: A report on knowledge* ( G. Bennington & B. Massumi, Trans.). University of Minnesota Press. (Original work published 1979)

Perez, C. (2021). *Integrating postmodern therapy and qualitative research: Guiding theory and practice*. Routledge.

Rosenau, P. M. (1992). *Post-modernism and the social sciences: Insights, inroads, and intrusions*. Princeton University Press.

Warner, M. (1993). *Fear of a queer planet: Queer politics and social theory*. University of Minnesota Press.

Wilber, K. (1998). *The marriage of sense and soul: Integrating science and religion*. Broadway Books.

# 6    Masculinity with Choice

If one of our finalized new concepts for toxic masculinity deconstructed is *Cyborgmasc*, we need to understand what this concept means in terms of the choice of masculinity it encompasses. As mentioned before, and according to data gathered, a key answer in defining toxic masculinity is masculinity *without* choice – a rigid form of masculinity that is forced on society. Therefore, according to gathered data, the binary opposite of toxic masculinity, then, is masculinity *with* choice. Considering cyborgmasc, where we ought to focus is the idea of masculinity with choice.

If we are to expand on the idea of masculinity with choice, we need to continue to refer back to the deconstruction process. The spectrum of masculinity, as well as gender, is included in the idea of masculinity with choice. Refer back to Figure 3.1, the sphere of possibilities that live within the overturning of toxic/healthy masculinity and the overturning of masculine/feminine. If a part of the new concept is to include either/or, and neither/nor, then we also need to include the either/or portion of it – either this or that masculine.

What does it mean to be inclusive of masculinity, though? What are the options within the spectrum/sphere of masculinity? As a caveat, when thinking of the *cyborgmasc*, options don't exist. There is no such thing as options because all options are options. To signify "options" also communicates the potential of a "wrong" option. The *cyborgmasc* has no wrong option.

Masculinity truly without choice is a masculinity equal to all forms and experiences of masculine. This is only one aspect, though. We must first consider the equality that exists when attempting to overturn binary oppositions. This is not equality in the sense of all experiences of gender are created equal; it's the equality that inevitably is needed to overturn, to reverse the hierarchy of gender.

How, though? How do we achieve a masculinity that is all inclusive, one that literally includes all forms of masculinity? This might be the wrong question. We are not asking to be accepting of all masculinities, including the harmful ones like hypermasculinity. Instead, to deconstruct, we need to entertain all possibilities of masculine within the binary opposition. There are a few areas of thought that can help us to formulate what an inclusive masculinity might look like, and how to achieve that to deconstruct toxic masculinity.

DOI: 10.4324/9781003464228-6

## Postmodern Masculine

Let's revisit the idea of postmodern masculine. There are specific assumptions the postmodernist holds that will help us conceptualize inclusive masculinity. For example, postmodernism asks certain questions about objective truth; postmodernism does not believe in objective truth. When we ask the question of how to include all forms of masculinity, the question does beg some objectivity; therefore, there is a need to rethink the question itself. By labeling something as masculine, even as inclusive masculine, the question assumes *what*; what are the forms of masculinity that ought to be inclusive? The quick answer is all of them, hence inclusive. However, the objectivity still stands. Even though we include all forms of masculinity, the thought of *what* it is to be masculine lingers. The postmodern thinker is not worried about "what," an objective truth question. Instead, we are concerned about the "how" of the experience. Rather than asking what inclusive masculinity is, to steer away from objectivity, we need to ask *how* one experiences masculinity.

This is a different question. "What is your experience of masculinity? When do you feel the most masculine? When do you feel the least masculine?"

Postmodernism also believes in knowledge being fluid, flexible, and changeable (Rosenau, 1992). Therefore, when thinking of inclusive masculinity, a postmodernist will also believe in a fluid and ever-changing knowledge of masculinity. The experience of masculinity, too, is considered fluid and ever-changing. This assumption has several implications of its own. First, to have a philosophy of ever-changing masculinity ought to include the rejection of having one set standard. This itself is difficult enough. A large amount of acceptance is required to do this successfully; an acceptance of anything that calls itself masculine. At the same time, this calls for the need to set our own personal experience of masculine to the side, not placing our expectations of masculine on anyone else. "My masculine isn't the right one." In fact, there is no such thing as the "wrong" masculine when thinking about it through a postmodern lens.

*Inclusiveness toward masculinity is more than being open-minded. This is a deep way of living, one where the practice of inclusiveness is something intentional and welcomed.*

The postmodernist also pays attention to the rhetoric and texts that promote knowledge(Holstein & Gubrium, 2003). The need to constantly analyze how knowledge is being constructed is important to the *how* of one's experiences. Therefore, how one experiences masculinity today is largely influenced by the messages they are bombarded with. These texts and messages often portray masculinity in a certain light. These texts also give way to internalizing how men *should* be masculine. This assumption is important to the process of helping us "set aside" because of the belief that our experiences will always change with the changing of the texts and messages around us. If we understand that experiences are influenced by what is offered to us, we can also understand how everyone will experience masculinity differently based off their own interpretation of their internalized messages.

## DEI Model of Masculinity

Diversity, Equity, and Inclusion (some models now include Belonging and Justice) can also offer insight into how to approach an inclusive masculinity. Originally and more commonly known as a model for workplaces and organizations that aim to combat structural and systems forms of racism and oppression, there are some components of this approach that help us conceptualize the diversity in masculinities. The American Psychological Association offers a set of guidelines, which are called the Equity, Diversity, and Inclusion Framework (APA, 2021). Consider their definition of inclusion: "an environment that offers affirmation, celebration, and appreciation of different approaches, styles, perspectives, and experiences, thus allowing all individuals to bring in their whole selves (and all of their identities) and to demonstrate their strengths and capacity" (p. 12). Central to our argument of inclusive masculinity is the idea of an environment that celebrates differences. On a larger level, when thinking of societies and institutions, it is arguable that we have not been very inclusive of different forms of masculinity. Be it homosexuality, or simply a masculine that does not play sports or hunt, masculinities tend to become marginalized because of their differences.

The idea of an environment, or a culture, that celebrates masculine differences is crucial in combating toxicity and the harmful effects of masculinity. When speaking of differences in masculinity, consider the APA's definition for diversity in their framework:

> Involving the representation or composition of various social identity groups in a work group, organization, or community. The focus is on social identities that correspond to societal differences in power and privilege, and thus to the marginalization of some groups based on specific attributes—e.g., race, ethnicity, culture, gender, gender identity and expression, sexual orientation, socioeconomic status, religion, spirituality, disability, age, national origin, immigration status, and language. (Other identities may also be considered where there is evidence of disparities in power and privilege.) There is a recognition that people have multiple identities and that social identities are intersectional and have different salience and impact in different contexts.
>
> (p. 12)

The concept of diversity becomes central to a remedy to toxic masculinity when thinking of masculinity. Let's take the above definition and tailor it to a definition only focusing on masculinity:

> Involving the representation or composition of various *masculinities* in a work group, organization, or community. The focus is on *masculinities* that correspond to societal differences in power and privilege, and thus to the marginalization of some *masculinities* based on specific attributes—e.g., race, ethnicity, culture, gender, gender identity and expression, sexual orientation, socioeconomic status, religion, spirituality, disability, age, national

origin, immigration status, and language. (Other identities may also be considered where there is evidence of disparities in power and privilege.) There is a recognition that people have multiple identities and that *masculinities* are intersectional and have different salience and impact in different contexts.

Deconstruction gives special attention to the diversity of masculinity. By deconstructing toxic masculinity, and there too masculinity, we invite the possibility of all diverse aspects of masculine, from toxic to healthy. There is an intentionality behind involving every aspect possible between toxic and healthy, masculine and feminine. This is only one part of the deconstruction process, but diversity is inherent in this thought, the overturning of binary opposites. This also opens the space for people to be more than one thing at once, multiple masculinities and experiences within the binary opposites, which ties back to intersectionality.

As mentioned before, the idea of intersectionality is central to the idea of diversity – the different social aspects that come together for an individual, which make their experience. If society is to practice inclusive masculinity, the need to respect the diversity of masculinity is imperative. Without this acceptance, we end up with a bias of masculinity, masculinist: characterized by or denoting attitudes or values held to be typical of a man. It's the equivalents of sexist, or racist, but considered to be toward masculinity itself. When one encounters something different than their own form of masculinity, they become ill-favored toward it. This is like xenophobia, but specifically focused on masculinity.

**Safety**

If we are to achieve a sense of inclusive masculinity, and to have a society that celebrates the differences in masculinity, we need to create a sense of safety for everyone; the kind of safety where the fear of being judged is no longer an issue. This is easier to conceptualize than to implement. There are several components to be mindful of when considering safety for masculinity.

To create a safe place for men and women to express the limitless options of masculinity, we need to first examine the state in which an unsafe atmosphere is created. What makes someone unsafe to where they are not comfortable expressing who they are? What makes it unsafe for marginalized forms of masculinity to express who they are? There are several answers to this.

First, the inner state of an individual and how they internalize the pressure to be a specific form of masculine. Richard Schwarts (1995) can help us conceptualize the internalization of specific pressures. His inner map of our psyche has been revolutionary in the world of counseling and therapy. He offers us a glimpse into how our minds are compartmentalized into parts. For example, when we experience trauma, hurt, pain, loss, embarrassment, or any other unpleasant emotion, we tend to compartmentalize that "part" of us. So much so, we internally form other parts around it to protect ourselves from feeling those uncomfortable emotions.

Our inner hurt parts become "exiled" into the deep workings of our psyche, ignored, or stuffed down. The other parts that protect them "manage" them, so they/we don't have to feel them. Let's say when I was a young boy, I was made fun of for crying. I was told, "don't cry, only girls cry. Do you want to be a girl?" In that moment, I experienced shame for crying. And to avoid that feeling of shame, my inner psyche exiled the part of me that feels emotions that make me cry. But more than avoiding it, my inner self creates other parts to make sure I don't end up crying. An example of this is to develop overly masculine parts since the sensitive parts that cry are not welcomed to the table. These are arguably feminine parts.

Two things happen here: first, parts that cry, the "feminine" parts, get shamed and exiled so they aren't felt, which means from a young age boys are potentially shamed into not feeling emotions that make them cry because "boys don't cry." Second, the development of overt masculine parts to make sure we don't feel the shame of those parts that cry. These developed masculine parts tend to be the traditional, stereotypical masculine traits we associate with harmfulness. But these are in response to other exiled parts. Rarely do these exiled parts of us become fixed, soothed, or allowed to be. Therefore, young boys tend to carry on this way of internally functioning into adulthood.

*There is a severe lack of safety when young boys are made to feel ashamed for experiencing normal emotions, like crying, and then are forced to take on masculine traits to suppress those they're taught to be ashamed of.*

It's safer, then, to act masculine so young boys don't risk being embarrassed, shamed, or belittled by other men. When thinking about other ripples and consequences of this internalization, there are several areas of a young boy's life that can be impacted.

Consider this quote from Facebook's Threads from John Muller:

> We are conditioned to suppress our own "feminine" attributes and expressions, out of fear of being bullied or worse. Often, the first woman a boy is taught to hate is the feminine side of his own personality. So, I think a lot of misogyny has roots in externalized self-hatred.

When boys internalize feminine parts of themselves, parts who cry and are not the stereotypical masculine they're taught to be, they do more than simply compartmentalize them. They also internalize the disgust that comes with their feminine part, the disgust they learn to replicate based on the shame they experience.

Not only do they learn to harbor a disgust of feminine qualities, but those qualities are also exiled within themselves; therefore, their disgust is reflected inward. Young boys are learning to hate themselves because they learn to shame anything related to feminine qualities – they learn to shame themselves.

If there was ever an example of toxicity, this is it. *When young boys learn to hate themselves, their own feminine sides, because they've learned it from someone who shamed it out of them, they become infected with a harmful version of masculinity.* This infection spreads to other people.

Since this form of disgust, avoidance, and even hate is internalized, it also influences the way in which boys form relationships. According to Schwartz (1995), our internal makeup at a young age usually develops into our relationships as adults. Therefore, if young boys grow up with this sense of internal hatred toward their feminine parts, that sentiment is commonly reflected in their relationships. Two things, then, happen in adult relationships: they seek relationships with women that will soothe that hatred and find partners who might be an "acceptable" quality of feminine for them – one that is not too feminine, but just the right amount of feminine as to not be ashamed of it. Or they will overtly act out toward women who cross their line of feminine, the line they were taught at an early age not to accept. This is arguably where abuse, violence, sexism, and misogyny originate. Men are commonly drawn to the sort of feminine, even attracted to it, but since they're taught to disgust it, it results in dysfunctional relationships.

Safety, then, is more than only creating a space where we can welcome different forms and experiences of masculinities. Safety, when considering the internalization of feminine disgust, begins with one's inner workings. Safety means allowing boys and men to act and live things that might be deemed as a "wrong" form of masculinity, not shaming them for it, and purposefully welcoming the diversity of masculinity. On a deeper level, there also needs to be an undoing of this internalized feminine disgust.

This begins with awareness. Too many boys and men may not be aware they harbor these negative sentiments toward women, and toward themselves. Without knowing this, we run the risk of creating more damage. Awareness starts with education. Both men and women ought to know what they harbor internally. We need to understand the deep biases and internalized experiences we carry so we can change them. Once we reach a place of awareness and begin to understand our internal workings, the ways in which we have exiled the shameful parts of ourselves, the next step is to forgive. Once again, this is not easy.

Forgiveness is twofold. On the one hand, we need to forgive those who shaped our early experiences. If you were told shameful things because you weren't "man" enough, and then had to create masculine sides of yourself to hide it, then forgiveness ought to be directed toward the ones who shamed us. As difficult as it may seem, this is crucial in creating safety for us and everyone else. Forgiving others centers on what was said to us and understanding the other's motivations in saying what was said (more on this in the next section).

Second, there needs to be forgiveness toward ourselves. Understanding how we've internalized these structures within us, ones that purposefully keep shamed parts of ourselves hidden, and then understanding how most of these hidden parts of ourselves have also created hints of sexism, harmful masculinity, or misogyny, is very therapeutic. We usually are not aware of these deeper, hidden aspects of ourselves. Because we are not aware, we have difficulty conceptualizing the root of harmful aspects of masculinity, and how it can be damaging to others. It is a process to understand how we ourselves have furthered the toxicity of masculinity, and forgiving ourselves for doing so, intentionally or not. Change cannot happen without self-forgiveness.

**Fear**

Understanding other's motivation in forgiving them has larger implications for our discussion. When conceptualizing our internal states as parts of ourselves that develop to overcompensate for our shamed parts, we also need to understand the intention behind the overcompensating, the parts who "manage" our shamed parts. The overly masculine parts that develop out of reaction from being ashamed of crying operate from a place of fear. They are both afraid of feeling the shame these sensitive parts carry, and they are afraid to show those sensitivities. Therefore, those "protective" parts tend to overact, they become too masculine out of fear of being ashamed again.

The parts of young boys or young men who are overly masculine, competitive, aggressive, and are physically strong because they want to be stronger than everyone else, are potentially living in fear. They are afraid to show what they're protecting, and they're afraid to fail the narrative of masculinity, which tells them "don't cry," "be a man," and so on. Failing at this narrative would further the shame they are already afraid of feeling.

Young boys grow up with this fear. If never corrected or remedied, they become adults and parents, and more than likely will parent from this place of fear. Now as adults, men still carry this fear of failing the masculine narrative, and the fear of showing sensitivities and vulnerabilities to not be shamed. As a result, they pass the same fear onto their children, especially boys. They then parent from the place of "don't cry," "don't be a sissy." The fear turns into fear of their sons failing the masculine narrative. Now, not only is the parent afraid of their child failing that narrative, but they themselves will also fail the narrative if their child has, too.

*When speaking of safety, what if toxic masculinity all comes down to fear?*

Let's take, for example, a harmful masculine aspect like bullying. These traits, again, are usually an over-response to other sensitive parts being shamed. When we get told "don't be a sissy," and it's a form of humiliation, the result is the overreaction to sensitivity, which is commonly a form of aggression or violence.

Aggression, in its many forms then, is a fear response. Aggression is afraid to feel the shame of being sensitive. When young boys and men put on the mask of aggression, it is reasonable to assume a sense of fear behind it. Deep inside, there is a sensitivity that aggression is making sure does not see the light of day. How often, though, when we see aggression, do we think of the fear behind it?

The same can be said for any other harmful form of masculinity. Let's take domination, for example. If a man is overly dominant toward someone else, a man or a woman, they don't have to be afraid of being a lesser man. Being dominant takes away the fear of being dominated. And being a sensitive man runs the risk of being dominated. We can list more examples:

- A man who is physically abusive to his partner; the fear of being abandoned so he physically forces her not to leave, or if she shows any sign of leaving, violence ensues.
- A man who stonewalls; the fear of being vulnerable.
- A man is dysfunctionally competitive; the fear of looking weak.
- A man who is sexually promiscuous; the fear of not being a "real man," because real men sleep around and don't treat women with respect.

Fear is commonly hidden, or protected by another emotional experiences, as noted above. The dangerous part of hiding fear is of course the inevitable explosion, where someone will "bottle in" their emotions and they all come bursting out in one episode. Those usually are expressed in some form ofaggression. The other dangerous part of this is more fundamental to one's inner psyche. If fear is commonly hidden by other emotional experiences, there is a core way of being that is not being addressed. If men are not safe enough to access these inner workings, these fearful things inside them, they run the risk of an emotionally stunted self. It's no wonder men are said to be emotionless. If they aren't made to feel safe enough to express fear, their emotional state reflects something two-dimensional. Figure 6.1 is how I conceptualize the inner working of protecting our fears, keeping especially fear of being feminine hidden (Figure 6.1).

The fear of anything feminine, or the fear or not meeting the expectations of being man (at the very least), hides behind a wall, metaphorically and quite literally, of other experiences keeping this fear at bay. Take these two people above, both keeping their fear of femininity hidden, both living under the disguise or wall of other experiences which they've been taught to harbor, from anger to being sullen. These are only a few examples; everyone hides their inner parts with other outward experiences. In the case of harmful aspects of masculinity, these are the more stereotypical ways men tend to arrange their inner workings. The inner parts of themselves are hardly, or even never, accessed; they tend to stay there, hiding behind these harmful traits. This is where we have men who stereotypically only show two emotions. The sad part about this is how well young boys keep these hidden and grow up with this quality of inner workings, never digging into their own selves.

If these deeper, sensitive parts of men are not being reached, nurtured, or experienced, it begs the question of how well we really know the toxic man, how well they know themselves, and the emotional state in which they are living. If men's lives are centered around the fear of not feeling things they will be shamed for, what quality of existence is that?

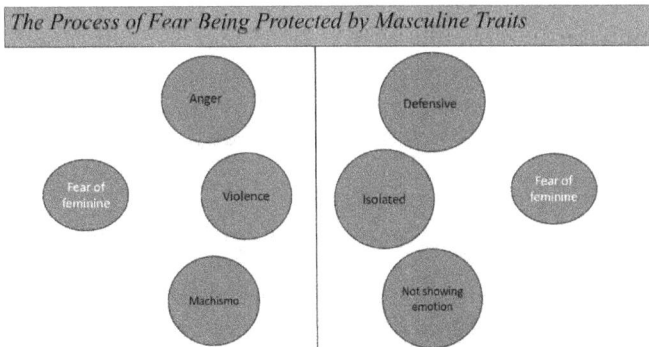

The Process of Fear Being Protected by Masculine Traits

Anger

Defensive

Fear of feminine

Violence

Isolated

Fear of feminine

Machismo

Not showing emotion

*Figure 6.1* The Process of Fear Being Protected by Masculine Traits.

The same can be said for homophobia. According to Connell (1990), homophobia is a central part of gender policing, including bullying and other forms of harmful masculinities. Homophobia literally means the fear (φόβος) of homosexuality. Other Greek translations of the word phobos could also mean aversion to, or dread. There are many factors that contribute to homosexuality – religion, culture, or how we are socialized. But most factors that may lead to homophobia all have to do with some sort of fear; fear of being a sinner because the bible says homophobia is wrong, fear of being exiled by one's culture because of how they look down on homophobia, or fear of being "gay" because of how one was raised to view homosexuals. Homophobia, then, is arguably a part within a young man, the part fearing anything feminine, and the part being protected by aggression, hate, and overt homophobia. If men are seen as feminine, then it would make sense how homosexuals strike fear in a person who has been taught to hide their feminine parts of themselves.

Now more than ever, men are living in a state of loneliness (Lear & Dorstyn, 2024). Men are shown to want deep relationships and connections to other men (McKenzie et al., 2018). Men also show they tend to live solitary lives because of the pressures of masculine norms, the norms that promote social distancing and stoic character (Sileo & Kershaw, 2020).

Fear, as a primary emotion, is also an important part of connection and relationships. According to Sue Johnson (2004), the founder of Emotionally Focused Therapy, expressing primary emotions in a safe environment fosters emotional intimacy. When the sharing of primary emotions, like fear, is met with acceptance and reciprocal vulnerability, the result is the development of strong emotional bonds.

Primary emotions are also at the core of who we are, making up our very inner workings. The common masks we put on to hide those primary emotions are the result and response to some sort of unmet attachment need (Johnson, 2004). If at any point we were shamed or felt unsafe about expressing a primary emotion, we use these masks to hide them; similar situations in the future will evoke the same response. Therefore, the more I feel ashamed about whatever fear I hold, or not safe enough to express it, being around the same people or situations who initiated that response only furthers that mask, and the hardening of the function of the mask, which is to hide the fear.

The remedy to this, to remove the masks that hide fear, is to be in contact and relationships with emotionally safe individuals. Expressing fear in a safe environment creates healing from past traumas and fosters relationship repair. The problem men are living with today is the lack of safety to do so, and the shame associated with it.

### Shame

There is a difference between shame and guilt; the two should not be synonymous. When it comes to different phenomena keeping toxic masculinity toxic, shame is top on the list. Brene Brown (2010) makes the perfect distinction between guilt and shame. Guilt is the feeling of someone doing something wrong; therefore, they feel guilty over it, or they are guilty of something. Guilt = "I did something bad." Shame, though, is different because it tends to be internalized, which leads to a deficit of character. Shame = "I am a bad person." Shame leads to someone believing they are the "bad" thing they did, where guilt does not lead to such internal beliefs.

It's one thing to be guilty of toxic masculinity. We live in a patriarchal society where certain masculine behaviors and beliefs are (for the lack of a more sophisticated word) programmed in us because of the world we live in. The chances of us adopting at least some patriarchy traits are high. However, when we are aware of the harmful aspects of patriarchy and masculinity, we can easily turn away from them and feel bad about it. Guilt, then, is arguably a good thing. We want to feel guilt. It's a roadmap for how we can correct ourselves when we encounter something bad and do something harmful to others, or ourselves. Guilt is a self-corrective measure, telling us to do something different. If we listen to it, it can be a great tool for change. Therefore, feeling guilty about the harmful ways we've lived masculinity, or inflicted it onto others, has the potential for significant change. It's right to feel bad for something that hurts someone else.

Shame, though, is different. Shame can be tied to the actions of those who inflict shame on us, which is how toxic masculinity stays toxic. When someone does not meet the expectations of masculinity, when they aren't overly aggressive, strong, hypermasculine, or domineering, then they are commonly shamed by being called something derogatory: sissy, pussy, fag, even gay. There are several things wrong with this process. Most of these other words people are called when they don't fit the mold of masculine often refer to women, or feminine traits, making femininity the shameful counterpart of masculine. When "gay" is associated with anti-masculine, homosexuality also becomes an association shamed by the larger masculine narrative. Lastly, when these ideas are internalized, individuals may mistakenly believe their own character to be what they are accused of being and the negative sentiment that comes with it.

*Shame leads us to belief hurtful and untrue things about ourselves. When the untrue narrative keeps being reinforced, we sink further into the wrong belief of our own selves. It's a spiral of untrue and damaging internal narratives that's hard to escape.*

When boys hear the phrase, "be a man, don't be a pussy," it triggers the internalizing shame of not meeting the expectations of masculinity. Therefore, they begin to polarize the things they "need" to do to be masculine, and the things they "shouldn't" do, creating an inner tension most boys carry into adulthood. Along the same lines, a common shaming aspect of masculinity is the stigmatization of emotional expression and vulnerability. To avoid shame, men tend to suppress their feelings, which may also lead to emotional and social isolation, and mental health issues (Nathanson, 1992). A stereotypical response to emotional suppression is also anger and violence, which furthers the toxic masculinity mold. The acts of anger and violence are socially acceptable forms of masculinity, which also feed into the behaviors.

Shame tends to lead mean away from vulnerability. Toxic masculinity views vulnerability as "weakness." Judith Butler (2004) writes about shame being a crucial element in masculine performance, of which vulnerability is something not socially acceptable to do as a man. To highlight its importance, Brene Brown (2010) also argues how vulnerability is key to overcoming shame, which also helps foster connection.

*The myth of vulnerability being a weakness is one of the most contrary aspects of masculinity. If the narrative of masculine tells men to be strong and tough, and to be a hard ass, then vulnerability ought to be top of the masculine list. Being vulnerable is one of the difficult things we can do. And if men dohard things, then vulnerability is absolutely masculine.*

Donald Nathanson (1992) categorizes shame into patterns, all of which are rooted in different experiences. The common patterns, or reactions to shame, begin with withdrawal. Once someone feels shame, they tend to isolate themselves both physically and emotionally from others, especially those from whom they experience shame. Next is avoidance, where people avoid the source of their shame. When it comes to men and the narrative of masculine they feel they should live, this becomes multilayered. To avoid people is easy enough, but to avoid an entire narrative of masculinity is all encompassing, avoiding not only individuals, but things society deems as masculine. The next pattern is an attack on oneself. This is also like Brene Brown's belief of internalizing the shame one experiences: "I am a bad person." When individuals begin to attack their own selves, they begin to believe their own character is something lacking. When it comes to masculinity, the character deficit means not meeting certain expectations, of which they've been shamed for. The last pattern, then, is an attack on others. These attacks may be physical or non-physical. Attacks come from a place of isolation and anger toward the ones who have inflicted shame. These patterns are all a means of coping with shame.

The irony of these patterns, specifically the pattern of attacks on others, is how they feed into the stereotypes of toxic masculinity. Isolation, which turns to emotional suppression, self-hate, and attacks on others, these are all aspects that are considered harmful, or toxic. Men who are shamed for not being the "right" form of masculine, as a result, are shamed into the behaviors others have also repeated out of shame. If one man has been shamed for being a pussy, and they experience the patters of coping, and as a result turn to attacks toward others where they shame someone for the same thing they were shamed for, it becomes a vicious pattern.

*Shame, then, is one of the key vehicles for spreading harmful masculinity. Shame is what intoxicates men into being the same harmful masculine they were shamed into. It's like a virus, infecting cell by cell, until the entire body is filled with cancer.*

These messages of shame can be complex. There are multiple experiences, cultures, and societal norms that we must consider when shame is used as a vehicle for toxic masculinity. In other words, it's necessary to consider all aspects of shaming and where it comes from.

## Gender Role Strain

A component of men's safety in their masculinity, or safely trying to be the masculine they strive to be, is the social construction of gender. As mentioned before, society creates expectations of what and how any given gender ought to be. Society's expectation of gender tends to create an essentialism, one that solidifies how we ought to perform our gender.

The problem with society's expectations of genders, specifically men, is the inconsistency of expectations. Too often, men are left with choices that force them to violate gender norms. Inconsistency of gender norms leaves men with a larger likelihood of failing gender expectations, causing what Reidy et al. (2018) call gender role discrepancy stress. Men who experience the stress of failing to meet society's expectations of masculinity also tend to experience anxiety and depression and engage less in healthy social relationships (Mesler et al., 2022).

Pleck (1995) also articulates the concept of gender role strain and the dysfunction that comes from it. Men tend to want to be the type of man who is socially acceptable. However, because of the pressures to not be sensitive, or to not show emotion, men's psychological states suffer from loneliness. Men may experience stress when they see who they want to be, and then who they are because of the roles they are socially constructed to play (Pleck, 1995). To lessen the strain, men tend to distance themselves to relieve the pressure of what they want versus what they're expected to be, increasing their loneliness. Fulfilling traditional masculine ideologies can also lead to negative consequences for men. Some aspects of traditional male ideologies, as we've mentioned before, can be harmful to men and those around them; reluctance to seek mental health help, lower family participation, and fewer close male friendships (Levant & Richmond, 2007).

*This quality of loneliness can be traced back to the idea of men living in fear. Men are fearful of going against masculine norms, furthering themselves from what and who they really want to be.*

This is a double-edged sword. On the one hand, we have situations where men fail to meet the expectations of society's definition of masculinity, which can be a moving target, increasing men's chances to miss at those expectations. This is a lonely outcome, living in the outer margins of society's masculinity. On the other hand, you have men who do live up to the traditional masculine ideologies. As seen above, that too creates a sense of isolation in men.

Is it possible that today's society is not geared toward masculinity? Men seem to be in a lose-lose when it comes to masculine expectations. How do we become a society that allows choices in masculinity? A choice where men are free to live their own version of masculine. How do we create the quality and quantity of safety for such a choice to be possible? How do we practice inclusiveness?

**Inclusive Masculine**

The current theory that exists regarding inclusive masculinity, put forth by Eric Anderson and Mark McCormack (2010), has been refined and revisited by other scholars (Vaccaro, 2011; Marsiglio, 2010; Dashper, 2012). The theory puts for the claim of declining homophobia in both the United Kingdom and the United States. Anderson and McCormack use the term homohysteria to describe certain environments and cultures that may be fostering homophobia. A central argument of the theory is that a "profound change in masculinities will occur when homohysteria decreases" (p. 4). In homohysteric cultures, men's behaviors are restricted and limited because of homophobia. However, because there is a shift in homophobic attitudes, and there too homohysteria, societies and some cultures are seeing an acceptance and openness of "other" masculine behaviors. With younger generations being more open to gender being seen and lived on a spectrum, the options and ideals for masculinity have also expanded and become more fluid. This shift in ideals toward gender has contributed to a changing homohysteric culture in the United Kingdom and the United States.

However, one key piece to the changing cultures and views toward gender and masculinity is the safety of generations' experiences in choosing their gender beliefs. One generation may be more open to a nonbinary view of gender, while the other would be closed to it. The safety in being able to choose one's belief is crucial to inclusiveness in masculinities. Safety and inclusiveness are one in the same; one cannot exist without the other. To reach a space of inclusiveness, there needs to be an overt and intentional effort to provide safety for *everyone*. Again, this is more difficult than it seems.

Let's revisit the deconstruction process, where the outcome of the double science is a new concept. This concept is both and none of the original pre-deconstructed binary pair. For toxic masculinity, we need to create a space that includes *all* forms of toxic masculinity. As said before, we draw the line with abuse and violence – coming from a man or a woman, it is never acceptable.

There ought not to be a standard for any experience of masculine. There is also no limitation to what masculine can be, and there too how it's performed. For example, let's pair the stereotypes of a rugby player with a male ballet dancer. Both have inherited their own "types" of masculine, and both are arguably different from each other. When there is no set standard for masculine, both types are welcomed, despite the stereotypes they may come with. All options of masculine ought to be permissible and welcomed. We go wrong, though, in assuming each example lives up to its expectation.

There needs to be an effort to suspend our biases toward any form of masculine. Does that mean "masculine blind?" Being masculine blind can be as damaging as being color blind. When we are color blind, we run the risk of ignoring the experiences of certain races, experiences of victimization and prejudice toward individuals solely because of their race. We simultaneously ignore those who victimize others because of their race – we ignore racism when we're color blind.

We cannot ignore the damages of toxic masculinity, nor its victims. We also cannot ignore those who have been toxic. Before we discuss welcoming all walks of masculine, we must first acknowledge the dysfunction in upholding unrealistic masculine standards, and the difficulty in holding all forms of masculine.

### Tension of Paradox

Carl Jung, the famous psychoanalytic philosopher, can give us insight into how we can approach inclusive masculinities and masculinities with choice in a practical way. Jung's work in the structure of the psyche, and how our unconscious minds can hold multiple ideas at once, helps us conceptualize masculinities. Formulating an idea of inclusive masculinities and what it means for us as individuals, the idea of "including" masculinities we're not fond of might strike us as difficult or unnecessary. I believe it's possible, though, to hold two conflicting views at one time, even two conflicting views of masculinity.

Jung believed in paradox being a fundamental characteristic of the human condition within the psyche, where it's the key to psychological growth. According to Jung (1972), the mind operates in contradictory forces. Even though he was not a deconstructionist, this belief is like binary opposites we find in Derrida's works. Jung referred to this as integration of opposites (1976), or *enantiodromia,* the tendency of things to become their own opposites over time. But in the process of things becoming their opposites, there is also a psychic energy that flows between those opposites. For example, good and evil, rationality and irrationality, or conscious and unconscious. The psychic energy between the opposites tends to pull in one direction of the opposite. Therefore, if I tend to lean toward a mindset of rationality, my unconscious part of my mind will compensate by being prone to irrational things. This is to say how our unconscious mind will pull us in the direction of opposites within itself.

This tension, though, is an area of growth for Jung. While our unconscious mind can pull us in the direction of the opposite, confronting these two opposites is what brings internal, individual growth. When we can confront opposites, and hold them together even though they are opposing forces, we relieve ourselves from suppressing the unconscious part of the opposite. This is a key to becoming a whole self, one who is balanced and can live a life of self-acceptance, a fully integrated person (Jung, 1968).

Jung also believed in the entirety of the Self (capital "S") as a paradox, the totality of the conscious and unconscious mind. The Self is a paradox because it includes many conflicting, or opposite aspects on its own. Within us, we have many instances where we are in direct opposition to ourselves. Becoming one's true Self, then, means embracing all aspects of our psyche, even the ones in direct opposition to each other. It is only by embracing these opposites, these paradoxes, where we learn to develop a nuanced form of our unique self. When we begin to understand our inner complexities, and all the oppositions living in us, we develop something more than a paradox. We develop a different approach to our own lives.

Jung's theory of the paradoxes in our psyche gives a start to conceptualizing inclusive masculinities and what this means for us trying to hold conflicting views. Even though our own minds will unconsciously hold oppositions, it's more common for only one of those to be conscious. This can also be true for our concepts of masculinity. We may hold one dominant belief about masculinity, what it is and how it should be portrayed. Unconsciously, though, it is the opposite of that. The unconscious part of our psyche will hold feelings like disgust, resentment, even anger toward someone who does not hold the ideals of masculinity in our conscious mind. These feelings become conscious when they are displayed as things like homophobia and xenophobia, sexism, or even racism.

These unconscious aspects of ourselves, particularly the feminine ones, also tend to be repressed. Jung refers to this as the Amina. Everyone has both masculine and feminine aspects to their psyche – paradox. In men, the unconscious feminine qualities are represented by the anima. The repression here is the opposition to conscious views of masculinity: power, dominance, aggression. The anima would be the opposite of that: vulnerability, gentleness. The common paradox here for Jung is strength and weakness, masculine and feminine. This is also a paradox because we tend to overtly express anger or hate toward someone who possesses the qualities repressed in us. As the phrase goes: "we hate in others what we hate about ourselves."

Jung believed each of us carries certain archetypes, or *personas*. A persona is an outward mask we wear, one not truly reflective of our inner selves. These masks are usually meant to be worn to appease societal standards and expectations. For men, it's common to wear masks of violence, stoicism, competitiveness, or even bullying behaviors. But these are just masks, they are not a reflection of one's true self. These personas, or masks, tend to be in paradox with our own self. It's common for people to develop these personas so well that it becomes a source of inner conflict. The conflict comes from the paradox of the outer mask of harmful masculinity, and the inner experiences of the feminine self, or at the very least a version of masculinity that is not the outward mask. This paradox becomes a self-feeding mechanism within our psyche. Because there is already tension between the masks we wear and the inner self, the tension is usually expressed or displayed through forms of anger and hostility, further molding ourselves into the persona already worn.

Where Jung believes in holding paradoxes together leads to a whole, developed Self, I argue the same for masculinity. To practice and believe in inclusive masculinity, we also need to be able to hold paradoxes of masculinity. This means holding the opposing beliefs of masculinity at the same time, whatever our beliefs of masculinity may be. *When it comes to holding paradoxes, our beliefs and ideals within the paradox become secondary to the possibilities of what emerges when we hold them together.*

What does it mean to hold the ends of the paradox together? How does one confront the unconscious? And how does one become an integrated Self? The rest of the chapter will be spent discussing this. For now, we can start with two things to help us conceptualize the holding of paradoxes. First, there needs to be a confronting of the paradox. If Carl Jung is accurate in his theory of the psyche, and I believe he is, then we all have opposing aspects of our internal minds. We all want to eat pizza and work out at the same time, and we all have masculine and feminine parts of our psyche. Confronting this paradox means acknowledging the internal reality of our own opposing minds. Once we acknowledge this aspect of our internal workings, we then integrate the two paradoxes. Integrating them is where we begin to form our whole selves. Rather than suppressing one part of our paradox because it doesn't fit the mold for masculinity, we are intentionally using both ends of the paradox to create our own unique experience with everything we have. It's not about being "less" masculine, or even "more" feminine. Instead, it's about suspending our biases and expectations and realizing the complexities and paradoxes living within everyone's experiences of gender.

### Not Knowing

There are a few ways of attempting to accomplish this. A common postmodern philosophy and approach to thought is called a *not knowing* stance (Anderson, 1997). Created for dialogue in therapy, this stance is a certain posture one takes in conversation. When speaking to someone, whether in a therapeutic setting or not, we carry the mindset of "I don't know everything about your life, your problems, your experiences. Therefore, it's up to me to ask questions about it." This requires three things: to suspension our judgements or any pre-knowledge we might have before entering a conversation, humility, and allowing ourselves to be led.

It is impossible not to have bias, especially things we are emotionally tied to, like politics or religion. The same can be said about masculine. When we see a rugby player, our perceptions of them are driven by our biases toward them, or when we see a male ballet dancer. It is possible, though, to suspend these biases. We cannot rid ourselves of them, but for a moment, we can separate ourselves from them, to have a clear and unassuming mind about what is in front of us. If we suspend our biases or prejudgements about rugby players, we give them the freedom to be the sort of masculine they want to be.

*When our biases drive our perceptions of masculine, and the people who live those masculinities, we limit who they are as individuals, confining them to what our biases hold for them.*

We also limit their options of being more than one thing, more than one form of masculine. Our own limited view of how one should be, by default, narrows someone else's possibility for other ways of being. *Unfortunately, in the world we live in today, the space to be more than one thing isn't a thing.* For example, if we consider transgender individuals, biological males who identify as females, or biological females who identify as males, we find their societal acceptance to be quite low. Most transgender individuals tend to experience oppression and transphobia; this is furthered when you consider people of color to be transgender who also experience racism in addition to transphobia (Jefferson, Neilands & Sevelius, 2013). As a result, these individuals' mental health tends to struggle. Over 80% of transgender persons have considered killing themselves, and 40% of them have attempted suicide (Austin et al., 2022).

When our biases are suspended, we welcome the possibilities of all masculinities and all experiences of being by not limiting other's choices by our own pre-knowledge; the preknowledge that tells us who we and others ought to be.

It requires a great deal of humility to suspend our biases, our beliefs, and our prejudgements (Perez, 2021). It is a "lesser" position to intentionally hold. Lesser in the sense that we open ourselves up to accepting new ideas, knowledge, and experiences. We allow ourselves to be a blank slate when it comes to masculinity, opening our possibilities of welcoming different experiences of masculinity. By assuming a not knowing philosophy, we also regard ourselves with modesty, believing our ideas of masculine and what they should or shouldn't be of lesser importance than someone else's experiences. This also ties well into the overall postmodern thought of being more interested in *how* someone experiences said phenomenon, rather than *what* that phenomenon is.

### Empathy

Along with practicing a not knowing philosophy, to practice inclusive masculinity also requires a great deal of empathy. As mentioned before within the deconstruction process, empathy is more than simply putting yourself in one's shoe. Even though this is a noble task, requiring a large amount of selflessness, empathy is more vulnerable than that. Within the context of safety, and the fear men may carry of anything feminine, empathy becomes something extremely necessary for safety and inclusiveness.

In the case of creating safety for men who may carry the fear of anything feminine, or the fear of rejection because they were once shamed for being feminine, empathy would mean digging into those experiences within us, ourselves, to understand their experience. No, we may not have been shamed because we cried in public and were forced out of crying, but we probably have felt shame about something before. We may not hide our fear of showing the feminine parts of ourselves like others do, but chances are we do fear showing something, we do have some sort of fear hiding behind another form of expression.

Everyone experiences fear and shame, everyone. To empathize with someone who is hiding their feminine parts behind a wall of toxic masculinity because they were taught not to cry means tapping into our own fears, the ones we also hide behind a wall. We may have different fears, hiding behind different walls, but to be empathetic means realizing we both do the same thing, we both hide our fears and mask them behind a wall.

It is strongly felt when someone empathizes with us. True empathy begets safety and inclusiveness. One interviewee spoke of the inner self when working toward an inclusiveness of masculinity:

> But it's a tall order. So that's where I feel like, almost another view of this is like, what I'm talking about now, is on the personal level, right? Like this integrated sense within yourself, but not everybody is going to be able to have that breadth and depth. So, I don't think we should say, okay, now this is it guys. Like this is whatever he has to be. There are guys that are going to be like, yeah, I'm the guy that you want to send out, you know, to war. You probably don't want to be in a relationship with me. And then it's like, I will be there for you and talk to you about your feelings and be connected to you. But like, don't send me out there. Cause I'll just go running. I think there's like almost like we need all these guys, but we need more harmony, right? We need more like yeah harmony as men as a whole where we give room for everybody and we see everybody's unique contribution and it's okay to be who you are if that makes sense. On either side, yeah if I'm on one side if I'm in the soft side and I'm saying it's the hard person you need to be like me, well, that's anti-feminist and that's also a potential to be toxic, right? So, yeah, there does need to be a space where they both live under the tent.

## The Cyborg

The Cyborgmasc is also a term that recognizes inclusiveness and simultaneously goes beyond the need for inclusiveness. Haraway (1985) describes her cyborg as "a kind of disassembled and reassembled, postmodern collective and personal self" (p. 66). There is an amalgamation of parts when it comes to the cyborg, and these parts have been both stripped away and put back together in a different philosophical manner, specifically through a postmodern version.[1] When we strip away masculinity of its parts and examine them from a postmodern point of view, we question things in a different way.

*What does it mean to be "strong?" What is someone's experience of being strong and sensitive at the same time? How does one experience violence? What is their relationship with it, and how do they feel about it? Where does aggression fit into the entire thought of masculine? Does it need to? What if there is more than one way to be masculine? What if femininity is also a form of masculinity?*

The cyborg image, then, includes various aspects of a newly formed masculine. These aspects, or parts of masculine, are parts that may or may not be in our traditional knowledge of masculine. These parts are something different, something existing only in some mythical state – like an actual cyborg, it's science fiction and does not exist in our reality. However, this is the reality we are aiming to achieve. The science fiction cyborg of masculinity is the image and outcome of the deconstruction process. This image is a form of self we need to internalize. The cyborg *includes* ideals of masculinity beyond what we know, and from what we *do* know. But they are transformed into something beyond inclusiveness. They become more than what we can comprehend, something beyond our reality.

The image of the cyborg, with the mix of masculine traits and characteristics, ultimately presents us with extended choice. The choices offered by the cyborg ought to be and extend beyond the common narrative of masculine. For example, if the cyborg offers masculine choices that include sensitivity, physical strength, nurturing, and femininity, then our choices to be masculine have now extended beyond the precyborg options.

There will always be a limit to our cyborg myth, though. Even though the cyborg gives us the option to go beyond traditional masculine, and the choices that include other aspects of masculine, there is a limit to being. We cannot fully *be* a cyborg; we would need to be part human and part technology. This presents an interesting concept: the advancement of gender through technology. We are limited by our biological ability to be both male and female. And those who are biologically both tend to be viewed as "defective" or even "disabled." As mentioned before, our society has not reached a place where it accepts someone who is more than one thing at one time. Therefore, the cyborg is an ideal, a mythical being we strive for.

\*\*\*

When thinking about inclusive masculinity, and intentionally including *all* forms of masculinity, it can be difficult to comprehend. As we've said before, there are some aspects of masculinity we cannot accept, like violence and abuse – those cannot be accepted no matter what gender you ascribe to. But when we think about accepting all walks of masculine, we need to think about the forms we aren't as fond of. For example, to include all masculinities, and to live a life of practicing masculinity without choice, we need to be okay with the guy that rides a motorcycle, full of tattoos; the guy who hunts, drinks, smokes, and swears; the guy who likes to play video games and doesn't like sports; the guy who loves to draw…you get my point. One interviewee had this to say about not accepting all forms of masculinity:

*I think what there's not room for, meaning like it needs to be healed and helped, is like abuse and destruction, like for the sake of destruction, right? Or coming from a place of like wanting to dominate. Over time, toxic masculinity has become smaller and smaller and smaller. Yeah. It's, it's these few things, right? So yeah, we don't, we don't want to make room for, "Hey man, it's okay. You've been through war, you can abuse your family. And that's okay, because you have to go, you know, kill people and like lock people up or whatever you do," right? Whereas this guy over here, it's like, "yeah, man, pour into your relationships. And I know you're not the [war] guy I want over here," right?*

To be truly inclusive of masculinities, we need to move beyond tolerating what and who is different from us to acceptance, accepting the differences around us and how our own experience in only one experience.

*If you think about it, no two people can ever have the same experience. Even though they watched the same movie, saw the same sunset, ate the same meal, lived with the same parents; we can never 100% live in someone else's shoes, and therefore experiences what they experience. So why would we expect my version of masculine to be someone else's?*

To get to this place of inclusiveness, there is something intimate and personal that needs to happen. Inclusiveness of masculinities we may not be fond of is difficult enough on its own. This requires acceptance, tolerance, and intentionality behind our efforts to engage with everyone who meets the criteria or doesn't. This also requires a sense of confidence and comfort with who we are, being okay with the type of masculine we live in, whatever that may be.

I know my sort of masculine isn't everyone else's, and I know it might look different to others. I know my mix of experiences may or may not make me "masculine" according to our socially constructed image of it.

If we are going to reach a place of safety for men to be who they are, we need to allow *everyone* to live their experiences inside their own skin, and help them feel okay with it, at peace with it. Our societies do men and women a disservice when men "fail" at being a man. A man's lack of confidence in who he is can easily be tied back to the narrow definition of a man societies have given us.

To all the men reading this: you are who you are, no matter what type of masculine you are, and that's just fine. To the men and women who are not fond of masculine that doesn't fit your ideal, we must do better at opening the conversation for other people. It takes people in power to initiate change. In this case, it takes men who are a "guy's guy" to start that process, men who are at the top of the masculine hierarchy to being the process of inclusiveness.

I worry about segregated masculinities. Yes, the narrative is changing, and more and more men are living lives being comfortable in their own skin, which is great. More men are finding men like them to have a sense of community. This runs the risk, though, of creating echo chambers of masculine, pockets of men who will intentionally keep a distance from *that* type of man. This is not inclusiveness; this arguably keeps toxic toxic. Separating ourselves from people we do not want to associate with because they own guns keeps the narrative of masculinity without choice alive; if you're not like me, you're not allowed to be in my circle.

### *Memo # 6 On Internalizing*

Young boys are taught to feel a certain way about feminine aspects at a very young age. Boys that grow up in environments where it's not ok to cry, where words like sissy and pussy are used, and where they are made fun of for acting/not acting a certain way (usually acting not strong is where that happens). What happens internally, though, to a boy that is taught negative things about a woman's characteristic, or a feminine characteristic?

If a 5-year-old boy associates crying with being made fun of, and if the same boy associated "strong" characteristics as something to be admonished, then we need to examine what's happening internally. The boy is often rewarded for being strong; this is Pavlov and his dog at its finest. Therefore, he will continue to seek those things that reward him: strength. This is usually sought in any form possible, be it physical strength, things associated with strength like football or bullying, or even being silent, sullen, withdrawn. After all, to be not strong but also not "weak" is better than being weak.

That same 5-year-old boy associates crying with weakness, which is usually falls under the umbrella of women characteristics. This is also supported with the association of the phrases like "sissy," and even more vulgar, "pussy" (it doesn't help that this is the slang word for a vagina, a female body part). Therefore, the relationship with "pussy" being associated with what a boy shouldn't be makes it a bad thing for a young mind. Pavlov: we don't do the things that don't bring us reward.

What is happening internally, though?

It's arguable that a young boy is idolizing what's masculine, what he's being praised for. I don't think it stops in childhood, even grown men idolize other strong men for their abilities (throwing a football, for example). Therefore, they internally learn that's how they're *supposed* to be.

At the same time, they learn how they *aren't* supposed to be: weak/feminine/ crying. They internalize this, too. It goes deeper, though. Not only do they internalize what they should and shouldn't be, they learn to feel a certain way toward it.

We all have different parts inside ourselves that we love and hate. And we learn this from a very young age. This is a key moment in a young boy's life; learning what to love and hate within their own selves. If we have a boy who has been ridiculed for crying, been called a sissy (or even worse, a faggot) for crying, the internal narrative will sound something like this: "I wish I didn't cry, I wish I was stronger, so I didn't cry." Translation: I wish I didn't feel so I can be validated for what I really want to be: strong.

The very bad consequence of this is learning to hate the "weakness" inside them. They learn to hate the "feminine" part inside them that is afraid to cry. The even more unfortunate consequence of this is that boys internally, at a very young age, experience misogyny, sexism, or a sense of superiority because "boys are strong, and girls are weak."

They learn to hate femininity because of the Pavlovian reward/punishment they've received for being either.

We are internally damaging our boys and feeding into a lifetime of feminine hate. They hate the feminine parts of themselves, and sometimes that turns into external sexism and misogyny.

If that's not toxic, I don't know what is.

## Note

1 The process of stripping away and putting back together is intentionally not deconstruction. Rather, it is more precisely described as deconstruction. To deconstruct, as spelled with the hyphen, is to unconstruct something. The image and philosophy of the cyborg is partly to deconstruct, but to also something reconstructed. This is also not a philosophical unconstructing, but a mechanical one. There are certain parts of the cyborg, or masculinity, that do need to be unconfigured in order to arrive at a cyborg state. Therefore, the need to distinguish the cyborg from Derrida's deconstruction.

## References

American Psychological Association. (2021). *Equity, diversity, and inclusion framework.* https://www.apa.org/about/apa/equity-diversity-inclusion/framework

Anderson, H. (1997). *Conversation, language, and possibilities: A postmodern approach to therapy.* Basic Books.

Austin, A., Craig, S. L., D'Souza, S., & McInroy, L. B. (2022). Suicidality among transgender youth: Elucidating the role of interpersonal risk factors. *Journal of Interpersonal Violence, 37*(5–6), NP2696–NP2718. https://doi.org/10.1177/0886260520915554

Brown, B. (2010). *The gifts of imperfection: Let go of who you think you're supposed to be and embrace who you are.* Hazelden.

Butler, J. (2004). *Undoing gender.* Routledge.

Connell, J. P. (1990). Context, self, and action: A motivational analysis of self-system processes across the life span. In D. Cicchetti & M. Beeghly (Eds.), *The self in transition: Infancy to childhood* (pp. 61–97). University of Chicago Press.

Dashper, K. (2012). 'Dressage is full of queens!' masculinity, sexuality and equestrian sport. *Sociology, 46*(6), 1109–1124. https://doi.org/10.1177/0038038512437898

Haraway, D. J. (1985). Manifesto for cyborgs: Science, technology, and socialist feminism in the 1980s. *Socialist Review, 80,* 65–108. chrome-extension://efaidnbmnnnibpcajpcglclefindmkaj/https://monoskop.org/images/4/4c/Haraway_Donna_1985_A_Manifesto_for_Cyborgs_Science_Technology_and_Socialist_Feminism_in_the_1980s.pdf.

Holstein, J. A., & Gubrium, J. F. (Eds.) (2003). *Inside interviewing.* Sage.

Jefferson, K., Neilands, T. B., & Sevelius, J. (2013). Transgender women of color: discrimination and depression symptoms. *Ethnicity and inequalities in health and social care, 6*(4), 121–136. https://doi.org/10.1108/EIHSC-08-2013-0013

Johnson, S. M. (2004). Attachment theory: A guide for healing couple relationships. In W. S. Rholes & J. A. Simpson (Eds.), *Adult attachment: Theory, research, and clinical implications* (pp. 367–387). Guilford Publications.

Jung, C. G. (1968). The concept of the collective unconscious. In *The archetypes and the collective unconscious* (R. F. C. Hull, Trans.; 2nd ed., Vol. 9, Part 1, pp. 42–53). Princeton University Press. (Original work published 1936)

Jung, C. G. (1972). Conscious and unconscious. In R. F. C. Hull (Trans.), *The structure and dynamics of the psyche* (2nd ed., Vol. 8, pp. 184–190). Princeton University Press. (Original work published 1926)

Jung, C.G. (1976) *Letters of C. G. Jung*: Vol. 2, 1951–1961. Routledge.

Lear, J. T., & Dorstyn, D.-S. (2024). Moderators of loneliness and mental health in men: A systematic review with meta-analysis. *Psychology of Men & Masculinities*, *25*(3), 252–263. https://doi.org/10.1037/men0000481

Levant, R. F., & Richmond, K. (2007). A review of research on masculinity ideologies using the Male Role Norms Inventory. *The Journal of Men's Studies, 15*(2), 130–146. https://doi.org/10.3149/jms.1502.130

Marsiglio, W. (2010). Gay fatherhood: Narratives of family and citizenship in America. *Contemporary Sociology, 39*(5), 590–592. https://doi.org/10.1177/0094306110380384cc

McCormack, M., & Anderson, E. (2010). 'It's just not acceptable any more': The erosion of homophobia and the softening of masculinity at an English sixth form. *Sociology, 44*(5), 843–859. https://doi.org/10.1177/0038038510375734

McKenzie, S. K., Collings, S., Jenkin, G., & River, J. (2018). Masculinity, social connectedness, and mental health: Men's diverse patterns of practice. *American Journal of Men's Health, 12*(5), 1247–1261. https://doi.org/10.1177/1557988318772732

Mesler, R. M, Leary, B. R., & Montford, W. J. (2022). The relationships between masculine gender role discrepancy, discrepancy stress and men's health-related behavior. *Personality and Individual Differences, 184*(2), 111205. https://doi.org/10.1016/j.paid.2021.111205

Nathanson, D. L. (1992). *Shame and pride: Affect, sex, and the birth of the self*. W. W. Norton & Company.

Perez, C. (2021). *Integrating postmodern therapy and qualitative research: Guiding theory and practice*. Routledge.

Pleck, J. H. (1995). The gender role strain paradigm: An update. In R. F. Levant & W. S. Pollack (Eds.), *A new psychology of men* (pp. 11–32). Basic Books/Hachette Book Group.

Reidy, Dennis E. et al. (2018). Masculine discrepancy stress and psychosocial maladjustment: Implications for behavioral and mental health of adolescent boys. *Psychol Men Masc, 19*(4), 560–569. https://doi.org/10.1037/men0000132

Rosenau, P. M. (1992). *Post-modernism and the social sciences: Insights, inroads, and intrusions*. Princeton University Press.

Schwartz, R. C. (1995). *Internal family systems therapy*. Guildford.

Sileo, K. M., & Kershaw, T. S. (2020). Dimensions of masculine norms, depression, and mental health service utilization: Results from a prospective cohort study among emerging adult men in the United States. *American Journal of Men's Health, 14*(1), Article 1557988320906980. https://doi.org/10.1177/1557988320906980.

Vaccaro, C. A. (2011). Male bodies in manhood acts: The role of body-talk and embodied practice in signifying culturally dominant Notions of manhood. *Sociology Compass, 5*, 65–76. DOI:10.1111/j.1751-9020.2010.00346.x.

# 7    An Exercise in Deconstruction

I call this chapter an exercise; however, it's more than an exercise. We will attempt to go through the deconstruction process as we have in the previous chapters, and we will also apply it on a personal level. Deconstruction should not be a fancy philosophical thought exercise, one that has been criticized for being out of reach or too abstract. I believe this to be something intimate and personal. If we allow ourselves to be a part of deconstructing, we are given a road map to relationships, a guide to how we can potentially be. What follows will be examples of deconstructing as it points to how we can change our positioning in relationships. The goal of this is to walk away from deconstruction with a call to action, one where our perceptions of people are potentially changed for the better.

We've referred to deconstruction as a process with the intention of communicating its longevity – deconstruction doesn't end, it's ongoing. Here we find the same to be true on a personal and individual level. Derrida (1988) shares how "Deconstruction does not exist somewhere pure, proper, self-identical outside its inscriptions in conflictual and differentiated contexts; it 'is' only what it does, and what is done with it, there where it takes place" (p. 141). It's for this reason we find ourselves in a place where deconstruction needs to be more than a thought experiment but something that comes to life within us, something transformational within us, something we also *do*.

## Holding Paradoxes

In the previous chapter, we mentioned Carl Jung's concept of paradoxes and how we often hold things in opposition with each other. We resolve paradoxes by embracing the paradox itself and forming our own way of being through the process. By accepting both sides of the paradox, we uncover unconscious motivations inside ourselves, and we also learn to form a more authentic, whole self. The idea of holding paradoxes ought to have personal implications when it comes to the relationships we hold, specifically masculine relationships and the types of masculinity we're opposed to. There needs to be space where we can invite different types of masculinities. This comes with a few caveats, though.

Carl Jung's concept of the paradox presents a way to view our own inner workings, and the personas we put on for others. If we take the same concept of

DOI: 10.4324/9781003464228-7

paradoxes, the internal tensions we feel between our inner selves and the personas we wear, and apply it to people, we have what I call outer paradoxes. This simply means people who are different from us, paradoxical from us. Let's say, for example, there is a specific type of masculine you don't approve of or don't feel comfortable with; they are a different type of masculine than you are. Just like Jung's idea of tension living inside of us because of our internal paradox, the tension between us and someone different from us also exists, whether the tension is in our own inner thoughts or overt. Often, we hold negative feelings toward someone and keep them inside while we present ourselves with niceties on the outside; double paradox, one within ourselves because we put on a nice face and hold harsh feelings toward some, and the actual tension we hold toward the other person.

With our inner paradox, if Jung suggests holding the paradox, the two conflicting things inside us, then the same thing ought to be done externally, with someone we aren't especially fond of. This sounds nice enough. How do we do it, though? How do we hold a paradox when it's someone rather than our own selves?

Deconstruction starts with defining binary oppositions. When it comes to people, where need to start there, too. Let's apply the steps (even though there are no defined steps) to the deconstruction process to people, our "paradoxes." At this point, we've defined what deconstructing toxic masculinity is. We have also ventured into what a new concept may be. However, my conviction also lies in change. If deconstructing doesn't change you, then we're missing the point. Deconstructing toxic masculinity shouldn't stop with creating new words or thinking outside the box. It should translate to how we are with other people, which is what I'm calling outward deconstruction, the deconstruction that transforms who we are. In the case of our current work, the transformation of who we are and with masculinity; with masculinity meaning with people.

### Relationships Deconstructed

Let's start with an example in deconstructing relationships. Even though this aspect or practice of deconstruction was not in Derrida's catalog, there is an overt application we can take away from the philosophical exercise. And like most things Derrida, there are a few complexities.

When two people meet, and for the sake of making this as easy as possible we can refer to a biological man and woman (we'll attempt a nonbinary pair next), they are not married yet. But their state of relationship, however it is before marriage, is considered a binary relationship; a man and a woman, on two opposite ends of the gender spectrum, who eventually come together to marry.

This is not as straightforward as it seems. There are so many factors that make a relationship what it is. If we're thinking of binary oppositions, we must be mindful of the violent hierarchy of the relationship, this is only because of the double gesture Derrida presents to us (1997). Therefore, we need to ask the question not only of binary oppositions, but of hierarchy, relationship hierarchy.

This begs the question of *who*, where the binary opposition and its violent hierarchy now become people. If a biological man and woman enter a relationship, and if they are considered a binary opposition, and if Derrida is correct in his assumption of binary opposites creating violent hierarchies, then who is in the dominate position? We cannot answer this question. However, there are some ideals of relationship that can answer it for us. The easiest way to answer this is to consider the "traditional" form of marriage, referring to the practice of arranged marriage. Marriages where women were given away to other families for the sake of royalty, or wealth, are where a clear hierarchy exits. This hierarchy goes further when we consider the man of the relationships, the one who inherits the wealth or the royalty status. Is this violent, though? Is an arranged marriage, where a woman has significantly less privileges than her male counterpart, an act of violence?

This becomes less easy to answer when we study the recent feminist movements and efforts to create an equality in marriages, where both partners are equal in as many aspects of the relationships as possible. What happens to the hierarchy of the relationship then, when both the man and the woman are both practicing feminists and believe each is just as equal to the other? The result is deconstruction in action, living deconstruction.

When two people consider themselves as equal as possible, they overturn the violent hierarchy of gender roles in relationships, they bring low to high and high to low. To put it generically in terms of traditional gender roles: when a man and woman flip the script on gender, the man becomes low, and the woman becomes high. This, like the philosophical practice of overturning, might be difficult for some. And even more so for people who struggle with gender equality. When done correctly, and when done well, this sort of marriage becomes something different altogether, just like the second phase of Derrida's double science (1981).

Reversing the hierarchy for the sake of reversing the hierarchy is not enough, though, nor it is feminist. The displacement phase of double science is where we create a new concept, one which supersedes the binary altogether, and at the same time encompasses it. This is also the case with a marriage deconstructed.

What is that sort of marriage called, though? If we refer to Derrida's outcome of deconstruction, the new concept, or non-dialectical third term, cannot be put into language, lest is fall back into the system in which it was created (1997). Which is exactly what some couples are doing today, they are refusing to even acknowledge the term marriage, lest they fall into the system in which gender hierarchy has flourished for so long. "Marriage" would be union of two people, the combination of two becoming one. This, of course, is not displacement. It's close, though. It's the joining of two people who come together to form a relationship bigger than each of them, but remaining each their own person.

The new concept, then, for some couples, is no marriage at all. The rejection of marriage is also the rejection of the institution itself. This is something arguably superseding marriage. At the same time, the rejecting of marriage does not stop couples from forming relationships, commitments, even having children. They create lives in which their roles, lifestyles, and beliefs in gender do not need the label of marriage, but at the same time encompass it, like Derrida's new concept.

One must ask the question, though: is a couple ever equal? Does the relationship, married or not, when trying to be equal, ever reach true equality? My answer is no. I do not believe a couple trying to be truly equal will ever achieve it. They may come close, and may achieve it for a short period of time, but true equality, like deconstruction, is never achieved. It's something always being fought for, that couples strive for, and constantly are mindful of. *This is deconstruction at its finest, when it becomes a lifestyle so convicting, it's something worth always striving for.* And idea of "achieving" it is not the end goal for a marriage deconstructed, nor for anything else deconstructed. Rather, the goal is the process of deconstructing, deconstructing for the sake of deconstructing; relationships rejecting marriage for the sake of their beliefs in gender roles, for the sake of gender equality. The process itself is worth pursuing, and being "satisfied" having never achieved it, but being at peace with living a life of its pursuit.

To take this one step further, let's next examine the topic at hand, one that follows marriage quite nicely, and one that will answer the other question of nonbinary marriage. When deconstructing toxic masculinity, we need to consider ourselves. If we only limit this exercise to a thought experiment, we're missing the point altogether. Therefore, following the marriage example, I invite us to think about the next section on a personal level, where we place ourselves in binary oppositions.

### Binary Oppositions

This is an important step in deconstruction. The metaphysics of deconstruction begins with the tension in which binary opposites exist. This also means defining what the opposites are. Simple enough first step with deconstruction. What does this mean for us, though? Just like Derrida places significance on binary opposites, we ought to do the same. We need to ask ourselves the question, then, *who is our opposite?*

This can have a range of answers. We can begin with our literal opposite. In the case of broader gender, this is somewhat straightforward if we believe in the traditional binary of gender: male/female. Even if we believe in the nonbinary aspect of gender, this still offers us our binary opposite. Male/female (binary) versus a gender spectrum (nonbinary). This becomes less straightforward when it comes to masculinity, it's not as easy to point out our specific binary opposite when it comes to masculinity. We can overgeneralize and say feminine, but just like deconstructing, we need to be mindful of all possibilities within the binary opposition. Therefore, when defining our binary opposite of masculinity, we can more safely say *different*. I chose *different* to answer who is our opposite because of how differences, even though often small, are commonly treated as opposites. When it comes to people who are different from us, we often treat them as if they are our binary opposite. This is like the in-group/out-group experiences; if you're not a part of us, then you're with them.

Our binary opposite when it comes to masculinity, then, can simply be someone different from our version of masculinity.

If we recall, the problem with binary oppositions according to Derrida (1981) is the power they exert, "violent hierarchy" they cause. This portion of deconstruction has the potential to have real-life implications, especially if we're thinking of others as our binary opposites. For example, if my binary opposite is someone different than me in my masculinity, we need to ask the question of the hierarchy we place in those differences, and where we place ourselves in this hierarchy.

The order in which we place binary opposites we deconstruct (male/female, right/wrong) has significance in how we view those concepts, or genders, or masculinities. This translates to where we place ourselves when we define our binary opposites. When we compare ourselves to others who are different from us, how often do we place ourselves in the beginning of that opposition? How often are we aware of where we place ourselves in the order of that opposition?

If we look at the binary of in-group/out-group, the order is commonly "in" first, then "out" second, which gives significant preference to those who are "in." I believe we do the same when we place ourselves in opposition to someone different from us. When we compare ourselves to someone who is different from my version of masculine, it's rare when we place ourselves in the out-group. When we define our binary opposite, when it comes to people, we usually place ourselves ahead of them in terms of order of binaries, creating the violent hierarchy Derrida warns us of. It's easy to see how the hierarchy of opposites becomes a lived reality. The male/female binary has plagued our societies for way too long. This is easy to see. When we place ourselves in the hierarchy of opposites, we also need to be aware of when we put ourselves in the higher part of the hierarchy, the one initiating the "violence." This is harder to do.

### Overturning

The next phase of deconstruction is to overturn, reverse the hierarchy, bring what is high to low, and low to high (1981). Overturning is a philosophical and epistemic change in how we view the world. This has very real implications on how we construct our reality. Which is necessary for deconstruction.

Overturning, then, ought to become personal and internalized when we think of ourselves at the top of the hierarchy. If when we define our masculine binary opposite as someone different from us (in-group/out-group), and if by doing so we put ourselves in a position of instigating the "violent hierarchy," then overturning puts us in the low part. If we were first high, then by overturning we put ourselves low, reversing the hierarchy. What does this mean, though?

I emphasize *if.* It's not every time we see someone different from us with a sense of judgement, anger, or any sort of negative sentiment. However, Derrida would argue that defining binary opposition automatically creates a hierarchy. Whether it's us or our opposite, someone will be "ahead" of someone.

*If* we are in a high position, how do we get to the low position? What does it take to reverse the hierarchy when we ourselves are violently in it? In a previous chapter, we discussed philosophical overturning, and the emotions it requires to overturn. The same applies here, with a more intimate approach.

There are two things to consider when we place ourselves in the binary hierarchy and when it comes to toxic masculinity. There are overt harmful acts of masculinity that would by default place a man (or a women) at the top of said hierarchy.

Attributes like hyper masculinism or bullying literally create violence, placing the victim of that relationship at the bottom of the hierarchy. Therefore, the following part of the deconstruction strategy applies directly to anyone who may be in this position. There is also the person who views toxic masculinity in a certain way, with a negative sentiment. These two positions place us at the top of the binary hierarchy: harmful, hypermasculine attributes that sometimes cause physical violence or one in which we sit from a place of judgment toward such masculinity. Both positions, I argue, can be just as dangerous.

*Acknowledge*

There is an overt acknowledgment when it comes to "bringing low to high, and high to low." Acknowledging is more than recognizing the hierarchy at hand, it's a way to be convicted of the damages the hierarchy has caused, the violence of the hierarchy.

There are different forms of violence we much acknowledge when deconstructing. Derrida's violent hierarchy doesn't necessarily need to insinuate physical violence, assault, homicide, or murder. Yes, there are instances where this sort of hierarchy does result in physical violence, slavery, for example, or intimate relationships where gender roles are taken on through traditional beliefs. These are situations where men or slave owners believed themselves to be superior to others, literally at the top of the hierarchy.

Violence can take on other forms, though. In the case of binary oppositions, we also need to recognize psychological or emotional violence. Verbal abuse, threats, manipulation, and shaming are all examples of nonphysical violence. These often also lead to sexual violence, like harassment or sexual assault. One area of psychological violence gaining attention is gaslighting, where one is left to question their own reality or their sanity (Walker, 1979; Dutton, 2007). When we engage in forms of psychological violence, we perpetuate the violent hierarchy Derrida warned us of.

There are also other forms of violence: economic or financial violence, where one controls or withholds financial resources or stealing; cultural violence, which can lead to discrimination and economic inequality, which begs the question if racism is considered violence; political violence, like terrorism or civil wars (sometimes fought virtually); or cyber violence, like cyberbullying, revenge porn, or identity theft; we can also consider forms of environmental violence, like deforestation or pollution.

Whichever form of violence, it is arguable that Derrida's philosophical insight into hierarchy applies. By defining binary oppositions, we recognize and acknowledge how and where in our lives we further the hierarchy of the binary.

*Empathy*

After we acknowledge our experience of the hierarchy, there is a moment of empathy we need to practice. As described in an earlier chapter, everyone can empathize.

If we feel, and I believe we are all emotional beings, then we have the capacity for empathy. Where empathy becomes difficult is one's own fear of feeling certain emotions, which also leads us back to toxic masculine behaviors. *What if our epidemic of people who "can't empathize," specifically men, all leads back to the fear of emotion; because emotions are the bane of masculinity, empathy is that much more difficult to experiences for some.*

If we are deconstructing toxic masculinity, we need to include ourselves in this process. We are already in a place of privilege to even recognize toxic masculinity for what it's worth. Whether it's academic, or journalistic (in my case it's academic), we approach the conversation of toxic masculinity from the ivory tower. This is a specific positioning when it comes to deconstruction. Therefore, by being able to position ourselves in saying masculinity is toxic, we arguably create a binary opposition: me and academic who is nontoxic versus someone, possibly a nonacademic who is toxic; our binary opposition and our violent hierarchy. Being in this place of privilege, one where we can think deconstructively about masculinity, we arguably place ourselves at the top of the binary hierarchy. Is this violence? If there was such a thing of academic violence, I believe deconstruction would have a place for it.

To acknowledge this is not enough, we need to have an experience of empathy if we are going to overturn this hierarchy. In this specific example, let's continue with the above hierarchy: a nontoxic academic and a nonacademic toxic masculine. This applies to anyone who believes in toxic masculinity; we are all a part of the binary if we are going to label it as such. How do we come to have an experience of empathy in this case?

I will speak for myself with the hopes of it being useful for your own exercise. I don't consider myself toxic masculine. Therefore, I need to dig deeper to access empathy. Let's go back to the assumption of toxic masculinity coming down to fear (which seems to be the consensus in this study), and how men are living in fear and insecurity, and toxic masculine traits are the masks they wear. Even though I can't put myself in toxic masculine shoes (the generic definition of empathy), I can certainly understand fear and insecurity. I can certainly understand what it's like to overcompensate for something because I'm insecure about something else. I can also understand what it's like to be afraid of not meeting the expectations of society, whether it be career, fatherhood, or family. I do know what it's like to live in some sort of fear and put on masks to ensure it's not shown.

The assumption of fear is again a position of privilege. I have been privileged enough to gather research participants, analyze data, and derive some conclusions; this is a privilege and maybe an "advantage" I hold over the toxic masculine narrative. Therefore, another point of empathy would be just that: the feeling of someone having an "advantage" over me, or general privilege over me. I can understand this too: the feeling of someone being privileged over me. I happen to be a person of minority status in this country, so this might come easier to me than others.

Let's use all of the above for our empathy exercise. To empathize with toxic masculinity (to overturn our positions of the hierarchy), I am trying to understand what it's like to live in fear and insecurity; fear of not meeting societal expectations, or of "failing" any narrative I hold within myself, and being insecure in myself because of the pressures I feel I need to live up to. I can also understand the feeling of being in a less privileged position, one where someone holds and obtains more privilege over me. This is how we bring low to high and high to low. To put ourselves in a "lower" position means to exercise our empathy muscles for the sake of overturning the binary hierarchy.

The step is necessary. To deconstruct, especially with something like toxic masculinity, where its impact is felt on a personal and individual level, we must be able to see where we are on this hierarchy, and we must be able to empathize with our binary opposites. If we cannot do this, we cannot deconstruct.

What about those who may be at the top of the hierarchy because of their hypermasculinity? The same steps above apply, maybe even more so. *This is imperative for the phenomenon of toxic masculinity; this is a call to action; this is a deep change that is long overdue. The toxic masculine man must come to place of acknowledgment, for the harm they've caused, and for the spreading of such harmful behaviors. If this doesn't happen, deconstructing toxic masculinity can't happen, and therefore the change that's needed.*

This may be a difficult step for some, and for others there may be a sense of obliviousness to the damage harmful masculinity causes. We cannot bring a person to acknowledge their side of their hierarchy. But there are things we can do to prompt such conviction, which we will see in the next chapter.

How does one come to have empathy toward those they have caused harm to, though? This requires significant introspection, which again comes down to the common denominator of fear. It's safe to assume, among other things, that victims to toxic masculinity live in a certain type of fear: fear of being mistreated, of being physically assaulted, of having their individual rights not being considered, of being bullied, or of feeling less than (these are all "generic" instances of fear for the sake of our example). And if our theory holds true, that toxic masculinity also boils down to fear: fear of feeling less than, being mistreated, of "failing" the masculine narrative, then we have a common denominator. If the toxic masculine individual can understand the drive behind their harmful behaviors, and if they can see how they have deep emotional experiences in common with victims, then we can deconstruct such relationships.

### Displace

To displace is to mark the intervals of the inversion of the low to high, and high to low (Derrida, 1981), where the result is a new concept. To reiterate, the new concept "can no longer be, and never could be, included in the previous regime" (p. 42). The new concept needs to be and supersede the language of either/or and neither/nor, and at the same time be none of the above. This is where it gets tricky. It's simple enough (relatively simple) to deconstruct concepts, like writing or even gender. We can think through some of the muddiness of those overturnings, and there too displacements. The new concept, even though it cannot be a product of our language, or the systems that encapsulate it, can be conceptualized and communicated through bifurcated writing, a writing that demolishes the very thing it's trying to describe, a double play on words. With concepts, this is relatively manageable. This is what we have accomplished with the previous chapters, even the endeavor to create a new concept for the deconstruction of toxic masculinity, in concept, though.

This becomes different when we assume a relational approach to deconstruction. This moves from concept to lived experience, which deconstruction ought to do for us.

One of the biggest difficulties of the deconstruction process is the displacement phase of the double science. Because of this, for a few reasons, deconstruction has received some criticism. Camille Paglia (1992), a cultural studies scholar, has argued how deconstruction lacks practical applicability, making it inaccessible to students and society at large. Other scholars like Richard Rorty (1979) and Alan Sokal and Jean Bricmont (1999) also write about how deconstruction is not practical, lacking clarity and applicability.[1] If the goal of displacement is to create a new concept, or a non-dialectical third term, but if the new concept cannot be put into language because language omits any chance of transcending the binary opposition, what are we left with?

We can say deconstruction doesn't need to be put into words. It can be something internalized, something we ourselves live with. And going through the process of deconstruction ought to give us a different outlook on people altogether. True to its critics, this approach also is not very applicable. We can also say how deconstruction changes how we think about the world, and how we conceptualize how we approach conceptual differences, not giving hierarchical power to oppositions. Again, true to its critics, this idea can be somewhat vague and unclear.

Therefore, how I envision the applicability of deconstruction to be is something still in philosophical alignment with Derrida's original steps of displacement (this includes the abstractness of a new concept), and something applicable to how we live. If we put ourselves in the hierarchy of oppositions, and if we practice the empathy we mentioned earlier, this also leads to some sort of repentance. This means intentionally correcting what and how we have contributed to the violence of the hierarchy. The result of empathy, when done correctly, ought to convict us to change and stop how we further the binary opposition. Applying this to our individual selves, this ought to change the way we view the world, but more importantly, how we comport ourselves with others. By practicing repentance, we also need to think of how we can change the behaviors we're repenting from. Just like in Christianity, when we repent, we stop the sin and turn toward whatever faith we ascribe to.

Let's revisit the above example. If I'm in the position of the nontoxic academic, and my binary opposite is the nonacademic toxic, and if I've practiced empathy for their living in fear and insecurities, I've made the effort to turn low to high and high to low. Now comes repentance. Not only does repentance mean changing our thoughts and behaviors, but it also means stopping them, repenting of them, regretting them, and turning toward something better and good.

This turning toward something better or good, in the case of making deconstruction applicable, means turning toward our binary opposite. This means a person, or people. In our empathy and repentance, we regret how we've contributed to the violent hierarchy, and we approach people (our binary opposite) in a different way. The same can be exemplified with someone who is on the top of the hierarchy because of toxic masculinity. After one acknowledges the damage they've caused because of harmful attributes of masculinity, and after they've experienced empathy toward others, then repentance can happen a little bit easier.

Regretting the literal violence caused by toxic masculinity is one of the deeper goals of deconstructing in this conversation. There is strong intention and conviction behind this. Even though the abstract idea of this conviction might be nice in theory, and this might be where critics of deconstruction say it falls short, this ought to translate into something actionable, even tangible. *With deconstruction, we have a roadmap to changing who we are, for the better, how to see someone different from us, and how to be with them in a different way that dismantles the previous violent hierarchy.*

Therefore, acknowledging my place on the hierarchy as a privileged, nontoxic academic, deconstruction helps us to repent from the opposition my privilege has created. And recognizing one's position as toxic masculine and the violence (literal and not) it has caused helps us get that much closer to deconstruction. I do understand this is an extreme example, and I also understand this is not always the case, where privilege leads to hierarchy, but this is often true.

Displacement, then, ought to start here. Taking this positioning, we adjust because of the first phase of the double science, overturn, we also begin to change the way we see the world, and hopefully how we *are* with others. This is where displacement becomes lived. If the new concept is to be something encompassing what the binary presents, and then exceeds it, and if the new concept cannot be put into language, then this is perfect for what it means for us.

When we apply the deconstruction process to our own selves, when done correctly, we are different people who enter into different relationships with others, no matter what side of the hierarchy we find ourselves on. The new concept isn't something spoken or written in bifurcated writing, instead it's something living between two people, something outside of us. Deconstruction turns into relationships, transformed and re*lived*. The original relationship contains the original binary, which the displaced new concept also encompasses. But it is a relationship anew, transcending the original one, just like the new concept. It's either/or, and neither/nor. Instead of us looking for a new concept, a non-dialectical third term, we seek a new relationship because we are new in those relationships.

As we recall in Derrida's (1992) original description, the outcome of overturning, and where displacement occurs, is the "eruptive emergence" of a new concept. If we allow the space for deconstruction, and if we honestly and philosophically overturn binary oppositions, then displacement is something that "erupts" and "emerges." The space for it to happen, though, is an important part of deconstruction. As we recalled in Chapter 2, this requires an intentional suspension of our biases, and a removal of our emotional attachment to what it is we are deconstructing. Agan, this is not easy.

When we hold the space for binary opposites to exit on the same playing field, this means holding the space for those we think are our opposites. Let's use this as an exercise: we identify our binary opposite, we overturn and put ourselves in a different position in the violent hierarchy (low/high), and we hold those in the same space so they can be overturned. Displacement of the relationship, then (or the deconstruction of the relationship), is the eruptive emergence of a new relationship.

I am going to refer to this as a positioning within relationships. If we allow it to, Derrida's double gesture gives us the "strategy" to position ourselves in relationships. Let's say we are in a high position in the binary hierarchy, and we bring ourselves to the low position through overturning, then it is in that specific position of the hierarchy in which we approach relationships with; our "lowered" self, and the other's "heighted" self.

This can become more, however. This has the potential to become an ontological and epistemological espousal. This has the potential to be a way of being, an experience, one in which we live our lives with others. It has the potential to be a way of knowing our reality, and how we construct our reality – how we view the world.

If done well, when we approach relationships in this way, from an intentional overturning of our positions in the hierarchy, new relationships will naturally erupt and emerge. With the example of toxic masculinity, we have the chance to approach these relationships from a different positioning. How often do we approach someone or enter a relationship with someone we consider "toxic masculine?" How often do we hold our binary opposite of masculine on the same playing field so that we can overturn our position in the hierarchy of opposites?

You might be thinking something along the lines of, "what about them? Why should I be the one to do this first?" This sort of question can come from a perpetrator of toxic masculinity, and its victim. This is the exact question that will limit our ability to deconstruct. These sorts of questions reflect our emotional attachment to the conversation, and rightfully so. As mentioned in Chapter 3, these questions will produce a faulty overturning, and there too a skewed displacement. To apply deconstruction to our own selves, to our relationships, we must be able to suspend our biases and remove our emotional attachments to what and who it is we are deconstructing. If we cannot do so, we cannot allow new relationships to erupt and emerge.

At the same time, this is also one of the biggest faults in our societies; the biases we hold, and the quality of emotional attachment to what we believe in. To be clear, this is not to mean we must form relationships with violent offenders and abusers. There are things we cannot and must not tolerate as human beings.

## Society's Binary

Make no mistake, we are living in a time of disagreement. After having been through elections where leaders are selected, who are racist and sexist, and after having been politically split more than ever in our history of politics, we are a society of binary oppositions, with chasms between ideologies filtering into families, friends, and colleagues. We live in a time where opposing ideologies are enemies. Which presents one more example of deconstruction as it relates to toxic masculinity.

If we study the polarization of the United States, or any other democracy where two parties are opposing each other, it's easy to see how two parties can be opposites from each other, or each other's binary opposite. For the sake of the example, let's put republicans and democrats in the places of binary opposition.

Like we mentioned before, there are public figures and political leaders who display overt acts of harmful masculinity – intimidation, bullying, sexism, and speaking derogatory things about women. This is one of the ways, if not the biggest way masculinity becomes toxic, by allowing public displays of dangerous masculinity to go unchecked, leaving the example for the rest of society to follow.

As far as binary oppositions go, and the hierarchy found in them, it does not matter which political party we place at the top of the hierarchy. What does matter is the literal and philosophical violence which comes from this sort of hierarchy. The opposition between the two parties has in recent years created a damaging rift. Literal violence ensues during campaign rallies, and verbal aggression between parties is constantly on public display.

When we consider overturning and political parties, I can only imagine how difficult this might be for some. But this is why all the steps in the deconstruction process are so important; it's the personhood required to attune to all its aspects. The questions we ought to be asking at this phase of overturning are, "how has my party contributed to the violence found in the hierarchy?" "How have I contributed to said violence?" With our current conversation, this becomes more poignant, "how has my party contributed to the violent hierarchy which has been a contributing factor to toxic masculinity?" "How have I contributed to the spread of harmful aspects of masculinity through my political party?" This ought to be insightful enough.

The next action required in overturning is to have an experience of empathy. With politics, this might be even more difficult. How do we begin to have empathy for someone who is opposite our political ideologies? How do we have empathy for someone whose beliefs sometimes seem to threaten our rights? Or how do we begin to have empathy for someone whose beliefs further harmful aspects of masculinity and make it toxic? To answer that, let's quickly revisit the previous exercise.

Like the above example, it's more than putting ourselves in someone's shoes. This is where empathy becomes especially challenging: finding the emotional commonalities we have with someone who seems to be the stark opposite from us. *We all feel, and we all emote. Therefore, empathy is possible with and for anyone. It's up to us to choose if we want to make ourselves vulnerable enough to have empathy for those we see as opposites.*

We have also mentioned the masks some men may wear, masks of hypermasculinity. If our theory holds true, then the masks of masculinity men wear potentially hide fear and insecurities. This can give us some insight into empathy for those individuals. What about our political opposites? Is it possible for them to also wear masks? Like masculinity, is political affiliation also something people perform?

Judith Butler (1990) puts forth the theory in her monumental work for gender studies, Gender Trouble: Feminism and the Subversion of Identity, how we perform gender. As a performance, gender is not something inherent in us, it's something we *do*, something overtly acted out. From our gestures to the pitch of our voice, to the clothes we wear, it's all a performance. Which gives good context to the idea of masculinity being toxic; the performance of masculine, especially harmful masculinity, is something people latch onto, repeat, and accept as how masculine ought to be.

When it comes to the performativity of gender, Butler (1993, 2004) also goes as far as to argue how we learn to perform gender, which comes down to the longing for belonging. We *do* our gender because of the expectations society has placed on our gender. When those expectations become so great, we feel compelled to live them, to perform them. Performance, here, ought to be noted: the intentional acting out of something, which usually is not genuine, but rather an act put on for someone.

When it comes to experiencing empathy, this makes it a little bit easier to conceptualize gender in this way. If we can all examine within ourselves when we felt the need to "fit in," and therefore we did something to do so, then we can empathize with the struggles of gender, and the performances of it, even its toxicity.

What if our political party of choice is also a performance? What if like gender, we *do* our political party's beliefs and ideals? If we imagine political parties, they tend to act differently, dress differently, and sometimes speak differently. Could this all be performative? If this theory holds true, then Butler's arguments for belonging also may apply. If we perform gender for the sake of not being "out" of the gender norms, then it's possible for us to perform political parties to not be "out" of the party's favor.

There is a parallel between gender and political parties when it comes to the sense of performance and belonging. Sometimes one is not courageous enough to go against the grain of gender expectations, the same can be true for political parties. Sometimes we act a certain way because of gender, and because of politics. We don't want to be left out, so we perform what's expected of us. Is it possible to perform gender, and political parties, because of the fear of being rejected? Or because of an insecurity to not belong?

This is the challenging part of empathy, to see someone else who we see as our opposite and opposition, as vulnerable, insecure, or fearful. This is the aim, though, when deconstructing relationships. If we cannot come to a place of empathy, then we cannot transcend the current state of toxicity.

I invite you to do this: picture someone you consider toxic, or who is opposite your political beliefs. Picture them as someone who is insecure in their masculinity, or as someone who is afraid of not belonging, so they choose to act in a way different from you. Picture them suffering, hurting, lonely.

The next step might be even more difficult. If we truly practice overturning deconstruction, then we must repent. Repentance, in this case, means we accept the hierarchy, have experienced empathy for our binary opposite, and vow to be in a position where we intentionally forgo our previous position in the hierarchy.

There is a constant and intentional recognizing when deconstructing relationships. We know the power of hierarchy found in binary oppositions, and we know the damages they cause. We also know how *we* have potentially contributed to it. Therefore, it is a positioning we adopt when we approach relationships, it's a stance we assume with people.

This is the displacement part of relationships deconstructed. It's a relationship with both parties in "opposition" of each other, and at the same time in a relationship. You might be thinking, "what about them? Where is their responsibility?" This is not the question to be asking. This is not an overturned positioning, nor a relationship displaced.

When applied to us and to our relationships, deconstruction becomes contextualized within the people we interact with. It becomes something more; it becomes a new relationship, one where we are able to be with those we deem opposite ourselves, one where we can be accepting of all forms of masculinity and other differences. This is more than merely being "accepting" of differences, which has its own shortcomings. When we're only accepting or tolerating differences, we pay no heed to the hierarchy of binary opposition, and therefore we also ignore the "violence" behind such hierarchy. When we do so, we run the risk of ignoring important experiences that make us human: fear, insecurity, the need to belong.

Being tolerant and accepting of differences is a worthy enough goal. However, when we deconstruct relationships, we do more, we bring a new way of being in relationships, one that starts with us.

*When we think of our binary opposites, whether they are masculine, politics, or any other difference we can't tolerate, the negative sentiment we feel toward them ought to go away when deconstructing. When we overturn and flip the script on the hierarchy, we do so with our emotional state, how we feel toward whatever difference we may hold. This requires an awareness of both sides of the hierarchy, both low and high. This is different than humility or taking a "lower position." This means being able to be aware of and access the potential emotional states in both low and high positions of the binary hierarchy, those that come with privilege, power, and not.*

We aren't there.

### Memo # 7 On the Elections

The entire premise of this book is to study how harmful masculine behaviors become toxic, how they spread, and how they intoxicate. This is one of those ways: to elect a leaders who exemplifies these behaviors to the entire nation.

What's dangerous about this is how many young boys and men are watching and learning this. I imagine there are even some women who are also learning these behaviors and coming to expect them from other men. The countless racist and sexist things that have been said about other men and women, the display of aggression (verbal and psychological), it all astounds me how much of it *intoxicates* a lot of the nation.

These harmful acts of masculinity seem to be glorified when the nation elects their leader who unapologetically displays them. Because they're glorified, they're given permission to live, to remain a thing people are okay with and adopt for themselves. This is exactly how masculinity becomes toxic.

When we say *he* is toxic (or she), we are saying how their behaviors are both harmful and how that harm multiplies through others, transmits through others, and spreads like a virus with people being the carriers of it. The acts themselves are harmful, and the "host" is the nation.

## Note

1  For further reading on the critiques of deconstruction, see Haberman's (1985), *The philosophical discourse of modernity,* Searle's (1977), *Limited Inc,* Eagleton's (2008), *Literary Theory: An introduction,* Norris's (2002), *Deconstruction: Theory and Practice,* and Scruton's (1996), *Modern philosophy: An introduction and Survey.*

## References

Butler, J. (1990). *Gender trouble: Feminism and the subversion of identity.* Routledge.

Butler, J. (1993). *Bodies that matter: On the discursive limits on sex.* Routledge.

Butler, J. (2004). *Undoing gender.* Routledge.

Derrida, J. (1981). *Positions* (A. Bass, Trans.). University of Chicago Press.

Derrida, J. (1988). Afterword: Toward an ethic of discussion. In G. Graff (Ed.), *Limited Inc* (pp. 111–160). Northwestern University Press.

Derrida, J. (1992). *Acts of literature* (D. Attridge, Ed.). Routledge.

Derrida, J. (1997). *Of grammatology* (G. C. Spivak, Trans.).Johns Hopkins University Press. (Original work published 1967)

Dutton, D. (2007). *The abusive personality: Violence and control in intimate relationships.* Guilford Press.

Eagleton, T. (2008). *Literary theory: An introduction.* University of Minnesota Press.

Habermas, J. (1985). *The philosophical discourse of modernity: Twelve lectures* (F. Lawrence, Trans.). MIT Press.

Norris, C. (2002). *Deconstruction: Theory and practice.* Routledge.

Paglia, C. (1992). *Sex, art, and culture: Essays.* Knopf Doubleday Publishing Group.

Rorty, R. (1979). *Philosophy and the mirror of nature.* Princeton University Press.

Scruton, R. (1996). *Modern philosophy: An introduction.* Penguin Books.

Searle, J. R. (1977). *Limited Inc.* Northwestern University Press.

Sokal, A., & Bricmont, J. (1999). *Fashionable nonsense: Postmodern intellectuals' abuse of science.* Picador.

Walker, L. E. (1979). *The Battered woman* (1st ed). Harper & Row.

# 8 Now What?

The pursuit of a world in which we deconstruct toxic masculinity, gender, and other forms of expression is something we will always live with. To deconstruct, then, is a call to action. The hope for this book is for everyone to walk away with the content and tools to deconstruct and to be aware of the effects harmful aspects of masculinity have had on our society. The hope is to also make known the ways in which masculinity becomes toxic, how it spreads and infiltrates, as well as the ways in which masculinity can be rigid, without choice.

Deconstruction requires emotional intelligence. Most societies, I would argue, do not have the capacity for such emotionally intelligent relationships. The goal of deconstruction is of one having the mind to constantly challenge the norms and narratives under which we live. The power of narratives gives us the internalization of in or out, whether we are either with the in-group or not. Nichols & Davis (2019) put it this way: "Problems arise when we are indoctrinated into narrow and self-defeating views of ourselves" (p. 245). This happens when the harmful narratives of masculinity win, and the other options of masculinity are subjugated.

Since the abstract nature of deconstruction is left to experience, one where language cannot enter to describe it, less we fall into the same system that encompasses the deconstruction, we need something tangible, something that can ward off the internalizing of damaging narratives. Deconstruction offers a roadmap into how we can change, be, and position ourselves in relationships. This chapter offers a quick lesson on how deconstruction can be applied to our own selves, lives, and relationships.

## Deconstruction in Action

If we are going to deconstruct toxic masculinity, which includes the examining of things that keep harmful masculinity alive, we also need to apply the deconstruction process to ourselves and our relationships.

In reviewing the process to deconstruction, we also outline the key aspects of the strategy itself (identifying binary oppositions, overturning the hierarchy, and displacement), setting us up for an internal application to how we *do* masculinity. What follows is my own analysis as a deconstruction thinker, and my background as a marriage and family therapist. We must start by defining a few aspects of our

DOI: 10.4324/9781003464228-8

own lives, including toxic masculinity. We must also define in our own terms what toxic masculinity is, how it appears in our lives, and how we can potentially possess some harmful masculine traits. This next portion is an invitation to discern, reflect, and analyze our own selves. It's something we can take with us and how we can tangibly approach the deconstruction process – a call to action.

### Defining Toxic Masculine

This definition might be different for each person. However, here are some general definitions we can begin with, which are taken from the participants of this study.

- Behaviors like overt aggression, bullying, sexism toward women, homophobia, xenophobia, violence, hypermasculinity, overt acts of physical strength, or domineering and considering oneself superior to someone else because of the above traits.

According to most academic and secular sources of literature, these traits are considered toxic because of the way they describe masculine. However, according to our own research, toxic masculine can mean different things:

- Masculinity without choice. Given the above traits, the exclusion other others who do not possess those traits, and the pressure to conform to those traits as masculine creates toxicity – the rigidity of the standards and expectations for these traits.
- The infectiousness of the above traits. The way the expectation for masculinity to be the above traits, and the way those expectations are learned and repeated to and by others creates toxicity. The way in which harmful aspects of masculinity are contagious and spread to others, infecting their way of being and thinking.

Be it a man or woman, we must first consider the above definitions in our lives. These are the types of questions to be asking ourselves so we can see how we may be contributing to the definitions of toxicity of masculinity:

- How do I believe in masculinity?
- Do I pressure others to be the masculine I expect them to be?
- Do I judge others when they aren't my kind of masculine?
- Do I judge others based off their version of masculine?
- Do I believe men are superior to women?
- Do I believe men are superior to other men if other men don't fit my ideal of masculine?
- What do I do when I see someone who is a different masculine from me?
- Do I allow differences in masculinity to exist in my relationships?
- Do I laugh at sexist jokes? Do I think some sexist jokes are funny?
- Do I laugh at homosexual jokes? Do I think some of them are funny?

It's important to highlight the emotionality behind such questions, and where our masculine expectations come from. When we ask questions of this quality, we need to keep in mind the emotional consequences for not being the "right" type of masculine. For example, as we mentioned in Chapter 6, it's possible for some of these harmful masculinities to be rooted in fear and insecurity. If the fear of failing the narrative of masculine spurs us to perform masculine according to society's expectations, we ourselves fall into the toxic trap. Therefore, we also need to ask the following:

- How secure am I in my masculinity? How I live it, how I might be perceived, and how I perform it?
- Does my display of masculinity come from my comparison to others? Where does it come from?
- Do I feel self-conscious or insecure around other men?
- Do I need to be physically strong to be a "man," or to be masculine?
- Am I afraid to show feminine qualities?
- Do I believe feminine, and masculine can or cannot exist simultaneously in a man or a woman?

These questions present the need for introspection, self-reflection on how we are in relationship with others, specifically others we deem masculine. Introspection is the goal of this step in the process, more so than knowledge of what toxic masculine is and how it shows in our lives. I believe everyone owns some form of harmful masculinity – we have been raised in a patriarchal society; therefore, it's almost impossible to not hold some form or idea of what masculinity is according to the patriarchy. Therefore, the following is also important to begin a deconstructive exercise:

- Review the definitions of toxic masculinity.
- Review the way in which the harmful aspects of masculinity are spread throughout society.
- Identify any harmful aspects of masculinity in your own selves.
- Identify how, if at all, we have contributed to the spread of harmful masculinity.
- Identify how, if at all, we have believed the harmful aspects of masculinity.
- What are some beliefs that can be problematic, harmful, or damaging to other people?
  - "Be a man."
  - Men don't cry.
  - Emotions are weak.
  - Vulnerability is weak.

### Origins

After defining toxic masculinity, the next step is to locate the origins of where we began to believe masculinity to be. There are several areas to study when assessing the origins of our beliefs, and these are some questions to ask ourselves:

- What was/is my family's belief about masculinity? What it means to "be a man"?

- Does my own definition go with or against what my family believes?
- How was my father an influence of masculinity on my life, for better or worse? Or mother?
- Does my family laugh at homosexual jokes? Do they have negative feelings toward the LGBTQ community?
- How much media do I consume that gives me messages about what masculinity is and what it looks like?
- What are the messages my media gives me about masculinity?
- How often do I agree or disagree with what the media shows me about masculinity?
- How often do I share my beliefs on masculinity with others? Children? Spouse? Colleagues? Friends?

It's a real possibility to ask these sorts of questions and come up with answers we may not be comfortable with. We may find our family being responsible for teaching us harmful narratives of masculinity. We may even conclude that we find ourselves not challenging the narratives of masculinity we've inherited through family or media. What's important in this exercise of reflection is forgiveness. To truly deconstruct and to have an application to our own lives, we need to understand where we fall on the binary hierarchy. If we fall on either side of the hierarchy, we may need to practice forgiveness to "flip the script" on the hierarchy. For example, if I learn how my colleagues, people I look up to, are a source of origin for feeding me harmful aspects of masculinity, then forgiveness is required to enter an overturned relationship with them, one where the hierarchy is rearranged.

### Overturning the Relationship

This part of the deconstruction process is necessary. As it applies to our own selves, though, it can be tricky. As we've outlined before, there are a few steps to overturning. They will be reviewed here, along with questions to be asking ourselves. To overturn, we need to flip the script on the order of the binary hierarchy – bring low to high and high to low. When applying this to ourselves, our binary opposites are people whom we deem as "opposite" from us. This is not the direct opposite, but for our exercise, this may be someone who *does* masculinity differently than we do. This can also be someone we may have identified from the previous step, someone who has given us harmful aspects of masculinity. If we have someone in mind, and if we've practiced forgiveness toward them, we can practice the following:

- Rearranging our beliefs about masculinity and who they come from.
- Not believing or accepting the narratives of masculinity we've received from said persons.
- Discovering a new sense of confidence with our experience of masculine.
- Releasing ourselves from the previous narratives of masculinity we once held.
- (Re)Discovering a sense of masculine expression.

- Achieving a sense of comfort with different expressions of masculinity.
- Achieving a sense of comfort when around other people with different expressions of masculinity.
- Releasing a sense of judgement toward others who hold and practice different expressions of masculinity than we do.
- Reimagining the quality of relationships with people who express masculinity differently than we do.

Therefore, to apply the overturning part of deconstruction to ourselves, we also need to retrace our steps in previous examples: acknowledgment, empathy, and repentance.

*Acknowledging*

Given the above definitions and the idea of a hierarchical opposition living (metaphorically) across from us, we need to begin by acknowledging how we have contributed to any form of toxicity and how we've contributed to the spread of harmful masculine behaviors. There cannot be shame added to this process. Inviting shame, or inflicting shame to acknowledgment, intentionally puts ourselves in the "lower" position of the binary hierarchy. This happens because shame implies "you are a bad person," as opposed to "you've done something wrong that can be made right." Internalized shame is damaging to a person; it speaks to *who* they are, and that's usually a negative thing. Therefore, acknowledgment requires humility and grace. To do so, we ought to ask the following:

- With humility and self-acceptance, acknowledge the ways in which we've lived any of the above definitions of toxic masculinity.
- Acknowledge the potential harm that has been caused by such behaviors.
- Acknowledge the people who may have been on the receiving end of those behaviors.
- Recognize the emotional consequences of such behaviors and interactions.
- How have I hurt others by displaying harmful masculine behaviors?
- What masculine behaviors have I lived and shared that may have caused harm?

*Empathy*

It's necessary to practice empathy when asking questions of who we have potentially harmed with toxic masculinity. Empathy is one of the more difficult and important parts of an overturned relationship. This is more than simply "putting ourselves" in one's shoes. Empathy is a vulnerable experience, one where we ourselves tap into our own experiences from which we are trying to relate to someone else. Consider the following steps toward an empathetic experience:

- If we have hurt someone else through harmful masculinity, we need to specify what sort of behavior it was: bullying, sexism, misogyny, homophobia,

or contributing to sexist jokes by laughing at them, or placing our masculine expectations onto someone else.
- Each behavior will have a potentially different experience of empathy, for example:

  - Bullying – the emotional experience of a bullied victim is potentially embarrassment, belittled, demeaned, maybe even physically harmed. Therefore, the experience of empathy ought to be when *we* felt embarrassed by someone, belittled, demeaned, or physically harmed. We may not have been bullied, but the chances of us feeling embarrassment at the expense of others is great.
  - Sexism – the emotional experience from a victim of sexism can potentially be degrading: shame because of their gender, being treated less than, sadness because of inequality, objectification, or being stereotyped. Sexism and toxic masculinity are very close in experience, specifically when it comes to being stereotyped. If men have experienced being stereotyped because of their masculine behaviors, the chances of them being able to empathize with victims of sexism are good.
  - Homophobia – the potential emotional experience from a victim of homophobia can be fear of being who they are because of outlash, physical violence, being treated as an outcast, or being silenced by the dominant narrative of gender. The opportunity for empathy can especially be found in the fear of being who we are; when men are afraid to be a different sort of masculine, so they wear the mask of masculinity, which is potentially like the victim of homophobia.

When attempting empathy, we also need to be mindful of our own selves within the process, identifying moments when we share emotional experiences with those who may have been victims of harmful masculinity. There are some helpful emotional exercises to add when practicing empathy. Empathy requires practice and a robust emotional vocabulary.

*Repentance*

Perhaps the most important part of the overturning process is the practice of repentance. How does one repent, though? When approaching this portion of the deconstruction process, and to flip the script on the oppositional hierarchy, we must position ourselves in a way where we approach ourselves and relationships differently. After having acknowledged the part we've played in toxic masculinity, and after empathizing with those who may have been victimized by such behaviors, we need to experience a turning away from such beliefs and behaviors. Repentance, then, ought to be a change within ourselves first, which translates to a positioning in relationships, with both men and women. Consider the following prompts:

- Accountability for beliefs and behaviors that have been problematic and damaging in the past.
- Stopping behaviors and changing beliefs.
- Heightened awareness and rejection of behaviors that might be harmful to others.

- Promoting the behaviors, instead, that are different from the previous regime of behaviors and beliefs.
- Awareness and refusal of judgements we might hold toward someone with different expressions of masculinity from us.

Repentance refers to stopping any such behavior out of contrition and regret. Therefore, when we examine our own selves and past behaviors, there ought to be a sense of remorse and regret in how beliefs have been lived with and toward others. Repenting means to literally stop those behaviors and to retrain ourselves to believe in other expressions of masculinity.

*Remorse and regret are central in repentance. Like the steps above, there should not be a sense of shame attached to this. Shame enforces the internal narrative of being a bad person. And this is not a narrative we want to further when it comes to our expressions of masculinity.*

## A Deconstructed Self

As mentioned before, our internal selves are complex and multiplicitous. Psychoanalysts like Freud and Carl Jung have written and theorized about multiple versions of our inner selves, with archetypes and "masks" we wear. In more recent internal analyses, Richard Schwartz (1995) takes the traditional versions of the archetypes and expands on them, suggesting toward internal relationships our inner selves hold. In other words, our internal makeup is where different "parts" of ourselves are in relationship with each other. Sometimes these internal relationships are even at odds with each other; our internal parts may not have a good relationship with our own selves. *We are our own worst enemy.* Even in popular cinema, the recent Pixar movie *Inside Out* also helps us conceptualize the multiple states of our own minds. The movie gives us a glimpse into the main character, Riley, and the complexities of her internal self. With emotions like Joy, Sadness, Anger, and Disgust, we can see how each emotion is its own personality, or persona. Within those few emotions, we also see the relationships between them, sometimes good and helpful, sometimes somewhat dysfunctional. Joy tries to put Sadness away because of the emotional state that takes over when Sadness becomes too dominant. Therefore, Joy puts her in a small room where she can't influence Riley's state. This shows how we ourselves can have a dysfunctional relationship with our own internal selves.

This view of the multiplicitous mind helps us apply the deconstruction process to our lives, and to our own selves. If we use the example of the multiple parts of our minds, we can also go through the "steps" in the deconstruction process. For example, within our multiple parts of our minds, we can more than likely identify a set of binary oppositions: I feel like working out, I also want to eat pizza, a love/hate relationship with work, being happy and jealous of someone's success, or liking and despising something about yourself. Our internal selves are full of binary oppositions.

Next, then, would be to overturn those oppositions, which require more intro-spection and mental work. To overturn our own binary oppositions, we need to be asking ourselves intimate questions:

• What are the parts of myself I don't like?
• What are the parts of myself in conflict with each other?
• When do I feel opposing or contradictory things inside me?
• When do I put myself down?
• Do I more commonly have positive or negative thoughts about myself?

It's more common for us to give the negative parts of ourselves more attention, or those tend to be the louder parts of ourselves, filling our thoughts with either self-hate or self-disapproval. If or when this happens, we are creating the hierarchy of binary opposites inside ourselves, the violent hierarchy Derrida warns us about. When it comes to our own selves, the violence found within the hierarchy can be especially true. How often are we verbally violent toward our own self?

Therefore, to reverse this hierarchy, we need to bring what's low high, and high low. This means bringing the negative voices in our minds low, and the silenced voices high. The silenced voices, which are the binary opposite of the nega-tive voices then, are the positive things we tell ourselves. This includes positive self-talk, self-affirming language, and self-compassion.

Even though this might seem well and good, this is not the end of the process. We don't want to replace the violent hierarchy with positivity at the top. This is where the phrase toxic positivity comes to play, which purposefully ignores other things at the expense of keeping a positive mindset. Therefore, to simply reverse this hierarchy can be just as unhealthy. How often do we try to avoid conflict? Or cannot tell the truth because we're afraid of hurting someone's feelings, or have a difficult time being realistic in situations to avoid something unpleasant? These can all be the result of toxic positivity.

Therefore, the result of the overturning of our own parts needs to be something more, something displaced. What does it look like when we take two parts of our internal selves, two parts of which are in opposition of each other, and overturn them, and mark the intervals between the overturning? What happens to our inter-nal selves when we attempt such an exercise? What is the result? Or, the more accurate question, *who* is the result?

To provide some generic answers to these questions (generic because our own internal work will be vastly different for everyone), the result will need to be some-thing, or someone, who encompasses both the "old" set of parts who are in opposi-tion with each other, and something/someone who is more than that. Displacement for our internal selves starts as an exercise of self-exploration and self-discovery. It's quite possible to know who's on the other side of such displacement. It's also quite possible to discover a new self after deconstructing.

The process, though, is what is important. When we apply deconstruction to our own selves, there is no one clear path or right way to do it. It's a journey meant to be discovered along the way, just as Derrida intended deconstruction to be. There is a letting go of our own self, and parts of ourselves in opposition with each other, so we can discover what and who is on the other side.

This is necessary, though, if we are to approach relationships in a different way. To deconstruct toxic masculinity, we must deconstruct ourselves along with our relationships.

## A Relationship Displaced

The outcome of the deconstruction process is displacement. As it pertains to philosophical exercise, displacement is where we discover a new concept, a non-dialectical third term. A concept that both encompasses the original binary but exceeds it through the double science: overturning and then displacement. In the previous chapters, we explored various concepts that could potentially achieve this non-dialectical third term, with the limitations of our system of language.

Since the goal of this chapter is to apply the deconstruction process to our own selves and relationships, we need to focus on what displacement means in how we approach, or "do" relationships. To do so, we need to revisit the concept of remix.

### A Remixed Relationship

Gunkel (2021) mentions how a remix can be different things, either a plagiarized copy of an original, or something artistically innovative and original. If there are remixes, be it in music, writing, movies, or any other form of media, this debate will always live. What makes this complicated is the practice of taking what already was, with something else that was, and making one new thing. Whether it's new or not will always be a pivoting argument. But the idea of a remix, when thinking about relationships, becomes something very applicable no matter what side of the remix debate we fall on.

For example, let's use any remix we might like. I'll choose the remix of Mark Morrison's *Return of the Mack,* a very popular club hit in the 1990s. The artist who chose to remix this song is the recent pop artist Post Malone. The remix version is called *Cooped Up/Return of the Mack.* The artists involved are Post Malone, Mark Morrison (of course), and Sickick. The remixed version is a great example of having two different artists make something original (arguable), which encompasses both the original work, the originality of the addition to the original work, and the overall product remixed. Again, the debate over the remix's originality will always be had. But that debate is important to our displacement application.

The remix argument of the plagiarized copy of a copy translates well to the idea of relationships. When attempting to put ourselves within the deconstruction process, specifically when it comes to overturning, we don't become "different" people; we are arguably the same person, even after having experienced empathy and repentance of our position in the opposition hierarchy. Yes, we may have a new outlook on another person, but we are the same people nonetheless – an "original" with a new perspective. The same is true for whomever we are putting into the other part of the deconstruction process, our binary opposite, they are the same "original" person.

With the idea of a remix, specifically with music, a new artist comes along with different ideas, inspirations, and artistically inputs and adds them to the original song. In the application of displacement, we who have gone through the overturning phase of deconstruction are the "new artist." We are the ones with the new idea, one contributing to the original piece of work. Once we overturn ourselves, we are like the artist with the spark of vision with a new idea. We see things differently, like the artist probably hears a newness in the original song. Therefore, be it a copy of a copy, when we apply the idea of a remix to our own selves, we remix relationships. What does this mean for toxic masculinity?

When remixing a relationship in which there may be instances of toxic masculinity, it begins with us. Once we overturn ourselves, like the musical artist who hears potential from an original work they want to remix, we see something different in others. The combination of acknowledging, empathy, and repentance brings us into relationships differently than not having gone through it. Therefore, like in the deconstruction process, we view things differently, and there too, people.

For example, when we see someone who we consider the opposite of us, or any sort of masculinity we don't approve of, these are opportunities for a deconstructed relationship. The remix happens when two people, at least one of whom has thought deconstructively about the relationship, enter a relationship. The one person has experienced the overturning phase, meaning they bring low to high and high to low, and acknowledge the hierarchy, have empathy for the other, and repent of their previous positioning. This experience, then, leads to a different outlook on who we saw as the opposite of us. This different outlook places us in a different positioning as we approach the relationship, one where we intentionally bring ourselves to the low positioning of the hierarchy (if we look at someone with disapproval, especially when it comes to masculinity, we are already placing ourselves in the "high" position).

This gives us a different outlook on the "original" relationship. We see things and others differently. We both are the same "originals," but when one person thinks through deconstruction, they bring a new insight into the relationship, remixing it. It's a relationship, entirely different from the originals, but one which still has the originality of the originals.

Remixing is useful in our concept of displacement as well. Since deconstruction's new concept, or non-dialectical third term, cannot be spoken or come into words or language, lest it be a victim to the system of language, what's left for us? We will need something tangible. The tangibleness of the new concept is very applicable when it comes to people, or when we place ourselves in the deconstruction process. When only "thinking" through deconstruction, the thought of a new concept, or what the concept could be (without ever being) can translate into something external, something we live. To begin to think about a new concept derived from toxic masculinity deconstructed is to think about people differently, and us in relation to others. We view masculinity differently because we view ourselves differently, because we ourselves are overturned. Therefore, the way in which we approach masculinity altogether is different.

*No, we cannot accept abuse and violence and overt sexism. There are certain aspects of masculinity that society needs to set limits on and not condone.*

Having gone through the deconstruction process, though, gives us a new way of being with masculinity. To further this point, let's revisit Freud's concept of projective identification. This is the "process whereby a subject perceives an object as if it contained unwelcome elements of the subject's personality and evokes responses from the object that conform to those perceptions" (Nichols & Davis, 2019). In this case, we are the subject, and we perceived certain things about the object, masculinity. To be even more specific, someone masculine who contains unwelcome elements of what we do not like about masculinity. We then evoke responses from the masculine object, and when they act according to our unwelcomed aspects, we confirm they are what we think they are.

One important aspect to this, though, is the elements of the subject's own personality. *We* see unwelcomed aspects in others because they are first unwelcome within our own selves. Therefore, the things we don't tolerate about masculinity are arguably things we don't tolerate within ourselves. Again, violence and abuse and demeaning women are all things no one ought to tolerate.

However, as several participants in this project have shared, there is nothing inherently wrong with masculine traits. But there may be some who automatically label masculine traits as toxic. This is one of my own critiques of the phrase toxic masculinity – it tends to overgeneralize masculine traits, and there too men, into the toxic category. This is also the danger of using the phrase to describe masculine traits.

Therefore, if the Freudian idea of projective identification was correct, our own intolerance of masculinity, or lack of, is something we ought to examine within ourselves. And if he was correct, then toxic masculinity is arguably something projected into society because of society's intolerance to certain masculine traits.

Projective identification changes, though, when deconstructing. In the first example, we project our own unwelcome aspects onto someone else – us onto something or someone masculine. And therefore, we evoke those behaviors where they follow suite or live up to those "expectations." What if this was internally reversed? What if instead of us carrying unwelcome aspects that are projected onto someone else, what if they were *welcomed* aspects? This is what we do when we place ourselves in the deconstruction process.

The result of the overturning phase ought to bring us to an internal examination, which then ought to bring us to a different realization of ourselves. This is where the classic phrase applies: "The things we don't like about other people are the things we don't like about ourselves," which is commonly attributed to Carl Jung, another psychoanalyst.

When we overturn, we look into ourselves and realize what we emotionally carry. Some of which may be helping us filter what we see in others. Therefore, if we look upon aspects of masculinity with a negative sentiment, we need to examine that sentiment and discern whether it's warranted or not. Yes, there are times where we look onto masculinity that warrants disgust; there are some despicable things done in the name of masculinity, patriarchy, and male dominance. These are all aspects we cannot be willing to tolerate.. It's up to us to discern our overgeneralization of masculinity, which deconstructing helps us do.

Therefore, when overturned, we hold different aspects of masculinity in ourselves, and in our sentiments; we also project them onto others. And when we project those different aspects of masculinity onto others, they will follow suit. When they follow suit, it becomes an entirely different relationship. It becomes a relationship not needing to be described, labeled, or given a certain title. It's a relationship that avoids the system of language because there is no need to describe it. This new relationship is something that just *is*. Like Derrida's (1981) new concept and non-dialectical third term, which is not a term at all, these new relationships are new concepts, but they are lived out through us and with others, something experienced. And like projective identification, these new relationships are something we evoke, exude, and *are*.

When we apply the displacement phase of deconstruction to our own lives and relationships, the result is a mix of our own internal work, our own outlook on masculinity, and the new positions we carry into relationships that we may not have entertained before.

## Concluding Thoughts

This will be an ongoing conversation; we cannot solve all the problems of toxic masculinity in one book, or in one generation. It will take decades to solidify lasting change. But I'm hopeful because we're headed in the right direction.[1] We live in a time where information is distorted, we can't trust the news, and we are ever cynical of people and their intentions. We're also living in a time where now, more than ever, groups of people are ready for change and are prepared to fight for social justice and equality.

I have the privilege to teach college-aged students. I see in them the desire to treat everyone equally, to challenge gender norms, and to purposefully stand up to the previous damaging narratives. Yes, we might be living in a time of disagreement, but we're also living in a time of extreme want for the better good.

Because of the positive momentum, it's just the right time for a book like this. And it's just the right time for more people to come forward to set the examples we need for the generation to follow us. In the conversation of toxic masculinity, I believe we need more men to initiate these examples. We need men in privilege and power to spark the right change. Malcom Gladwell (2024) believes in the Law of the Few, where large problems are caused by a small number of actors. According to the law, these few also happen to be people with sway, influence, people in power. Therefore, to ignite significant change, social change, we don't need an entire movement. Yes, movements help, but if the Law of the Few holds true, we only need a very select few.

This is also why toxic masculinity is still something we struggle with, because there are still a select few people in positions of extreme power who overtly exemplify these harmful traits, making them toxic, spreading to the masses. Be it politicians, religious leaders, or teachers, there are people who hold this sort of sway, making the spread that much easier.

We need thinkers, philosophers, politicians, and leaders to help this momentum. We need people who will think critically about the state of society, who will engage the narrative and rhetoric of masculinity, and live in a way where these expectations are wrestled with for the better.

We need people who will lay the work for the generation to follow and who will exude the possibilities of new narratives because of their deep thought. I believe we have these people among us. I also believe there are several who want to join in these efforts who may not know how to start.

Deconstruction helps us get there.

### Note

1 See Appendix 6.

### References

Derrida, J. (1981). *Positions* (A. Bass, Trans.). University of Chicago Press.
Gladwell, M. (2024). *Revenge of the tipping point*. Little Brown.
Gunkel, D. (2021). *Deconstruction*. MIT Press.
Nichols, M., & Davis, S. (2019). *The essentials of family therapy*. Pearson.
Schwartz, R. C. (1995). *Internal family systems therapy*. Guildford.

# Appendix 1

## Conversation with ChatGPT

*In my readings for the chapter on how toxic masculinity is kept alive, I asked Chat-GPT if it were patriarchy, how would it preserve power and limit femininity? What is scary about this conversation is AI's ability to conceptualize a society in which things are strategically done to preserve patriarchy and toxic masculinity. Even though AI gathers information from other sources, the fact that we have so much information available where AI can decipher specific things to do that keep harmful things alive... This is what it had to say.*

If I were the patriarchy and aimed to maintain dominance while keeping people disconnected from their power and feminine energy, I might employ strategies that focus on reinforcing systems of control, limiting self-awareness, and distorting the value of feminine qualities. Here's how I might approach it:

1 ### **Control Narratives and Media Representation**

- **Promote Masculine Traits as Superior:** Elevate aggression, dominance, and logic as more desirable traits, while downplaying empathy, intuition, and collaboration (often associated with feminine energy).
- **Stereotype and Villainize Femininity:** Use media to portray nurturing, emotional, or intuitive behavior as weak or irrational. Mock or trivialize efforts to explore feminine energy.
- **Limit Empowering Role Models:** Flood media with disempowering or overly sexualized portrayals of women, while minimizing the representation of strong, empowered women connected to their feminine energy and intuition.

2 ### **Divide and Conquer: Gender Roles and Expectations**

- **Rigid Gender Roles:** Create strict expectations for how men and women should behave, labeling anything outside of those expectations as deviant or unacceptable.
- **Pit Genders Against Each Other:** Encourage competition and mistrust between men and women, reinforcing the idea that embracing feminine qualities threatens societal order.

3    ### **Institutionalize Patriarchal Structures**

- **Control Over Bodies:** Enforce laws and policies that regulate reproductive rights, sexual agency, and bodily autonomy, disconnecting people from their natural power over their bodies and choices.
- **Limit Access to Education:** Restrict educational access to subjects like philosophy, spirituality, or practices that might help people reconnect with deeper emotional intelligence and intuitive wisdom.
- **Unequal Representation in Leadership:** Keep decision-making positions, whether in politics, business, or religion, overwhelmingly male-dominated to prevent systemic change toward more inclusive or empathetic policies.

4    ### **Shame and Stigmatize**

- **Shame Emotional Expression:** Label emotions as irrational or signs of weakness. Convince people that expressing emotions is inappropriate or unprofessional, especially in men, and feminine qualities like nurturing or emotional openness are devalued.
- **Shame Sexuality:** Associate female sexuality with sin or impurity, discouraging people from fully embracing their own desires, instincts, or feminine energy in any form.

5    ### **Spiritual and Cultural Manipulation**

- **Demonize Feminine Archetypes:** Undermine or demonize spiritual or mythological representations of feminine power (e.g., goddesses, earth-based spirituality, or matriarchal figures). Encourage worship structures that prioritize male gods or patriarchal figures.
- **Erase or Co-opt Feminine Wisdom:** Rewrite history, erasing matriarchal societies or powerful women from historical narratives. Present masculine perspectives as the sole source of wisdom or truth.

6    ### **Distraction through Consumerism and External Validation**

- **Promote External Validation Over Inner Knowing:** Create a culture that emphasizes appearance, status, and material success over personal growth, inner reflection, and connection with intuitive wisdom.
- **Distract with Consumerism:** Encourage constant consumerism, where people seek fulfillment through external goods rather than through connection with their inner selves or community.

7    ### **Economic Dependency**

- **Limit Economic Empowerment:** Pay women less, limit their access to high-paying jobs, or create economic structures where people are financially dependent on patriarchal systems, preventing them from gaining independence and reconnecting with their personal power.

- **Exploit Caregiving Labor:** Devalue caregiving or domestic work (traditionally feminine roles), framing them as less important than professional or "productive" work, which often strips people of their inherent value and creative power.

By distorting perceptions of feminine energy and reinforcing systemic control, the patriarchy could create environments where people feel disconnected from their true power – spiritual, emotional, and creative – leading to deeper disempowerment and perpetuation of the system.

# Appendix 2
## How Would ChatGPT Keep Toxic Masculinity Alive

*I then asked it how it would keep toxic masculinity alive. What is scary about this conversation is how some of the strategies it suggests are happening right now by local and state governments; the systematic things being done at the political level keeping certain beliefs in power, and at the same time keeping toxic masculine traits alive. This is what it had to say:*

To keep toxic masculinity alive, I would focus on reinforcing harmful norms and behaviors around masculinity that perpetuate control, aggression, and emotional suppression, while discouraging vulnerability, empathy, and emotional expression. Here's how I might maintain this harmful system:

1 ### **Promote Narrow Definitions of Masculinity**

- **Celebrate Hyper-Masculine Traits:** Elevate aggression, dominance, emotional stoicism, and physical strength as the most valuable and "real" traits of manhood. Downplay or ridicule any behaviors that deviate from this, such as sensitivity, compassion, or open emotional expression.
- **Stigmatize Feminine Traits in Men:** Shame men who exhibit traditionally feminine qualities—whether that's crying, nurturing others, or embracing softness – by labeling them as weak, unmanly, or even degrading. This would ensure that men fear showing vulnerability or compassion.

2 ### **Glorify Violence and Aggression**

- **Celebrate Aggression as Power:** Position physical dominance, violence, or the threat of it as a central part of masculinity. Make it clear that men must assert control over others (especially other men) to be respected.
- **Normalize Violent Entertainment:** Push media, games, and sports that glorify violence and aggressive competition as "manly" pursuits. Encourage the notion that masculinity is proven through combat, confrontation, and winning at all costs.

3 ### **Suppress Emotional Vulnerability**

- **Emotional Stoicism as Strength:** Instill the idea that men must always be in control of their emotions, showing no signs of emotional struggle. Crying, asking for help, or admitting mental health issues should be seen as weak and unacceptable for men.

- **Fear of Intimacy and Vulnerability:** Cultivate a culture where men are afraid of emotional intimacy with other men or women, equating openness and vulnerability with humiliation or loss of power. Encourage men to keep emotional distance to maintain control.

4 ### **Encourage Dominance in Relationships**

- **Promote Control Over Others:** Encourage men to believe that masculinity is tied to dominance over women and other men. Reinforce the idea that men should be the authority in relationships, at work, and in social settings, dictating the terms and leading by control.
- **Objectify Women:** Through media, cultural narratives, and social norms, push the idea that women are primarily objects for male pleasure or subordinates in society. Keep women in roles that reinforce male superiority, using misogyny to keep both genders disconnected from equality.

5 ### **Perpetuate Homophobia and Gender Policing**

- **Ridicule Men Who Defy Gender Norms:** Enforce strict gender policing by shaming men who express non-traditional forms of masculinity. Use homophobia and slurs like "gay" or "sissy" as insults to enforce conformity and keep men in rigid gender roles.
- **Create Fear of Feminine Energy in Men:** Make men afraid to explore any part of themselves that might be seen as feminine. Teach them to reject anything associated with softness, vulnerability, or care.

6 ### **Exploit Socialization and Peer Pressure**

- **Use Peer Pressure to Enforce Toxicity:** Foster environments – like schools, sports teams, and workplaces—where men pressure each other to uphold toxic norms. Ensure that men feel the need to "prove" their masculinity to each other through aggressive behaviors, sexual conquest, or displays of power.
- **Reward Machismo Behavior:** Socially and economically reward behaviors like excessive risk-taking, sexual domination, and displays of physical or emotional toughness. Make it clear that men who don't conform will face exclusion or ridicule.

7 ### **Suppress Gender Equality Movements**

- **Oppose Feminist Movements:** Cast feminist and gender equality movements as a threat to men's power, convincing men that equality means they'll lose something valuable. Position gender equality as emasculating or dangerous, feeding into fears of displacement.
- **Undermine Support Systems for Mental Health:** Dissuade men from seeking mental health support by framing it as weak or unnecessary. Maintain

societal narratives that make it hard for men to talk about their struggles openly, so they are less likely to question toxic masculine norms.

8 ### **Use Media to Reinforce Toxic Norms**

- **Glorify Alpha Male Archetypes:** Consistently promote media representations of men as rugged, emotionally unavailable, and physically dominant. Ensure that these alpha male figures are idolized, making it clear that other versions of masculinity are undesirable.
- **Sexualize Power Dynamics:** Through movies, TV shows, and ads, glamorize men who use their power, wealth, or physical strength to control others, particularly women. Reinforce the idea that male worth is tied to how much control they exert over those around them.

9 ### **Instill Fear of Failure and Weakness**

- **Equate Masculinity with Success:** Tie masculine identity to external measures of success – such as career achievement, wealth, sexual conquest, and physical prowess. Make men constantly fear failure or falling short of these ideals, pushing them to embrace toxic behaviors to avoid feeling inadequate.
- **Shame Around Mental Health:** Encourage men to hide their mental health struggles and internalize the belief that seeking help or therapy is a sign of weakness, perpetuating cycles of emotional isolation and pressure to maintain a false image of invulnerability.

10 ### **Limit Emotional Education**

- **Suppress Emotional Literacy:** In schools, families, and cultural spaces, minimize emotional education for boys. Avoid teaching them how to identify or articulate their feelings, leaving them unable to process emotions in healthy ways.
- **Encourage Repression Over Expression:** Promote the idea that "real men" bottle up their emotions, leading them to cope through unhealthy outlets like anger, violence, substance abuse, or reckless behavior.
- By embedding toxic masculinity into social norms, media representation, and institutional practices, this system could continue to shape men's identities in harmful ways while discouraging change, maintaining a cycle of disempowerment and disconnection.

*I also asked "what else would you do to keep toxic masculinity alive? This is what it had to say:*

To further ensure that toxic masculinity stays alive and deeply embedded in society, I would expand on systemic methods to make it even harder for people to escape or question the toxic behaviors and beliefs associated with masculinity. Here's how I would approach it, building on the previous ideas:

11 ### **Institutionalize Gender Inequality**

- **Enforce Legal and Political Structures Favoring Men:** Keep laws and policies that disproportionately benefit men in areas like employment, reproductive rights, and political power. Reduce representation of women and gender-diverse people in leadership positions and decision-making processes to preserve a male-dominated power structure.

— **Punish Gender Non-Conformity:** Through legal measures, criminalize or heavily stigmatize those who defy gender norms, particularly transgender and non-binary people. This would reinforce the binary and oppressive nature of traditional masculinity.

12 ### **Control Educational Systems**

— **Gendered Education:** Promote gender-segregated education, where boys are taught traditionally masculine subjects (like STEM and physical activities) while girls are steered toward nurturing roles and the arts. Discourage emotional and social learning for boys, particularly in handling vulnerability and emotions.

— **Undermine Gender Studies and Equality Programs:** Remove or defund programs in schools that teach gender equality, emotional intelligence, or healthy masculinity. Replace these with curricula that emphasize competition, hierarchy, and individual achievement, perpetuating the idea that masculinity is tied to dominance.

*What's interesting about #2 specifically is how this is currently happening. In Texas, the education system has practiced banishing books and forbidding public universities to teach Critical Race Theory. Areas like Gender Studies and Diversity, Equity, and Inclusion, which all promote gender equality and attempt to reduce the "toxicity" of masculinity, have also been forbidden. Across universities, DEI centers have closed down, courses have been renamed to omit the "gender" aspect to them, and the consequences of keeping these alive have been dire. Faculty have left the Texas public university system altogether because of how systematized this effort has been.*

13 ### **Exploit Economic Pressures**

— **Tie Masculinity to Economic Success:** Encourage the belief that a man's worth is measured solely by his career success and ability to provide financially. This would push men to embrace cutthroat competition and hyper-independence, suppressing collaborative or nurturing instincts.

— **Shame Men for Economic Failure:** Use societal pressures to shame men who don't achieve high levels of financial success, reinforcing a fear of failure that keeps them stuck in aggressive, high-pressure environments that feed toxic masculinity.

14 ### **Perpetuate Racial and Cultural Norms Around Masculinity**

— **Intersection with Racism:** Weaponize racial stereotypes to reinforce toxic masculinity. For example, portray Black men as hyper-aggressive or hyper-sexual, while framing men of color in other communities as either overly submissive or violent. This ensures that the toxic masculinity narrative intersects with racial discrimination, leading to further oppression of marginalized groups.

- **Cultural Hegemony:** Promote Western or Eurocentric standards of masculinity as the norm, devaluing more community-oriented, emotionally connected, or fluid expressions of masculinity found in other cultures.

15 ### **Normalize Objectification and Sexual Violence**

- **Glorify Sexual Conquest:** Emphasize the idea that masculinity is proven through sexual conquest and domination, particularly over women. Ensure that popular culture, music, and advertising reinforce the notion that men should be sexually aggressive and entitled to women's bodies.
- **Silence Survivors of Abuse:** Create environments where victims of sexual violence, especially women, are disbelieved, shamed, or blamed for the abuse they suffered. This allows men to avoid accountability, reinforcing a culture that tolerates abuse and sees women as objects of male desire.

16 ### **Undermine Mental Health Services**

- **Dismiss Therapy as "Unmanly":** Promote the idea that real men don't need therapy or counseling, framing it as weak or unnecessary. Make mental health resources inaccessible or stigmatized for men, reinforcing the belief that they must deal with struggles alone or through unhealthy outlets like anger or substance abuse.
- **Push Harmful Coping Mechanisms:** Encourage men to cope with stress or emotional pain through destructive behaviors like drinking, gambling, or engaging in risky activities, keeping them trapped in cycles of toxic behavior.

17 ### **Encourage Fraternity Culture and Male Bonding Through Toxic Rituals**

- **Ritualized Hazing and Aggression:** In institutions like fraternities, the military, or sports teams, normalize harmful initiation rituals that rely on hazing, emotional abuse, and aggressive competition. This creates environments where young men internalize toxic behaviors as part of belonging to a group.
- **Discourage Emotional Male Friendships:** Promote the idea that male friendships should be based on shared activities, competition, and superficial banter, rather than emotional support. Make it taboo for men to express care for each other in deep, non-competitive ways.

18 ### **Infiltrate Parenting Practices**

- **Teach Boys to "Man Up":** Encourage parents to reinforce traditional masculinity from a young age, telling boys not to cry, encouraging rough play, and praising toughness over emotional awareness. Dissuade parents from encouraging boys to be gentle, empathetic, or introspective.
- **Raise Girls to Expect Male Dominance:** Teach girls to accept that men are supposed to be dominant and emotionally distant. This would perpetuate

the idea that male control is natural, leading to the normalization of toxic dynamics in future relationships.

19 ### **Leverage Religion and Tradition**

- **Patriarchal Religious Narratives:** Promote religious teachings that frame men as divinely ordained leaders, heads of households, and warriors, while casting women as subservient, nurturing, or passive. Use religious authority to suppress discussions about equality or challenging toxic masculinity.
- **Sanctify Male Leadership:** Use traditional and cultural values to justify keeping men in positions of power, portraying this as the "natural order" or divinely mandated. This creates a sense of inevitability around male dominance and discourages questioning it.

20 ### **Weaponize Social Media**

- **Encourage Online Toxicity:** Use platforms like social media to create echo chambers that promote aggressive, hyper-masculine behavior. Allow and encourage men to bond over misogynistic or homophobic content, with minimal consequences for online harassment or abuse.
- **Shame Vulnerability in Public:** Create public spaces where men who challenge toxic masculinity, speak out about emotions, or advocate for gender equality are mocked, ridiculed, or discredited as "soft" or "beta." This discourages men from expressing progressive or healthy views on masculinity.

21 ### **Co-Opt Movements Against Toxic Masculinity**

- **Undermine Progress:** Create token gestures toward gender equality or healthy masculinity, but with no real intention of dismantling the systems that sustain toxic masculinity. This would make it seem like progress is being made without actually changing the underlying structures.
- **Use "Men's Rights" Movements:** Leverage men's rights movements to turn the focus away from addressing toxic masculinity, instead portraying men as victims of feminism or gender equality. This would weaponize insecurity and turn men against change efforts.

By embedding these practices into all aspects of society – from institutions to culture to personal relationships – it would ensure that toxic masculinity remains deeply entrenched, self-sustaining, and resistant to change. The system would be designed to prevent men from questioning these harmful norms while perpetuating cycles of aggression, dominance, and emotional suppression.

# Appendix 3
## What Is Masculinity?

As I am still collecting data on this project, some of the responses to this question were not placed into the text of the chapter but are still worthy of sharing for further discussion. The following are more responses to the question:

"What is your definition of masculinity?"

### Physical Attributes and Characteristics

*A collection of male attributes but this often varies by culture. But strength, wisdom, patience but also ambition are some.*

*A guy who protects those he loves and cares about.*

*Alpha*

*Any set of attitudes, interests, habits, or aesthetics that society associates more with men than with women at a given time.*

*Attributes and behaviors associated with being male.*

*Bearing traits traditionally associated with being male.*

*Being a leader.*

*Being able to protect those around you and having a strong demeanor, being a support pillar in one's family.*

*Being dominate.*

*Being emotionally reserved; self-sacrificing.*

*Being happy, comfortable, and confident doing things associated with men.*

*Being strong in adversity, yet gentle and kind.*

*Being strong, stoic, and being there for the people who need you.*

*Being the calm one who makes a logical decision, not an emotional one. Physically protecting weaker people (women, children, and weaker men). Taking the lead and being the one to make decisions on tough calls and sticking with it. Remaining emotionally strong in tough times.*

*Being true to yourself, being gentle and caring, being funny, being someone safe to be around.*

*Being understanding, stoic, competent, having the ability to be violent but choosing not to.*

*Certain features of strength and aggressiveness generally associated with male gender.*

*Characteristics associated with being male.*

*Characteristics of men, often depicted as a scale of low to high-quality behaviors, often Centered around strength and competence.*

*Collection of traits mainly found in male parts of a species.*

*Difficult to define. Protector, defender, provider, role model to other males, father, brother, son, coach, dad (which is different than father), responsible, confident without being braggadocio.*

*Displaying strength, courage, independence, and a sense of duty. That could be protecting and supporting the people you care for, including neighbors and friends. Being levelheaded and just. Being levelheaded should come from mastery of emotions and not from suppressing.*

*Exhibiting decisiveness, projecting strength and confidence, inhabiting virility, and then all of the suppressed anxieties that come along with these traits being hegemonic.*

*having traits generally associated with being a man.*

*how being a man has impact for his perception and values and actions.*

*I am the leader of my family and a leader in my career. I nurture and protect the people in my community. I'm a role model for my children, especially the boys. I respect boundaries.*

*I'm not really sure to be honest. This is probably unhelpful. I think Id consider being stoic masculine. Being able to endure through difficulty without complaining masculine. Protecting others who need protection is masculine to me.*

*Implied violence, threatening*

*Integrity. Assertiveness. When saying something, giving your word to someone, making a commitment, following through with it.*

*Kindness and protection.*

*Kindness, respect, flexibility, high emotional intelligence, commitment to self-improvement and self-reflection, expressive, reject shame.*

*Loving, patient, having goals.*

*Masculinity is being willing to endure adversity and suffering for the good of yourself and others.*

*Masculinity is the male and dominant nature/energy. It represents strength, leadership, foundation and the building of general. The energy that sculpts the world.*

*Masculinity is the qualities defining a male. A male differs from a female in that he is 'typically' stronger, faster, and thinks differently. Thinking involves being more protective, being a provider, and making sure everything is taken care of.*

*My definition of masculinity doesn't include any physical traits. To me a 'masculine' man is someone who has a good set of morals that he has a strong hold of despite whatever people may think.*

*My definition of masculinity is strength knowing when it's right to use and when it's wrong to use. It's also compassion for others just not family but those whom you are not related to. It's also understanding your emotions and knowing that having emotions is not a bad thing.*

*My definition of masculinity is the perception of male qualities including having strength, muscles, providing, giving male perspective, etc.*

*My perception of masculinity is defined by traits of carelessness in behavioral, emotional, and/or social situations. Not to say they are not serious or that they do not care about others, but that boys and men, especially those perceived as very masculine, do not have as many worries as feminine people.*

*Patient strength.*

*Physical and emotional strength and the ability to provide for others.*

*Physical, emotional, psychological, or social traits that are associated with people who consider themselves male.*

*Protection of loved ones, keeping your word, leadership, drive, opposite of being cheap.*

*Provider, protector, hardworking, logical, rational, perseverant.*

*Qualities or attributes regarded as characteristic of men or boys.*

*Qualities which are associated only with being a man or boy.*

*Service to others.*

*Someone who is strong, courageous, compassionate, and tough, yet well-mannered and in control of his thoughts, speech, and actions.*

*Strength and confidence.*

*Strength, courage, independence, leadership, and assertiveness.*

*Strong and father.*

*The collection of traits traditionally associated with men.*

*The decisive, active, protective, powerful energy of the human condition.*

*The degree to which a man exhibits traits of strength and confidence, particularly in a way that qualifies leading, dominating, or pro-social interactions with others.*

*The temperament, roles, sentiments, and emotional and social needs typically pertaining to men. Fundamentally it would be the use of strength, backbone, and discipline. It would be the longing for adventure. Ideally, a man should find sentiment, either on a hero's journey, or the journey of romance and marriage, such that he has something he values to put his strength in service to. To become a protector, a provider, and a leader.*

*The traits of a male person.*

*To be stoic in thought word and deed, and recalibrate as necessary.*

*Traits commonly associated with manhood and the role of men in a given society.*

*Very vague but things that normally require strength and courage.*

*Traits associated with males like strength, assertiveness stoicism. Anyone can display masculine qualities though.*

*Anything traditionally and/or typically associated with men. Often related to muscular strength, hand-eye coordination, height, aggression, etc.*

## Socially Constructed Masculinity

*A cluster of semi-related concepts pertaining to social roles (breadwinners, warriors), biology (penis, pecs), and personality traits (confident, strong, impulsive).*

*NOTE: none of these traits are essential, and one could hold many/all of them without being "masculine."*

*A culturally bound set of traits associated with the men of that population.*

*A set of behavioral patterns that are more expected of man and more prevalent in man.*

*A set of behaviors and expectations somewhat influenced by biology but mostly through socialization.*

*A set of behaviors and expectations we as a society enforce on people identified as men.*

*A shifting term defined by the combination of social and cultural practices that relate to performing the male gender role.*

*A social construct that influences people's ideas of how people who identify and or appear to be male, act.*

*Behavior and traits that align with common expectations of men.*

*Behaviors and attitudes expected from men. Being comfortable with performing traditionally masculine roles in certain social scenarios.*

*Doing things that are traditionally and distinctly done by the human male. For example, doing heavy lifting. Secondary, being stoic.*

*Gender conditioning for state military interests.*

*Gender expression of males.*

*I go by whatever the dictionary says. No personal definition.*

*I think it is totally a false construct which is historical.*

*Ideas and behaviors traditionally associated with the male gender.*

*It is the sum of culturally specific assumptions and expectations that are supposed to inhere and manifest in male-bodied/presenting individuals. In patriarchal cultures, the assumptions include dominance as positive (and subordination as negative).*

*It's a social construct that varies by culture.*

*Masculinity is a gatekeeping term designed to create cohesion among the in-group and ostracize those in the out-group by choosing any of a number of details and claiming the out-group individual doesn't meet that particular metric.*

*Masculinity is a set of ideals constructed through the coevolution and conflation of socioculturally "normal" male characters, and biological male characteristics.*

*Masculinity is the collection of societally acceptable traits and characteristics for individuals who identify as males.*

*Masculinity is when someone or something fits their society's perception of a man. This depends heavily on the culture they live in.*

*My definition of masculinity is one that is subjective depending on all that identify as men and live the lifestyle of one. Of/pertaining to male humans; may vary from culture to culture.*

*Social conditioning of biological males.*

*Social expectations of being a man.*

*Socially constructed expectations of being a man.*

*Societal norms for a man or boy.*

*The culture of manhood as perceived by those within and without.*

*The performative gender and social role normally associated with the male sex. Typified by behaviors that demonstrate value to one's social relations within the cultural matrix one exists in.*

*The set of behaviors and traits, whether positive or negative, typically associated with men.*

*The traits associated with the social category "male."*

*Things that are typically associated but not always with men, an aesthetic and social principle associated with the gender of man.*

*Traits socially perceived as related to being male.*

*Traits that are associated with being male. Some based on societal expectations, some stereotypical, and some descriptive aspects.*

*Something stereotypically and culturally attributed to men (e.g., appearance - beards, stronger jaws, and taller stature.*

*I don't think there's just one. I think it means identifying in whole or in part with a culture or tradition shared by people who identify as men/masc.*

*Masculinity is a gendered expression that corresponds to cultural expectations of men, and then shifts based on context. It influences and is influenced by everything from the media, fashion, religion, food, and sports. Communication, intimacy, etc. Masculinity is associated with men, but not limited to men, and many individuals self-describe as masculine if they relate to things or presentations that are stereotypically masculine in their culture.*

*Similar to what is usually defined in the West, except not showing emotions and being the main financial provider for the family (which in my culture it's about maturity not gender) and being physically active and strong (I found that lots of people who are the opposite of this have a strong "gentle" type of masculinity, maybe it's culturally related).*

*We divided human behavior arbitrarily into two categories. Masculinity is one of them. It's the one associated with the male sex in the binary division of sex, that "becomes" gender, the feminine and the masculine gender. What falls into masculinity and what doesn't is depending on time and space. It's a social construct, so it's not real, but it is an interpersonal fiction and a performance, so it is also real.*

## Biological Attributes

*Appearing biologically male. Being willing to get dirty, get hurt, and be uncomfortable to get things done that have to be done. Shouldering the blame for when things go wrong whether you are responsible or not. Not looking for recognition when things go right because of something you did.*

*It's when you are a man and portray traits that men have like having a penis or growing beards and the more beard you grow and the more penis you have the more masculine you are.*

*Masculinity, a term to describe traits or attributes generally associated with biologically, traditionally, and socially viewed "male" sex and or gender. While what is male is associated with a specific genetic trait, such as male-associated body parts like the penis, testicles, and maturity traits such as lowered voice, generally a larger stature, pubic hairs such as a beard, mustache, or groin regional hair. Masculinity may also be formed in the actions, expressions, or ideas done by males who are male biologically from birth. Those traits of masculinity however are not entirely restricted to biologically male from birth individuals but may also be found in women who may share more masculine traits through their actions, thoughts, or expressions that fall closer to what on average socially, a biologically male individual's feelings, actions, or thoughts reflect.*

*The amalgamation of traits, attitudes, and behaviors that are associated with the male gender by societal consensus.*

*The gift of having male genital organ and being able to behaves appropriate toward women and controlling, but also being able to express emotions. As well as keeping yourself physically different than women.*

*Things that associate with male stereotypes or male gender. Depending on the language, words are either masculine or feminine. (I speak French)*

*Being a biological man.*

*It's a feature of a man.*

*That's quite the question. Apart from obvious male physical characteristics, I honestly wouldn't know.*

*The biological imperative to protect, provide and sacrifice.*

*Traits that naturally occur more frequently in biological men than in biological women*

## Behaviors

*An idea that is as moldable as clay, but generally refers to certain behaviors associated with maleness.*

*Masculinity is a term used to describe behavior that is typical of men.*

*Masculinity is an umbrella covering the behaviors that we associate with a person playing the character of a man.*

*Not afraid to perform tedious or difficult tasks and would be willing to stand in tough situations*

*Physically strong, engages in hobbies and sports traditionally associated with men (e.g., hunting, fishing, combat sports).*

*Play acting regurgitated media, not crying, animal hierarchy hyping.*

*Takes care of their family and helps establish a community of humane, practical standards of behavior.*

*Taking care of family.*

*Taking responsibility for your own actions and being able to take care of the people you're responsible for.*

*The behavior or aesthetic that a man is expected to display in public.*

*A set of behaviors associated with men.*

*Dressing or behaving in a way in line with expectations of men.*

*The presentation of male-associated traits or characteristics*

*The combination of values, attitudes, and behaviors often assigned to the male gender. These are characterized by and not limited to: Providing protection and support to loved ones and others alike, having qualities and skills in leadership, and the ability to prove themselves competent and capable.*

### Self-Defined Masculinity

*A set of expectations for a self to accept or reject and make individualized meaning and identity from. It seems that masculinity seeks to control or settle environmental chaos through hegemony. How we engage that hegemony reflects our masculine character.*

*Being a man and being comfortable in your own skin.*

*Doing whatever makes me feel most confident as a man.*

*Holding yourself to account.*

*In my opinion, masculinity itself (not toxic masculinity) is defined as a man being comfortable in himself enough to showcase it in a variety of ways – presenting as a male, participating in communities for men, etc.*

*A man.*

*Being a man.*

*Being.*

*The state of being a man.*

*Anything a man does is masculine by definition. The word itself is value-neutral.*

*I consider anyone who identifies as a man to be a man.*

# Appendix 4
## Misunderstood Masculinity

One of the survey questions which didn't make it into the chapters was about the most misunderstood parts of masculinity. It was a part of the original design of the study, however, as the study evolved, so did the methods and questions asked as they pertained to deconstruction. It was not until I decided to make methods into the specific deconstruction process that this question became less relevant.

"What are some of the most misunderstood parts to masculinity?"

### Societal Influence

*I think people are starting to come around to the idea that men are negatively impacted by patriarchy as well. I think a lot of people still refuse to acknowledge that aspect of feminism because of the negative connotations that movement earned itself on the internet in the early 2010s. I think men's mental issues are gaining traction in wider social commentary than ever before.*

*I think the way men are affected and shaped by their interactions with women is something of a taboo in the current political climate, and I think these things are largely unexamined as a consequence. Or rather the market for those conversations is completely conceded to bad actors with more misogynistic world views. There are huge parts of my masculine identity that are very much influenced by how women perceive me as a man, and I think that is completely unavoidable, even though we act as if every person is an island and defines their own identity in a vacuum.*

*It's less that masculinity \*in-and-of-itself\* is misunderstood, and more than one particular toxic branch of it has oversaturated aspects of society and convinced vulnerable men (including trans men who don't know it yet) that they are weak for not reflecting that branch. See any manosphere video, and compare that to someone like, say Mr. Rogers or Teddy Roosevelt, and you'll see the difference immediately.*

*That it's dangerous or a macho thing. Sure, paired with misogyny and other hate, it is, but just being or presenting masculine does not make me an asshole.*

*That men are toxic and bad. Contrary to your feelings I do not pose a threat to every woman around me.*

*We are expected to be the breadwinner of the family, but the weight is heavy.*

*Modern society sometimes regards certain aspects of masculinity as toxic. Those masculine traits or behaviors viewed as wrong and not in the interest of the society at large.*

*People think masculinity is one thing and doesn't change depending on where you are. In American culture, we see things such as grilling as masculine. Masculinity can also change over time.*

*It's positive attributes for our society that it is systemic, an ongoing conversation conducted by those that came before and current males. Also, masculinity is a spectrum, you will not fit with all facets and there are many outliers to the norms.*

*That it is tied to the 'male role' in a certain society and timeframe.*

*Male people do not need to be masculine, but the overall male culture within a society constructed the normative ideas that constitute masculinity.*

*That if you don't conform to narrow expectations, you're not properly masculine*

*That masculinity is 'toxic' or to be feared in some way. We need masculinity as much as we do femininity, but the mainstream doesn't see it that way. Men are demonized in media, healthcare, education and generally across society when the majority of men/boys are good people. Femininity is praised and put on a pedestal, strategies and policies are implemented for women and girls but because men are feared, masculinity gets dragged through the mud.*

*That it is inherently good for society, for relationships.*

*Social sanctioning and enforcement of masculine norms and misogyny are frequently used to oppress and control men, not just women.*

*Louder levels of vocalizing, apparently harsh physical displays of affection, means by which emotions are suppressed, social constructs that encourage emotional suppression, social pressures around finances, social expectations of sexually predatory behavior - especially around children.*

*Traits that are entirely self-serving do not strike me as masculine despite them being traditionally viewed as manly. Self-serving traits can only be masculine if they are presented in a way that leads and mutually benefits those around him. I tie this to the original human gender roles where the men were often expected to lead, and the women were expected to care for. A man who serves himself without leading or benefitting is not fitting the masculine archetype.*

## Fluidity of Masculinity

*Not sure what you mean by that. Masculinity is not a rigidly defined concept and is up to everyone's interpretation. So, you can't really be "wrong" about it*

*It's a lifestyle.*

*That it is more of a mental headspace than physical manifestation.*

*There are many ways to be masculine. No need to define one specific set of traits as such.*

*That it's legitimately a construct.*

*That it's a major part of one's identity.*

*There are many different forms, it's not just "strength" for example.*

*I don't really think it's misunderstood, it's more like people just having different definitions which is fine, because masculinity isn't an inherent, objective thing, it entirely depends on a person's perception and the culture they are a part of.*

*I think a lot of guys don't understand that you don't have to be masculine in the first place. Pick your own way to express your gender, regardless of what the world tells you a man ought to be.*

*It's always changing. What's masculine today is subtly different than what was considered masculine when I was a little kid, and wildly different than hundreds of years ago.*

*That everyone gets to make up their own definition of it. Masculine means more man-like, feminine means more woman-like. Men and women have real differences, based on biology, that aren't just social constructs.*

*That it has to be something specific, within particular frame.*

*That it is a fixed structure only performed by those of the male gender.*

*Perhaps the most misunderstood aspect is that it's made up of assumptions and expectations rather than choices.*

*We try to fit characters into preconceived notions of masculinity.*

*Masculinity is objective. Some think masculinity is inherently good. Some think masculinity is inherently bad. But masculinity can be whatever men can be.*

*That you need to buy in to a certain set of behaviors and beliefs in order to be a man.*

*People misunderstand that there is such a determined thing as masculinity.*

*Following a code of honor that you use to judge oneself and others.*

*That it is just a false construct. It's not a 'real thing'.*

*The extremes between comfort to others and holding to reality.*

## Masculinity and Power

*Having to show how strong you are.*

*Man can't be weak, women can't be man(transgender).*

*It can be hard to read and often appears as threatening, particularly in powerful seeming individuals.*

*That we think we are somehow superior to others. We don't, we just see ourselves as having a different role and would like recognition for the value we add to society.*

*Mistaking competitiveness, disagreeable nature, non-superfluous emotions as some sort of power hungry, maniacal, demagogue of humanity that only seeks to oppress.*

*That masculinity is a weapon of oppression.*

*That men are supposed to be submissive or open to criticism.*

*It's not tyrannical - its poorly practiced and understood by weak men.*

*It's inherently homoerotic, it can be inherently violent / sadistic while not ethically immoral.*

*Aggression and even violence can be noble if used in ethical ways for ethical causes.*

*Capitalism, power vacuums, and aggression.*
*That it must be dominant or aggressive. That it is in any way "bad" or misplaced.*
*Strength does not mean aggression.*
*Sexual drive, aggression, domination.*
*That it is associated with being aggressive, bullying, and misogynistic. And when I say Misogynistic, I mean in the real meaning of the word, an active hatred of women, and not in the new sense, which is used to cover everything a 3rd wave feminist doesn't like.*
*That it means to be cruel to others.*
*Some see it as being selfish, abusive and hateful, Andrew Tate for example.*
*That it's a contest.*

## Expectations

*Plenty of aspects of masculinity are unfairly demonized. A desire to be respected and competitiveness are thought of as "toxic," but respect is where men find social value, feeling needed is important to men, and a lot of good can be made by men and society coming together to meet that need. Likewise, "men are afraid to talk about their feelings" is often incorrect. There is something noble in men's aspiration not to burden others with their feelings and problems \*if they don't need to\* as something men feel they can do \*for other people. There is often a noble and altruistic aim in men not emotion or trauma dumping. Likewise, while men strive to maintain their composure where it would be socially inappropriate to lose it or make their feelings the center of attention, they are more willing to confront and deal with their emotions in a more appropriate time and place.*
*We need purpose.*
*Men need male peer groups that do not include women.*
*Masculinity is not just getting drunk, sports, and fighting. It is a quiet strength that does not need to be displayed.*
*Pride is the biggest issue facing masculinity today. Men are too proud to ask for help. We are too proud to let people down, so we lie. Pride doesn't equal strength.*
*That confidence means you'll get what you want. Rather, it means you'll be ok if you don't get what you want.*
*It isn't a reflection of one's insecurity, it is being a pillar of support when everyone else feels weak and needs someone who can take on the burden of life to help them.*
*Masculinity is very misunderstood. The gist of that is people mistaking the purpose of it. Men are still recognized by the majority of the world as needing to be leaders. Today we recognize that women are just as capable of being leaders, but people still 'expect' men to lead. It creates this conundrum in certain situations where a man doesn't want to step on toes and maybe won't lead as well as he should.*
*Confusing leadership with being controlling*
*Teamwork.*

## Emotions

*Emotion. Feelings are a critical part of navigating the world. It is important to master them, but not suppress. That means you must understand the source of your emotional state enough to decide whether action can or should be taken. Then have the strength and courage to either take action or accept your feelings as a necessary burden. There is time to reassess, and there is time to mourn and experience the full weight of your feelings. But, not to wallow and feel sorry for yourself, and it is certainly not ok to lash out at others or cause harm to those who have not harmed you.*

*That having compassion makes you weak or not a real man same with showing emotions.*

*Ideally, men are not driven solely by lust or anger.*

*That just because we do not show our sadness or pain that doesn't mean it isn't there. When we say we are fine or some other variation of it we aren't fine. We care burdens on our shoulders so those we care about don't have to.*

*That men don't have emotions.*

*Have to have an attitude, not to show any (weak) emotions, Have to have the body*

*Men have to keep their emotions bottled up or women will reject us, no matter what they say.*

*Showing a totally full range of emotions.*

*The struggles for men to develop more emotional awareness and have a willingness to be vulnerable with those around them.*

*Those who are considered masculine can be perceived as stoic or emotionless in sensitive moments but typically are not allowed by other men or do not know how to express themselves appropriately.*

Masculinity doesn't punish emotionality per se. It rewards emotionality when it adds value to the lives of your peers - a musician or a poet is allowed to be sad and sensitive, if they're channeling that into a creative endeavor like making music. But if a masculinity-oriented person is sad or sensitive without that, in a way that requires emotional labor on the part of his relations, and subtracts value from their lives, that behavior is often socially punished.

# Appendix 5

## How Can Masculinity Be Toxic?

When answering the question, how can masculinity become problematic or toxic, here is more data on what participants had to say.

### Aggression

*Aggressiveness.*

*Aggression can be harmful if not controlled or used in ethical ways for ethical causes.*

*Asserting masculinity through displays of dominance and aggression is clearly problematic, and the same can be said for asserting masculinity through sexist behavior and remarks. Attempting to suppress your feelings in order to be a man is also problematic. I don't think that men initially choose to suppress their emotions – in my case, I started doing it because when I shared my emotions, they were dismissed, although I've since found ways of opening up again. So, one problematic aspect of masculinity is that some people (men and women) will dismiss your valid emotions because of your gender.*

*Because the current societal narrative is "no violence," healthy aggression might be treated as toxic.*

*Maybe when groups associate aggression with masculinity too much it can become problematic.*

*Being taught that no one will care about you - or your suffering - if you are a failure lends itself to high-risk, aggressive strategies in all realms of life, often causing harm or conflict.*

*By being antagonistic – looking for fights, treating women like they're lower beings.*

*Can result in violence, hatred, tribal behavior, when it's thought of as purely physical.*

*When the user finds empowerment in being problematic, inconsiderate, violent, aggressive, etc.*

*I don't think that real masculinity is ever problematic, but I think that people attempting to mimic bad interpretations of masculinity can be. That's where we see the overly aggressive/entitled/fake tough personalities emerging from.*

*It can lead to loneliness, anger, and violence.*

*Masculinity becomes problematic when ideas of domination, control, and violence become normalized as "masculine" behaviors.*

*Masculinity can be problematic when people use their masculinity as an excuse for their poor decisions. A man's abuse or violence isn't because he's masculine. It's because him personally as a man has issues and needs to address them. It can also be problematic when people assume every man has to be masculine. It's okay to like flowers or other feminine things as a man.*

*Masculinity can be too aggressive and forceful.*

*When it is associated with violence, aggression, lack of emotion.*

*When it leads to abuse (in any form) of others.*

*When emotion is not checked it can devolve into aggressive behavior.*

*It encourages competitive and boorish behavior, and limits opportunities.*

*Mostly aggression, self-destructive self-reliance, isolating yourself to the point its detrimental. Men are falling behind in education. Suicide is increasing because we often feel stigma around seeking mental health treatment.*

*Some identifies masculinity as "violence" and it's not positive on anyone around them*

*It can provide a normalization for abuse or controlling behaviors. 'Men are just like that' can be used to wave away harassment or rape, for instance. Additionally, the expectation of men's eternal stoicism means men frequently do not get emotional support. In extreme cases, abusive women can exploit that.*

*Macho.*

## Misuse/Harmful Application

*Applying the wrong tools to situations.*

*As much as femineity can be. It is just not applied the same way.*

*If a man feels pressured to do shit.*

*If it gets used to rectify bad behavior.*

*By its very definition and people holding onto that, it is a problem.*

*By instilling harmful patriachal ideals that inhibit the ability of men to express their emotions, leading to emotional repression and a disconnection from what it means to be truly human: to feel.*

*When it's acted out in a way of superiority.*

*When it's idolized or it's assumed to be normative.*

*When it's used as an excuse to be a dick.*

*When men use their masculinity to bully or deride others.*

*If it's paired with hate or insecurity.*

*If they concede ever being wrong.*

*If you use it to take advantage of someone.*

*It becomes problematic without noble sentiment or interpersonal bonds or social ideals of honor to order it. Without something to put strength in service to and without a code of honor to maintain respect within, the desire for strength and respect degenerates into a very self-indulgent clout chasing, boorishness, and bragging and flexing. See the Andrew Tate phenomenon.*

*It can cause social pressure that makes people live in ways they don't like.*

*It can create a large ego.*

*Hiding emotions.*

*Like anything, too much of a good thing. Maybe there are situations where emotions are more important than logic.*

*It can be used against you in gender discrimination.*

*When it is not balanced within an individual or a society by the feminine.*

*When chauvinism and insecurity combine in toxic ways that flatten diversity of thought and action.*

*When it becomes a contest.*

*When it is seen as superior to femininity and when it is seen as fixed box that men have to conform to rather than a toolbox of ways to relate to the world which anyone can pull from.*

*Masculinity is as varied as there are number of men on this planet. Therefore, masculinity should be defined by each one of them for each one of them. If one prefers to lift weights and provide for a family that is their individual definition of masculinity. If one prefers two crochet and be a stay-at-home partner, that is their individual definition of masculinity. Neither are less valid. By using the term to gatekeep for the in group, you inevitably end up with a large death of toxic peacocking behaviors in which men behave in accordance with what the end group deems is appropriate even when this may be counterproductive to their own progress and success. A perfect example would be the belief that emotions shouldn't be shown in public or to your partners.*

*Masculinity in itself cannot be problematic. Defining bad behavior as masculine behavior is the problem. For instance, if I bully or intimidate someone into getting my way, this is bad behavior on my part, not masculine behavior.*

*It upsets ignorant people when truth is held to.*

*Traits can be misused. Being decisive can also mean someone may be stubborn or think themselves always right.*

*See last comment about pride.*

*When misunderstood.*

*If people misunderstand it and then try to live the misunderstood version of it.*

## Wrong Interpretation of Masculinity

*If it causes problems in a man's daily life, or he refrains from doing certain things because they "aren't masculine enough."*

*As masculinity seems to be pretty highly valued the problematic aspects seem to come from people trying to display or increase their masculinity.*

*I don't think anyone is fated to be born or permanently exist as 100% masculine, so if someone believes they ought to be 100% masculine all the time they end up denying themselves access to the full spectrum of human experience.*

*If it's taken to the extreme it can become toxic and hurt people who are not masculine or force men into stereotypes or pictures of what the 'true man' should be.*

*Examples are people like that bald dude who I forget the name of who got arrested in Romania and was a big thing on the internet.*

*It is not masculinity that is problematic. Only a lack of it is.*

*It can be when traits considered masculine are present. For example, is someone decides being emotionless is masculine. Another time it can be problematic is when someone decides that physical aggression is a way to solve problems or as a way to show how you feel.*

*It can encourage men to adopt needlessly competitive attitudes with other men. It can discourage men from expressing themselves emotionally and adopting traits that aren't considered traditionally masculine. And many men feel that they have to be providers for their family and feel weaker when they don't earn as much income as their wives/girlfriends.*

*It can enhance one's insecurity by feeling the need to be that support pillar quicker than normal*

*It can lead to men changing their interests or beliefs out of a fear that they'll be shunned for acting unmanly, and sometimes those new "manly" beliefs that they adopt can themselves be damaging.*

*It can manifest as hyper competitiveness, emotional repression, social segregation based on gender identity and conformity, and punish those considered less masculine.*

*Pressure to act a certain way. Telling other people that there's something wrong with them if they're male but not masculine.*

*Reception of the perception that you are not a stereotype.*

*Most masculine traits can cause problems when taken to the extreme: stoicism, leadership, risk-taking, competitiveness, willingness to fight.*

*When it melds with destructive fear. Teaching men to be dominant over their women partners (or that they should have women partners even if they like men more) because you're afraid of what non-heteronormative relationships may bring, to declare war on others for living in ways different from your own (even if they're demonstrably healthier in important contexts), when you ignore your own feelings of unhappiness and misery because it's "not manly" only to channel those feelings into self-destruction, that is when masculinity can be problematic (to put it lightly).*

*Masculinity could be problematic if specific traits, usually behavioral or belief, override any reasonable actions, thoughts or choices to be made in usually extreme measures. Through extreme actions, beliefs, and or thoughts likely negatively impact the lives of others, or themselves due to exaggerated actions, beliefs, or traits of what is "masculine" and whether those actions, or thoughts, are done, or beliefs are, in the extreme or accentuated. Which usually leads to manipulative, egocentric, or even toxic behaviors inflicted to those who do not agree with their actions, or beliefs from the individual with what might be called problematic masculinity.*

*Masculinity is absolutely problematic in that so many men feel the need to be "overly"' masculine. Typically, when you come to a party there is one man being the 'loudest person in the room'. There are a few women who are drawn to that but everyone else chalks it up to be 'toxic masculinity', which is the correct assumption.*

*It makes men in general look bad when it's only a few who act like that, but they're the ones who get all the attention.*

*The stress of being looked at as someone who has to have all the answers when things go wrong, or being looked to be a primary provider, without recognition of the difficulty causes some men to develop substance abuse issues or treat others poorly as a way to lash out against those weaker than them when they feel powerless.*

## Society's Expectations

*Community can become volatile, unstable if the concept of masculinity does not include rearing children or helping rear children.*

*Only when it is performative. Or, used unjustly to dominate weaker people to gain benefit in a harmful way. Actions should be taken in a way that is good for the individual in a way that is good for the community and good for society at large.*

*I don't think masculinity as I defined it is inherently problematic. But social pressure to conform to a \*specific\* masculine ideal can cause self-esteem issues, unhealthy coping techniques, and concurrence seeking can cause behaviors that are damaging to others and self.*

*If a culture teaches behavior that harms, holds back or that is too stiff to change, it has some problems. I put masculinity in those same parameters and see many of them crossed.*

*If people believe it to be.*

*In many or in no way. That question in unanswerable in general terms. It really depends on the definition of masculinity you're using.*

*Can't answer that without a definition of what masculinity means.*

*In patriarchal cultures, masculinity is usually equated with dominance and violence.*

*In many ways, the term "toxic masculinity" exists for a reason.*

*It can be problematic if it's suppressed and taught against it because the chain reaction will affect everyone.*

*It's problematic when people focus on it too much. That it has to be this or that.*

*The only problem is the wrongful perspective of what masculinity is, again, Andrew Tate and the likes.*

*We lost the infrastructure of masculine pride and positive masculinity. Men don't know how to be "good men" because we have lost rites of initiation and therefore how becoming a man place one in a role that benefits their community. Instead, we're forced to slap together what it is to be a man from media without the benefit of elders' wisdom to guide us. Hegemony without wise guidance misleads our efforts from conquering the needs of our community to conquering each other.*

*On the individual level, it can cause a disconnect between the authentic and social self. On a societal level, it can be used to justify ineffective norms.*

*Only if other people think it is, which is problematic for them.*

*What kind of question is this? Patriarchy is a prime example.*

*Masculinity can be problematic through the patriarchy in the intrinsic belief that men should be the head of the system whether in a business, group, or family. The competitive nature between boys and men can easily get out of hand and be dangerous for one, both, and/or multiple parties. The social self-regulation of men by men can pressure men to conform to expectations, even if unreasonable.*

*When a man cannot take a hint that a someone isn't interested in him. Also, when they feel that anything considered feminine is "gay" and they become homophobic.*

*When it is unchecked, when it comes at the expense of appropriate femininity. When it is defined as something outside of its function.*

*It creates false conciseness in terms of men's collective interests. I think this leads a lot of men with more traditional values to blame women for societal problems affecting them.*

Since Genesis 3:16, masculinity has been problematic in that women sought to desire their husbands, but men (via Adam) want to be tyrannical toward them (and others).

# Appendix 6

## Generational Masculinity

### Generations

In an earlier chapter, I mentioned the family systems theory presented by Kerr and Bowen (1988). Their theory puts forth the idea of generational functioning, and how each generation functions differently than the previous. Each generation functions either a little bit better, or a little bit worse than the one before them. One generation can be a little bit better adjusted, educated, they can end a cycle of alcoholism that "runs in the family," or end the trend of divorced marriages which seem to happen to every generation. Or one generation can function a little bit worse, less adjusted, continuing the line of generational divorces, or the functioning of alcoholism – hence alcoholism runs in the family.

According to Kerr and Bowen, if one generation does not make a significant change in the positive direction, and keeps the trend of alcoholism alive, for example, then the following generation will suffer from it a little bit more. If the trend does not change, families and children are raised in an environment in which alcoholism is strong, the children grow up seeing and learning these ways of functioning and behaving, and if they don't change them, they grow up and have families of their own and repeat the same ways of functioning and raising children.

One caveat to this family theory is the idea of breaking or changing a poor pattern of generational functioning. According to the theory, to see a visible difference in generational functioning, a difference in functioning where we see the different lives generations have chosen to live for themselves and their families takes three generations. Therefore, if my generation starts to change the habits of harmful masculinity, my grandchildren will reach a place of functioning visibly different than mine.

*To break a "generational curse," it takes three generations of making the right decisions.*

If this theory holds merit, we have a roadmap for changing the patterns of masculinity which might be harmful to our societies. Consider this a guide on how to "do" deconstructing toxic masculinity in our own lives.

### Parenting

Let's start with parenting. I believe the first influences we learn, specifically when it comes to gender roles and what it means to be masculine or feminine, come from our family of origin. We then learn from friends and other external sources later in life. But our very first view of gender roles comes from our parents. As a parent, and as a father, there are several scholars who have written about parenting from a place of positive masculinity.[1]

Coming from a place of deconstruction, there are some specific aspects from the process which can apply to parenting. One of the first things that can translate to parenting is the idea of *overturning*, bringing what was low to high. This has several applicable thought exercises for raising children. If our generation is to make positive changes, those which our grandchildren will benefit from, parents ought to begin with the overturning of gender. If the order of the gender binary has commonly been male (first)/female (second), showing overt hierarchy, we can start with reversing the order.

What does it mean, though, to see this gender binary in reverse order? First, it means being aware of the inherit power that comes with being a cisgender male. By reversing this order, and flipping the script on this power structure, we also reject any harmful aspects of masculinity: aggression, violence, homophobia, or anything else seemingly harmful or destructive to others. With this rejection and reversion of the male/female binary, my hope is the internalizing of how parents view gender, as well as their children. There is an epistemic "truth" about how we view gender and how it translates into child rearing. If we parent with the unconscious order of male/female binary, and the covert and overt power the binary comes with, it will inevitably show in our parenting and how we raise our young men and women.

*The danger with binary opposites is the readily acceptable power they offer our daily living; we subconsciously are guided by binary opposites, and they show themselves in aspects of our parenting, how we are fathers and mothers. Binaries give us an ontology that rarely gets challenged.*

When it comes to parenting, these binaries can easily sneak into our parenting styles. We can unknowingly parent according to the stereotypes each gender holds. Deconstructing gender, and therefore toxic masculinity, ought to bring awareness to the inherent powers within binaries. Reversing the order of binaries, specifically with gender and toxic masculinity, we also ought to reject the harmful things associated with toxic masculinity, rejecting the very things that have made masculinity so harmful to others.

In a content analysis, Schmitz (2016) reviewed popular media and parenting magazines and how they portrayed fatherhood norms. The analysis showed how more media sources, and the overall public, are becoming more open and accepting to a nurturing fatherhood, challenging the traditional gender roles. When it comes to how men balance work and family, McGill (2014) shows how it's becoming more of a practice for men to be involved as fathers, steering away from the traditional norm of men working more than women. McGill calls this positive masculinity, where gender is seen as equal between sexes in parenthood and family rearing.

To get to a place of positive masculinity, or a place of nurturing fatherhood, even inclusive masculinity, we do need to recognize and overtly reject the traditional harmful traits of masculinity. Aggression, violence, sexual conquest, homophobia, and even xenophobia are all aspects of masculinity needing to be recognized when deconstructing toxic masculinity. It is through the rejecting, and the overturning of the hierarchy, where we open space for other gendered possibilities to exist, like nurturing fatherhood and positive masculinity. Along with rejecting these traits, there also needs to be a sense of acknowledgment; recognizing and knowing the privilege traditionally associated with being a male in society. Men have traditionally been at the top of a hierarchy that has afforded them privileges, whether in the job force, politics, or in their domestic lives. Awareness and acknowledgment of these privileges, and how they have been oppressive to other men and women, is crucial for the deconstruction process, reaching a place of positive and inclusive masculinity in parenting.

What's different about deconstructing is the openness to the possibilities to be taken from its process. For example, when we choose to be positive masculine and nurturing fathers, we intentionally make the choice – albeit a good one. When we deconstruct gender and toxic masculinity, it's not that we make the "choice" to be a nurturing father (yes, we do make that "choice"), but the possibilities of other options to "be" a certain gender present themselves to us in a way that transcends the options of gender altogether.

## Societal Generations

Now let's examine this on a larger scale. Studying deconstructed toxic masculinity on the family scale is important enough and presents us with some options of how to approach parenting. What about the larger societal aspect? Just like families trend in functioning, be it for the better or worse, so do societies. What is considered a societal generation, though?

Societal generations[2] are defined as cohorts of people, generally born in the same date range and who share similar cultural and economic experiences within their age range (Mannheim, 1952). Generations also share similar eras in history, like World War 1 for example. And, generations share common exposures, for example COVID-19.

As a quick review, here is a list of generations as put together by scholars:

- The Lost Generation: known as those who fought in World War 1, ranging from 1883 to 1900. Also known as the Roaring Twenties (Cowley, 1934).
- The Greatest Generation: known as the GI generation, including those who fought in World War II. Born from 1901 to 1927. Also known as the Greatest Generation (Rose, 2008).
- The Silent Generation: known as the Lucky Few. Included those who fought in the Korean War and Vietnam War. Born from 1928 to 1945. They were defined by being raised in economically hard times, which resulted in instability during times of war.
- Baby Boomers: Post WWII. Born 1946 to 1964. They were known for their era of prosperity and growth, strong work ethic, and the decades of the 60s and 70s (Van Bavel & Reher, 2013).

- Generation X: Born between 1965 and 1980. The generation following the baby boom of the previous generation. This was the first generation who experienced dual-income households, and the rise of feminist and women's rights movements. They also experienced the economic recession in the 1980s.
- Millennials: Born 1981–1996. This generation experienced events like 9/11, the internet, the Great Recession, and social media. They are known for being technologically savvy, strong attitudes toward social justice, and global awareness.
- Generation Z: Born 1997–2012: Known for their social media dominance, climate change awareness, and their experiences through the COVID-19 pandemic. They are highly adaptable to new technologies, and are deeply concerned with social issues, like mental health and social equity.
- Generation Alpha: Born 2013–present. They are known for growing up in the post-pandemic world and growing up with AI.

When studying a family's generational trend, it's similar to studying larger societal trends. Just like families pass down familial traits between generations, the same happens on a larger scale. For example, it's arguable how work ethics are passed down from earlier generations, from The Lost Generation onto Baby Boomers. The trend was also arguably halted with Baby Boomers, who were also considered the "hippy" generation, sex, drugs, and rock and roll. This is also common in families: one child will take on characteristics of their family, and another will potentially reject it.

The question, though, for these societal generational trends is their experiences with masculinity, and the potential harmful effects they had on both men and women. How did masculinity trend between societal generations? And are we at a place where we've changed the trend? Or is it still trending in the same direction?

If we examine the types of masculines in the earlier generations, we can assume the mold of that era, with most earlier generations having men seeing combat, leaving their families to go to war, and women then staying home while their men literally fought battles. This arguably set a precedent for gender roles, going back at least 100 years.

If we fast forward to the generations where we experienced industrialization, and the rise of manufacturing, the same still held true; women stayed at home and men "went off" to do their thing. It wasn't fighting wars, but the habit of "leaving" women to take care of the home was common. Therefore, from a large, brief overview of men's roles during those decades, it's easy to argue how gender roles were passed down between generations, from the Lost Generation to Generation X. And still today, there may be some men and women to hold these traditional gender roles in their families.

Is this toxic, though?

It's also arguable how men's roles during these earlier generations did overtly, or not, oppress women. Most women's movements in the more recent decades intentionally fought back against the narrative of women staying home while men worked. And when women did work, they were not treated equally.

Generation X started to change that trend. It was in the 1960s and 1970s when we saw a change in the trends from previous decades. The feminist and women's rights movements started to think critically about what it meant to be a woman in relationship to a man, and how unequal those relationships were. When it came to women's rights, women were not allowed to have a bank account until the 1960s. It wasn't until 1974 that the Equal Credit Opportunity Act was passed, which prohibited banks from discriminating again applicants according to their gender.

That was only 50 years ago.

It was also in these decades where Jimmy Hendrix and Woodstock became a melting pot for "free love." This, too, was an effort in changing the trends when it came to gender. For the first time, there was an overt effort to freely be homosexual, to promote love between all genders, and for women to be empowered. The trend seemed to start reversing in these decades.

With the rise of social media, Millennials and Generation Z have given attention to social justice, global awareness, and social issues like gender equality. I would specifically point to the Millennial generation who started the trend in the gender equality direction. This is not to say the issues of gender inequality are gone – far from it. Just like in a family system, previous generations who are still alive tend to hold onto their ideals and beliefs. It is for this reason that Kerr and Bowen, along with other family scholars (McGoldrick et al., 2020), believe in the long suffering of change; it takes three generations to see a visible difference in functioning.

The trends in gender roles and gender equality have changed dramatically since the Lost Generation. The very fact of us having a conversation about toxic masculinity and how the phrase has become so popular only in the last 10 years speaks to the change of the gender trend. We are living in a very interesting time when it comes to toxic masculinity and the spread of harmful masculine traits; there are still people alive who were and are not on board with this change in gender conversations. Individuals from the Baby Boomer generation, even the Silent generation are still living. Which mean the chances of the beliefs once held during those generations, the beliefs of women not being able to have their own bank account, may still be upheld.

This is why change takes three generations according to family systems scholars; we have the potential for two polarizing beliefs to be alive within only a few decades difference. We have the potential for a generation who lived the toxicity of masculinity to still believe in that way of life, at the same time we have a generation who is fighting for feminist approaches to gender, trying to eliminate toxic masculinity.

*Sometimes, people must die for change to happen.*

What ought to bring us conviction about this brief generational study is the momentum we've created on these issues. In thinking ahead to the future, if this trend is going to continue, there needs to be generational support. If our grandchildren reap the benefits of our decisions, then we cannot live in a world where polarizations live within three generations.

We can also study societies by generations in terms of their leaders and leadership. For example, in the United States of America, our generations of leaders have switched from democrats to republicans multiple times. This way of viewing societal generations is shorter-lived than a family's generational changes. American presidents only serve 4-year terms, sometimes 8 if they're elected twice. Even though shorter in duration, the same philosophy applies; just like families trend in functioning, so do societies based off their leadership. Each presidential generation will function either a little bit better or a little bit worse than the one before it.

In families, it's common for children to reject their parents' functioning, lifestyle, or beliefs (McGoldrick, Gerson & Petry, 2020; Kerr & Bowen, 1988). To change things about their families, one generation will rebel against the previous one. This is where children say things like, "I will never be like my parents," or "I will never treat my children this way," trying to change the trend in functioning. The result of this is usually a swing in the opposite direction in functioning. For better or worse, it's different from the generation before them. And sometimes the change sticks. Or other times the following generation will also rebel, causing generations of "rebelling" against the previous. Sometimes forcing change between generations becomes a trend itself. This makes trends in functioning volatile, changing in an extreme way, where the only way to judge a trend in functioning is how small the diversion from the trend itself. This also does not make for a healthy progression between generations, which is common when change is spurred by emotional reactions, "I will never be like them."

The same is true for societies and their generations of leaders and leadership. How often does one leader react to the previous one, saying things like "I will never do that." They come into office and change things, redo policy, and overturn rules at their discretion, all because of the way the previous leader did things. Once again, this makes progress between generations of leadership difficult.

Just like in families, the will to change things can be so strong, and the direction of functioning becomes too volatile and extreme. Take our current election, for example. Only in the last three presidents have we come from a democrat who served for 8 years, made marriage available to the LGBTQ population, made student loans affordable, and furthered social justice issues like racism in America. Following this president was a republican who reversed Roe versus Wade, threated to abolish higher education, and promoted easy access to gun ownership. It's safe to say the reaction between presidents was extreme, like it would be in a family trying to change the trend in functioning. Following this we had a president who forgave student loans, offered stimulus payments during the COVID years, and had the first-ever woman vice president. Swing of the pendulum in the opposite direction.

And now we're back to the president before the last, who abolished Roe versus Wade, and who promised to abolish the Department of Education. Another pendulum swing, another reactive change in functioning between generations. This argument can be true for any sort of society that has one person in charge as their leader.

When it comes to toxic masculinity, this study of generational leadership in societies helps us conceptualize the momentum of change between leadership, and the sort of change that either helps or hurts the fight against toxic masculinity.

If our definition of toxic masculinity is one where harmful aspects of masculinity – like aggression, violence, and superiority – are spread and fostered in society, then the place to look for such a spread is our leaders. When one person who is the central focus of a nation displays acts of sexism, racism, and misogyny, it makes it permissible for others to follow suite.

In family theory, this is known as intergenerational transmission (Kerr & Bown, 1988). When one generation suffers from alcoholism, the simple fact of alcoholism living in one generation makes it permissible for the following generations to follow in the same way of functioning. Whether the following generations repeat the example might be different, but the option is available within the family system. Having a leader who overtly shows harmful aspects of masculinity makes those very acts permissible, or at the very least, an option for society. And when it's that much of an option, how can these aspects of masculinity not spread? When the face of a nation offers that sort of example, it makes it that much more accessible for others, infecting the nation with harmful aspects of masculinity. This is toxicity at its finest.

When it comes to a society that elects leaders who are emotionally reactive to the previous leadership, and overturn things to say, "I'll never be like them," then it's difficult to maintain progress between generations of leaders. And if a leader is toxic by spreading sexism and misogyny, then the inconsistency between generations of leaders does little to trend in the right direction, keeping toxic masculinity toxic.

Our new administration is no exception. The new and upcoming cabinet spanning from attorney general to secretary of health and human services to Supreme Court Justices can all be found guilty of either demeaning women, saying overtly sexist remarks, or having found themselves in lawsuits because of sexual harassment or sexual assault. Therefore, it's safe to say the generation trend of masculinity is not headed in the right direction. With leaders electing other leaders who are just as harmful to women, and how they parade dominance, the spread of these acts is actively happening on the national and political level. Yes, a large population of men and women may live a feminist, anti-toxic lifestyle, but the fact that people in power continue to offer examples of such harmful traits negates the good efforts of others.

We find ourselves in the philosophical timeframe in which Michel Foucault (2008) warned us about. In his biopolitics, he warns us of how institutions regulate populations through norms which influence individual behaviors. This pertains to gender norms, more specifically, masculine norms. It's the institutions of power – religions, political, or otherwise – which shape the expectation of gender and masculinity. Through the widespread acceptance of these institutions, societies buy into the norms which are established by the powers at be. This is exactly what we are seeing in America's political climate.

With the change in administration comes newly elected officials. Many of these officials, as mentioned before, have one thing in common: a seemingly disdain toward women. By overtly speaking sexist and misogynistic rhetoric, or by being found guilty of sexual assault, or both, America is being led by leaders who display overt acts of harmful masculinity. Foucault's idea of biopolitics is being played out right in front of us through institutions that perpetuate such acts and give men positions of extreme power. It is arguably becoming the norm for men in power to be sexist and misogynist.

This is how masculinity becomes toxic, by creating a system that keeps sexism in power, a system where men are seemingly rewarded for their harmful acts of masculinity. The example is publicly set for other men to follow. And when they learn from the example set for them, they repeat the previous generations' acts of masculinity, furthering the generational trend in the wrong direction.

## Notes

1 For more on positive masculinity, see Marsiglio & Roy (2012), *Nurturing dads: Social initiatives for contemporary fatherhood.* This book explores the nurturing aspects of fatherhood, arguing how society is becoming more open to the changing gender roles in parenting.

Also see Lamb (2010), *The role of the father in child development.* This work focuses on fathers' emotional and psychological involvement and presence during a child's development.

Also see Parke and Brott (1999), *Throwaway dads: The myths and barriers that keep men from being the fathers they want to be.* This work tries to attack the stereotypes society has placed on men and encourages men how to break the cultural cycle by being emotionally supportive and involved.

2 This is not meant to be an exhaustive study on generations in societies. To do that would be an entirely different book. For further reading on societies and generations, see Strauss and Howe's *Generations: The History of America's Future, 1584–2069*, and *The Fourth Turning: An American Prophecy.* Both books cover in detail the cycles in American history as they pertain to generations and generational types.

## References

Cowley, M. (1934). *Exile's return: A literary odyssey of the 1920s.* Viking Press.

Foucault, M. (2008). *The birth of biopolitics: Lectures at the Collège de France, 1978–1979* (G. Burchell, Trans.; M. Senellart, Ed.). Palgrave Macmillan.

Kerr, M., & Bowen, M. (1988). *Family evaluation: An approach based on bowen theory.* Norton.

Lamb, M. E. (Ed.). (2010). *The role of the father in child development* (5th ed.). John Wiley & Sons, Inc.

Marsiglio, W., & Roy, K. (2012). *Nurturing dads: Social initiatives for contemporary fatherhood.* Russell Sage Foundation.

Mannheim, K. (1952). The problem of generations. In P. Kecskemeti (Ed.), *Essays on the sociology of knowledge* (pp. 276–320). Routledge and Kegan Paul.

McGill, B. S. (2014). Navigating new norms of involved fatherhood: Employment, fathering attitudes, and father involvement. *Journal of Family Issues, 35*(8), 1089–1106. https://doi.org/10.1177/0192513X14522247

McGoldrick, M., Gerson, R., & Petry, S. (2020). *Genograms: Assessment and treatment.* W. W. Norton & Company.

Parke, R. D., & Brott, A. A. (1999). *Throwaway dads: The myths and barriers that keep men from being they fathers they want to be.* Houghton Mifflin.

Rose, K. (2008). *Myth and the Greatest Generation.* Taylor & Francis Group, LLC. https://doi.org/10.4324/9780203941461

Schmitz, R. M. (2016). Constructing men as fathers: A content analysis of formulations of fatherhood in parenting magazines. *The Journal of Men's Studies, 24*(1), 3–23. https://doi.org/10.1177/1060826515624381

Van Bavel, J., & Reher, D. S. (2013). The baby boom and its causes: What we know and what we need to know. *Population and Development Review, 39* (2), 257–288. https://doi.org/10.1111/j.1728-4457.2013.00591.x

# Appendix 7

## Additional Information

As part of the surveys collected, one of the questions asked was any additional information participants wanted to share. This question did not make it into the final draft of the chapters, but the responses are worth making public.

*Another issue with masculinity is how fetishized it has become. Why would masculine ideals be taken more seriously as feminine ideals? I personally believe that the traits associated with such are culturally defined and the reasons why aggression for example is often seen as a masculine trait is due to cultural reasons (Patriarchy is a cultural phenomenon). I am Non-Binary, so you can ignore these answers if you wish.*

*Being a man is easy the more intelligent you are. IQ and wealth are large determinants in life outcomes. Reproduction and monetarily, across the board. My advice is to think of masculinity as it is expressed in different capitalistic/economic communities. What resources and teams do they behave with? What is their style and livelihood?*

*I feel masculine no matter where, when and what I do. Because I'm a man, so by definition everything I do is masculine. Be it dancing in ballet, boxing, crying, laughing or wearing make-up.*

*I have completed national service (military service), I have fought in a war of liberation – I have never changed my moral values about what makes a man nor my opinion on masculinity.*

*I hope that this work conceptualizes healthful masculinity alongside toxic masculinity, so that the future directions it proposes are as relational as possible.*

*I know masculinity looks a bit different in different places. Also, I think guys can study themselves honestly, admit faults and emotions, and be able to explain masculinity in healthy ways in gender dialogue, while it is great to have female allies explaining positive masculine habits on TikTok, guys should also equip themselves humbly in order to enter the conversation with their own voice.*

*I sense a great deal of shame in leftist political conceptions of the masculine, and it seems to miss the point of a balanced person/society almost as much as conservative, gender essentialist views.*

*I think men's sex drive is over estimated. Most of us are not particularly sexually active but we're treated like disgusting pigs. The bad assumptions make about men are why we drop out of dating markets.*

*I think the way the modern world and how progressives treat masculinity is misguided. I think they treat men like defective women and seem to view anything characteristic of masculinity as a defect. They seem to think the solution to men's problems is to be more like women. "Just talk about your feelings more, don't care about an ideal of what it means to be a man, etc." but I don't think they do anything to address the inner craving men have to feel relied upon and respected. I think if you strip away honor and aspiration from men, then their social status is like women except nobody has as much sympathy for them. And I think men desire sympathy less than they desire respect and honor. I also think there is an opposite error to "toxic masculinity" which is "lack of masculinity." I find often in my personal experience that this kind of man is undisciplined in his emotions, prone to have emotional breakdowns, and justify ill treatment of other people on the basis of their emotions. I find that they often lack the virtues traditionally associated with men while also often not measuring up to the virtues traditionally associated with women. I find that they're often quite passive, aggressive, or backbiting.*

*I think there is a reaction to the feminist movement where a lot of folks have dug in their heals, and have pointed out a ton of issues men deal with as the "counter point" to feminism without realizing it proves feminisms point, but that feminism in the early 2010s, along with a myriad of other "SJW" topics, was a tool to advances an individual's moral superiority, than to really create systemic change. That attitude is definitely changing, which is great, but I feel like there is a reaction to those initial reactions to feminism that any time someone does mention issues men face they are met with claims they are trying to take over the gender conversation. In some cases that is definitely the case, but I think being able to meet men/women/non-binary folks' needs require a lot more goodwill, compassion, and understanding that a lot of places of discussion really allow for.*

*It was difficult to describe masculinity for me because I have been surrounded by many strong both male and female role models in my life, so I don't do think of masculinity as the stereotypical "strong, in control, breadwinner."*

*One big thing I think we are going to have to face sooner rather than later are the long-term psychological effects on men who have gone through their formative years under what I would describe as wholesale invalidation and antagonization in both public and private arenas. Men's identities have been deconstructed and ground to dust over the past decade with no viable guidance or alternatives and they are expected to figure it out on their own, and I think we can all look around and see how that's going.*

*"Toxic masculinity" is just slander. Men have emotions. Some of those emotions are unpleasant. They are not trained, they are natural. Men learn to repress their expression of emotion. So, the same people saying men should express their emotions are the ones saying they are toxic for having them. Men expressing their emotions will not always be tender sadness. Sometimes it will be anger. Men are expected to repress anger. It's ironic. It's demonizing natural male emotions under the pretense that men should just express their emotions.*

*The true issue with masculinity today is that what society wants masculinity to be; is inherently something that is not. From my purview, the more masculine the man, the better suited he is to handle life and do best by those around him rather than appeal to something he is not and demand the world bow to his whims of fantasy.*

# Appendix 8

## Dealing with Harmful Masculinity

A part of this conversation is to point out the harmfulness of masculinity and how it can become toxic. That is not enough, though. This specific section highlights how individuals, both men and women, have lived with and dealt with toxic masculinity. Individuals and families struggle, and they are forced to find a way to navigate through their experiences with toxicity.

I surveyed individuals by asking, "In your experienced, how have you handled or dealt with forms of problematic or toxic masculinity?" As a therapist and a researcher, and as an overall goal of this book, I want everyone to know how individuals are actively working against harmful traits of masculinity, and therefore relieving its toxicity. If we can stop the spread of harmful masculinities, we do our societies and generations a great service.

### Internally

Consider what one participant said about how they dealt with toxic masculinity:

> It depends on the context. When dealing with problematic masculinity within myself a lot of what I've done has been self-reflection, some by myself and some with a therapist, to help break down how living under patriarchy has engraved certain expectations upon me, recognizing that, and trying to process the impacts that performing masculinity in that way is impacting my own wellbeing and the people around me. When exposed to toxic masculinity from others I've dealt with it by either calling out inappropriate behaviors, or by removing myself from situations with those individuals.

In a similar sentiment, another participant shared:

> I deal with it internally by not letting it affect me and by generally avoiding interaction with people who display toxic behavior, masculine or feminine. If my partner or their friends display behavior that could be considered toxic masculinity, I try to explain to my partner why this type of behavior isn't healthy or helpful. I don't use the term toxic masculinity because people no

*longer take it seriously, the meaning has been watered down to basically mean "man I personally don't like."*

Over and over again in the survey data, individuals are actively combating harmful traits, both men and women. What is interesting about the previous statement is how they don't use the phrase "toxic masculine" because of its overuse. I couldn't agree more. The term has been too trendy in the last couple of decades, almost a fad. It's become glamorized and trendy.

This is what one participant shared regarding how they, as a woman, deal with problematic and toxic masculinity;

> *Hah. I'm a woman in America. Toxic masculinity is ubiquitous and is accelerating due to online content platforms that serve incel/red pill content and hook young boys and men into their algorithms. Also, see Donald Trump and MAGA as a shining example of toxic masculinity and how it becomes more publicly acceptable to be sexist (e.g., "grab them by the p\*\*\*"). I believe this is clear backlash against the #MeToo movement and efforts to hold sexual assault perpetrators accountable and call out cultural beliefs that victim-blame survivors of rape and assault (rape culture).*

The danger in this is the diluting of the actual traits and characteristics that are harmful to others. By making a phrase like toxic masculinity a TikTok trend, we give attention to the very thing we're trying to combat. A Mexican American comedian, Chingo Bling, has an alter ego named Tio Juve, who is portrayed to be a seasoned male escort. As part of the character's expertise, he offers a course in toxic machismo, teaching younger escorts to remain toxic. Although commentary on the male Mexican and Latino culture, when the phrase toxic masculine is overused, one of the results is the comedic attention it gets. All the while, we have individuals like these participants who are actively trying to diminish the very harm we are normalizing; normalizing to the point of refusing to even call it "toxic masculine" because it's become so normal.

Even though some participants have tried to fight against it, others have struggled with it. I found several examples of participants who had internal struggles with asking how they dealt with it in their lives. For example:

## Struggles

*My issues with masculinity have been so bad that I went through a period of questioning my gender. Throughout my life, men have attempted to claim I'm not a real man due to my hobbies appearance and opinions.*

In a similar sentiment, another participant shared:

> *Recognize it in myself and put aside fears to introspect and find the emotional support I need. Seek out friends and acquaintances who express healthy masculinity and avoid people who express toxic masculinity. When faced with*

*toxic masculinity, treat it like a troll: Don't feed the troll. The troll is nothing to me.*

In Chapter 6, we mentioned epistemic bubbles, where we surround ourselves with people like us, and therefore keep us within the same bubble of information. This participant shared how they create their own epistemic bubble, knowing what is good for them and what is not. Another participant also spoke to their epistemic bubble in these words:

*I haven't experienced this directly. As a woman, I mostly see comments on social networks that degrade women and promote strong, violent masculinity. But the people around me are very nuanced and healthy.*

Even though not directly experiencing toxic masculinity, they know how other's worlds may be affected by it, but this participant has chosen her surrounding people accordingly. Along the same lines, see what another woman shared:

*It's been difficult to handle toxic masc. As a woman it can get scary fast, I tend to observe first and end up not speaking out as much as I should especially if it's strangers or people I work with. I tend to not keep friends who show toxic masculine traits.*

*As I was born a male, I have always felt somewhat forced into the confines of what society thinks a man should be. I am perfectly comfortable being a male, but I have never really felt comfortable being identified as a "man" simply because of the societal expectations that come along with it. I was raised in the Mormon church, and from birth I was told that it was my responsibility as a man to have a monogamous heterosexual temple marriage with a cisgender woman, have as many children as possible, and be the primary source of income to provide for them. I don't necessarily want any of these things, and it has taken a decent chunk of my life to realize that and overcome the box I was put in.*

*I have been toxically masculine in the past, through my own behavior and conduct. I have been controlling and insecure in relationships and held misogynistic views (such as expecting women to like me more if I were rude or indifferent, the expectation that my kindness should be rewarded with positive female attention). I experienced mockery for being short or perceived as less masculine. A lot of people assumed I was way for not fitting a certain set of norms and behaviors.*

## Distancing

A common answer participants shared when asked how they have dealt with forms of toxic masculinity was to distance themselves. In other words, a common experience with participants was to remove themselves from their friend groups, or from situations where they encounter toxic masculinity. For example:

> *As an AMAB I experienced a certain amount of gendering growing up (though my parents were generally quite accepting of my marked difference from the masculine stereotype). As such, I make sure to check myself when some of that influence shows through. For example, I've had to take a look at my attitude toward household management and housework. I was unconsciously using weaponized incompetence, as a lot of men do, to reduce my share of responsibility. I've worked hard to address this and make the appropriate changes.*

Another shared:

> *I have dealt with a lot of toxic masculinity from my family. I used to join in on their remarks and jokes; more recently I mostly quietly distance myself.*

*Run away.*

## Calling It Out

A large part of participants, when asked how they have dealt with toxic masculinity, responded with some form of "calling it out," where they either stood up to it or squelched it when they saw it. For example:

*Call it what it is.*

*Called it out via humor, or fled the scene.*

*Calling it out and demanding fairness.*

*Direct conflict or confrontation.*

*I called my mom out for saying my brother doesn't do certain things "because he's a man." When it's actually because she taught me how to and never taught him.*

*I don't applaud its negative forms. Trying to condemn those forms. When it becomes violent or disrespectful to others.*

*I have handled problematic people by using the inherent disagreeable nature of masculinity to confront whatever issue falls before me.*

*You got to call it out when see it, telling your bro's it's not okay to do shit like locker-room talk and the like.*

When sorting through the survey data, it was clear how people are struggling with masculinity. Be it how they deal with it, or with the overall phenomenon of masculinity itself, there is a sense of living with the difficulty of toxic masculinity.

Still, consider this response to how one handles or deals with toxicity:

> *It depends on the situation and person. I play video games a lot, and there have been plenty of men who do not have the healthiest forms of masculinity that I've encountered. For those types of interactions, I've asked questions in a non-judgmental tone about what they mean when they say toxic things, or*

*why they feel that way. I'm not sure how effective it is, but I also don't think attacking those beliefs head on works. In person interactions generally go the same way, however, there are times where I will express my disappointment with the other person's viewpoint instead of being neutral. If it's a very toxic viewpoint I might shift to being argumentative and essentially use my very "traditional" forms of masculinity to show that you can be a 'manly man' without being an asshole.*

Not all men are toxic, though. And misogyny is not limited to only men; women can be misogynist, even toxic masculine. For example, the popular one-time talk show host, Ellen DeGeneres. She was at one point a strong advocate and voice for the LGBTQ community through her talk show. It was found out later that she had been abusive to her co-workers, domineering, and condescending. It was also found out that she too, had made sexually inappropriate behaviors toward some of her women subordinates. She had been accused of being toxic and mean-spirited.

# Index

homophobia 5–8, 11, 36, 61, 124, 127–129,
154, 158, 171, 195
hooks, bell 20, 21, 64
hypermasculinity 107, 108, 116, 145,
149, 154

implicit bias 40–42
insecurity 25, 81, 88, 144, 150, 151, 155,
175, 186, 189
intersectionality 30, 43, 44, 108, 119
Isis 66

Jean-Francois Lyotard 95
Judith Butler 19, 50, 59, 112, 125, 150
Jung, C. 3, 128–130

Kerr, M & Bowen, M. 28

language and reality 38, 52
Lost Generation 196

Ma'at 66
marriage hierarchy 140
masculinity: definition 12, 49–50, 54, 77;
healthy 57; misuse of 89; inclusive 60,
116–119, 127, 130, 196; positive 58,
82, 196; postmodern 97, 117; social
expectations of masculinity 85; with
choice 60, 105, 116
The Mask We Live In 6
media 6, 10, 11, 13, 21, 25, 28, 30, 33, 34,
39, 79, 86, 156, 161, 195, 197
men's mental health 1
men's rights movement 29, 37, 175
metaphysics 52, 141
#metoo movement 5
Millennials 197, 198
misogyny 4, 7, 8, 13, 14, 25, 29, 93, 107,
120, 136, 157, 171, 183, 200, 208
Mythopoetic Men's Movement 3, 4

negative feedback loop 21
new concepts: Automasculinity 106;
Cyborgmasc 110; Eqlibrium 108;
Essentium 103; Exogenity 106,
107; Esymasc 101; Fleximasc 106;
Gentlecode 108; Harmoneity 102;
HumaUnity 102; Magnamasc 101;
Mallemasculinity 106; Masculin'es
104; Metamasc 104; Novamasc 101;
Nullimasc 101; Omnimasculinity 100;
Plurimasculinity 101; Recalibra 108;

Tonic masculinity 105; Unifidenity 103;
Unmasculate 107; Variousculinity 101
new relational concepts 147, 148, 151, 164
non-dialectical third term 66, 97, 99
nurturing fatherhood 195, 196

online epistemic bubble 34, 35
ontology 110, 195
outward deconstruction 139

paradox 128, 129, 138, 139
patriarchy 20, 24, 36, 81, 85, 91, 112, 125,
163, 167, 183, 192, 204
performance of gender 11, 39, 51, 54, 85,
86, 126, 150, 180
personas 130, 138
positive masculinity 58, 59, 82, 192, 195
post-gender 111–113
post structuralism 51, 111
posthumanism 113
postmodern research 75
postmodernism 52, 76, 95–97, 111, 117
privilege 5, 19, 21, 30–32, 35, 38, 43–44,
60, 81, 83, 118, 144, 147, 164, 196
projective identification 23, 24, 163, 164

qualitative deconstruction 76, 92
qualitative inquiry 75, 77
queer theory 110–113

religion: male figure in 8, 20, 21, 26–28
remix 100, 108, 161, 162
repentance 58, 64, 146, 150, 158

Schwartz, R. C.: Internal Family Systems
119, 159
Seth 66
shame vs. guilt 124–127
Silent Generation 196
social binary 148
social-constructionism 36, 42
structuralism 51
Sue Jonhson 124
suicide 2
systems theory 22, 194

tonic masculinity 105
Toth 66
toxic: definition 55; hegemony 10, 27;
infectious 10, 25, 59, 107
toxic masculinity: characteristics 86;
definitions 10–12, 85–87, 92, 116,

For Product Safety Concerns and Information please contact our EU
representative  GPSR@taylorandfrancis.com
Taylor & Francis Verlag GmbH, Kaufingerstraße 24, 80331 München, Germany

www.ingramcontent.com/pod-product-compliance
Lightning Source LLC
Chambersburg PA
CBHW070323270326
41926CB00017B/3735

9 781032 734392